DELTA WINGS

Convair's High-Speed Planes of the Fifties & Sixties

Motorbooks International
Publishers & Wholesalers Inc
Osceola, Wisconsin 54020, USA

CHARLES A. MENDENHALL

The Greek capital letter D (Δ) is *delta*. In engineering parlance it means difference. For example, *delta t* is usually understood to mean elapsed time, say the minute difference between 2:18 and 2:19. In the case of the radical-winged aircraft created by Convair between 1948 and 1956, *delta* also meant a difference, but this time, it went back to the Greek letter's triangular shaped symbol.

Most aircraft are shaped like birds, natural to be sure. Convair's unique progeny can only trace their ancestry back to the schoolboy's paper dart. However, a look at today's ultrasophisticated Mirage 2000 and Israeli Kfir fighters confirms the soundness of the early engineering decision by Convair to go the delta wing route with design studies beginning as early as 1945.

© Charles A. Mendenhall, 1983
ISBN: 0-87938-172-8
Library of Congress Number: 83-12184

Printed and bound in the United States of America.
Book and cover design by William F. Kosfeld.
Cover photo of the B-58 Hustler courtesy U.S. Air Force.

Motorbooks International is a certified trademark, registered with the United States Patent Office.

1 2 3 4 5 6 7 8 9 10

Motorbooks International books are also available at discounts in bulk quantity for industrial or sales-promotional use. For details write to Marketing Manager, Motorbooks International, P.O. Box 2, Osceola, Wisconsin 54020.

Library of Congress Cataloging in Publication Data

Mendenhall, Charles A.
  Delta wings.

  1. Convair airplanes—History. 2. Delta wing airplanes—United States—History. 3. General Dynamics Corporation. Convair Division—History. I. Title.
UG1243.M45 1983   358.4′183   83-12184
ISBN 0-87938-172-8 (pbk.)

ACKNOWLEDGMENTS

Writing the story of Convair's deltas was not a one-man task. Without input from companies, organizations and over a hundred individuals, this book would have been a slender volume indeed.

Z. Joe Thornton of General Dynamics, Fort Worth, Texas, and John F. Isabel of Convair, San Diego, California, provided information and photos in abundance. Likewise, Mike Pollack and Kearney Bothwell of Hughes Aircraft Company came up with a wealth of data about that company's weapons control systems and Falcon missiles as they applied to the F-102 and F-106 aircraft. The story of the PQM-102 target drone system was furnished by Brent Hosage of Sperry Flight Systems.

Organizations that were of major assistance were the National Air and Space Museum, Library; the USAF DAVA Still Photo Depository at Arlington, Virginia; the American Aviation Historical Society, with its negative collection; and the USAF Museum Archives at Dayton, Ohio.

A letter to the editor of *Air Force Magazine* concerning my intentions of writing a delta book brought forth over a hundred responses from readers of that magazine, all having flown or worked with Convair's array of triangle-winged aircraft over the past three and a half decades. Several invested a fair degree of time and effort to help this book along by providing pages of information and even voice recordings of their recollections. Tom Hull, a flight test engineer at NATC Patuxent River, went to great lengths to provide photos, data, and other information about the Sea Darts, one of which he was restoring at the Naval Air Test and Evaluation Museum. John M. Fitzpatrick, an engineering test pilot who joined Convair at the start of the YF-102 program and remained until becoming chief engineering test pilot during the last years of the F-106 program, provided many fascinating facts and experiences. R. Cargill Hall, deputy command historian, Headquarters, Military Airlift Command, produced more information about the B-58 than I believed could exist in one place, a veritable treasure trove of unusual facts for use in the book's chapter on that aircraft. Joseph M. Kovac, Jr., who spent many hours in Thule, Greenland, wrote (on seventeen closely typed pages) his recollections of B-58's when he was a staff weather officer for the 43rd Bomb Wing from the time the Air Force had three B-58's until September 1962. Wilbur R. Wortham, Jr., Lt. Col. KSANG, also produced nearly a chapter of interesting experiences about flying the F-102A. I list these names and contributions not only to thank them, but to illustrate the caliber of contributors who helped make this book possible.

Space limitations make it impractical to mention all contributors in as great a detail as above. However, I would like to mention the names of a few others who made contributions, large and small but always important and interesting. (The order of the names is the order in which I have retrieved them from my somewhat random files.) Jack Sullivan, Maj. Charles E. Townsend, Walter D. Allen, Ken Myers, G. R. Hennigan, W. H. Lawton, George Cockle, Garry Sanger, Dustin W. Carter, Joseph Dodyk, Lt. Col. Park D. Waldrop, Col. Gerald de la Cruz, James A. Dykes, Maj. Thomas M. Hammons, Daniel R. Kistler, Don Loewen, Jim Monaco, Leslie J. Prichard, John Vadas, 1st Lt. M. J. Kasiuba and Joseph Adams Shortal.

Last, my thanks to Mrs. Karen L. McManus, who has typed her way through the manuscript, at least twice, as I vacillated about trying to figure out how to make this book informative, readable and interesting.

INTRODUCTION

OF AVIATION HISTORY'S NEARLY EIGHTY years, it took almost fifty of them to learn to build and fly a delta wing; which is quite strange, because the design has been flown out second-story windows in paper dart form since the invention of paper itself! Indeed, a patent for a delta wing aircraft design was granted to two Englishmen, J. W. Butler and E. Edwards, on July 19, 1867, almost forty years before the Wright brothers fluttered their *Flyer* across Kitty Hawk's windswept sands. In addition to the triangular wing configuration, the Butler-Edwards concept was jet-propelled using steam, gunpowder, rockets or compressed air jets as thrust providers. Nothing came of it. The delta wing was one of those great ideas that had to wait until its time would come—in this case, the jet engine and the Cold War drive for speed.

Supersonic in level flight—that was the way to go if you wanted to win a fighter plane contract in the early fifties. The idea of going supersonic was not all that old. With World War II finished in 1945, General of the Air Force H. H. Arnold was advised by Theodore von Karman, a renowned aerodynamicist and chief scientific counselor to the Air Force, that with continued effort future aircraft would "move with speeds far beyond the velocity of sound." Prior to this, about the only things around that had broken the sound barrier were artillery shells, and many responsible aero-engineers believed a stone wall separated subsonic and supersonic flight. As a result, the Air Force began a vigorous program to prove von Karman's optimistic viewpoint—and it did.

At age twenty-four, Major Charles E. (Chuck) Yeager, USAF, rode the orange Bell X-1 (Glamorous Glennis) through the sound barrier over the Mojave Desert on October 14, 1947, for a minute or two. For his trouble, he had the hell shaken out of himself as he passed through the transonic range and over Mach 1, and he got no immediate public glory. The Air Force stamped the flight "secret" and did not even talk about it until June 1948.

Even then, it certainly was not all that routine. The X-1 had to be air launched from a B-29, and a powerful but dangerous four-tube rocket motor was required to provide the massive thrust needed to do the job. Range of the aircraft was much too short to be of any military use. And luck still played a part in completing successful supersonic test missions, as the new high-speed technology sometimes fell short of predicting aircraft flight characteristics in the high stratosphere where the experimental planes careened along above Mach 1. An example is the later slick Bell X-2, which came unstuck from a programmed flight plan and dashed its struggling test pilot, Captain Milburn Apt, to the ground. Pilot control was, at best, marginal, and maneuverability was almost a joke—just enough to keep the aircraft straight and level and not crash. This was *not* the stuff dogfighting fighter planes should be made of.

Yes, there were many rocket-powered research planes close on the heels of the X-1: the X-1A, the X-1B, the X-2, the Douglas D-558-2 Skyrocket and, in England, the D.H.108—all still very experimental. By the late forties, the fairly new, powerful turbojet was deeply entrenched as *the* military powerplant to use. Myriad jet aircraft designs, fighters and bombers, appeared both in the United States and abroad. The engines worked well and were generally reliable. Several successful military jets came on the scene in quantity—Lockheed P-80, Republic P-84 and Boeing B-47. Their speeds were a quantum jump over the World War II piston-engine machines, but what the military really wanted was a supersonic level-flight capability. Swept-wing technology was then applied, having been acquired from captured German data developed during the war. Soon, North American's swept-wing F-86 Sabrejet was regularly breaking the sound barrier in dives. It first did so on April 25, 1948. Also, the introduction of afterburners to the turbojets provided a monumental increase in thrust from the same engine, but with unfortunate monumental fuel gulping.

Since it was a foregone conclusion that the turbojet with afterburner would be the plane required for supersonic flight, the fuselage shape and proportions were, in many respects, defined by the long, cylindrical powerplant. True, the placement of engine air intakes was "a six of one, half dozen of the other" choice. The direct through-the-nose intake design route was straightforward but required long duct work to reach the engine. It was efficient but the system had the disadvantage of using precious fuselage space that could better be used for equipment, and it also made the nose mounting of the upcoming fire control radar more difficult. Using bifurcated fuselage shoulder ducts cut down the distance the engine intake air had to travel and provided more fuselage volume for avionics and an uncluttered nose for the fire control radar. The tradeoff, however, was greater fuselage cross-section and, of course, more built-in drag due to the increased frontal area. Fuselage design was pretty much confined to those two choices.

However, the *real* place for change when going after the supersonic golden ring was in wing design. Aspect ratios (wing chord-to-span ratios) similar to those used on piston-engine fighters were, along with straight wings, carried over to the first generation of production jets. However, the U.S. aviation industry soon digested wartime German research on high-speed flight, and added some technology of its own that was hoped would make the second generation of jet fighters supersonic in level flight.

By that time, three types of new wing planforms had emerged as front-runners in the quest for high fighter speeds: the relatively high aspect ratio swept wing (North American F-100), the ultralow aspect ratio straight wing (Lockheed F-104), and the triangular delta wing (Convair F-102).

The swept wing, due to its relatively high aspect ratio, structurally required a wing thickness-to-chord relationship similar to previous straight-wing fighters, but it demonstrated good success in the high subsonic and transonic speed ranges. Indeed, it is still used today on nearly all jet-powered transports save the supersonic Concorde and the Soviet TU-144, which are both essentially deltas.

The ultralow aspect ratio wing, due to its short span, was able to exhibit a comparatively low thickness-to-chord ratio, that is, the airfoil was quite thin compared to the airfoil width—which, of course, was ideal for high-speed flying, due to low frontal area and lack of drag. Also, the straight or slightly tapered leading and trailing edges allowed for leading edge slats and trailing edge flaps to be fitted, providing high lift and relatively low airspeed landings and takeoffs. The main problem—if there was one—was that there wasn't enough thickness to allow landing gear retraction into the wing. Carrying fuel in the wing was also a nebulous possibility. However, the landing gear could be retracted into the fuselage, and fuel tanks could be situated there as well. Extra range could be accomplished by the addition of large wing-tip tanks. Clarence (Kelly) Johnson, Lockheed's chief engineer, used this option successfully in the design of the Lockheed F-104 Starfighter. It was certainly a fine enough design, and it was built and used by several NATO countries in addition to the United States.

The last wing type, the delta, was by far the most radical. It offered exceptional area, a low wing loading and a short span. However, due to the sharp, sixty-degree back-sweep of the leading edge, high-lift devices on that portion of the wing were of little use. (The French are now using such devices on the new Mirage 2000 and 4000 aircraft, however, and with success.) The superlow wing loading, because of the inherently large area, helped offset that drawback. Due to the extremely wide wing chord at the fuselage side, even though the airfoil height-to-width ratio was minimal, a reasonable wing thickness could be obtained. This allowed room for landing gear retraction and fuel tanks while still maintaining all the high-speed flight characteristics of the swept-back and ultralow aspect ratio wings.

It was surmised early that large angles of attack would blanket a delta-winged aircraft's vertical tail surfaces and result in a minimum degree of directional stability under such conditions. (The monstrous vertical fin and rudder on the Convair XF-92A demonstrate this early fear and the designer's understandable reaction to it.) With experience, this was found to be untrue and, as succeeding models of Convair delta fighters evolved, the vertical tail surfaces became ever smaller. With the B-58 Hustler, the vertical tail was proportionally no larger than a conventional aircraft's. The National Advisory Committee on Aeronautics (NACA) also did a great deal of experimental work in the late forties and early fifties to iron out some final delta wing design details and, as a result, the delta-wing shape became more than fully competitive with other wing shapes for supersonic aircraft.

As speeds have continued upward to Mach 2 and even Mach 3, the delta wing now appears to have won out as the ultimate supersonic wing. Examples of more recent aircraft designed to operate at high Mach numbers include the North American B-70, the Concorde and the Russian TU-144 supersonic transport. Lockheed's SR-71, while not a true delta, approaches that planform and it *was* developed under the leadership of Kelly Johnson, who earlier had substantial misgivings about the delta configuration. The French Mirage series and the Russian Sukhoi fighters were Europe's version of the delta, along with such British offerings as the Gloster Javelin and the Avro Vulcan. The Convair F-106 still flies with the U.S. Air Defense Command as an all-weather interceptor, a front-line aircraft, while the stub-winged F-104 Starfighter has nearly seen its day.

This book will attempt to cover the history and usage of the delta wing planform from its inception with the Butler-Edwards design to the latest Mirage fighters of today. Most of the book will cover Convair aircraft. That firm courageously laid its resources, financial and engineering, on the line to back the delta when most others were afraid to take a chance on it. The XF-92A through the B-58 and F-106 aircraft were Convair/General Dynamics' very important contribution to aeronautical science.

CONTENTS

CHAPTER I
△ *PAPER DART TO FIGHTER PLANE*

△——————————ALONG WITH THE MANY other "dreamt of" flying machines in the nineteenth century there was the Butler-Edwards design of 1867. The proposed aerial vehicle was delta-winged, with a propulsion by either gunpowder-fueled rocket, steam jet or compressed air. Control, for climbing or descending, was to be accomplished by the aeronaut pushing his seat forward or backward on rails, moving the center of gravity rearward to go up and ahead to go down, truly flying by the seat of his pants. Of course, neither this design or any of the other fanciful flying contraptions of that period ever flew. The Wrights were finally successful in 1903. Their design became the benchmark from which aircraft design stemmed for the next forty some years, with more or less straight, birdlike wings. Soon other designers, following on the Wrights' heels, had moved the directional controls to the far aft of the aircraft—and there you had basic airplane design, carved in stone.

However successful this evolution was, there was always room for renegade thinkers. The Scroggs Dart, with a ninety-horsepower OX engine, was actually built in 1929 as an interpretation of the Butler-Edwards design. It was not successful. Even the Russians got in the delta act with their Tscheranovsky machine—a half-circle wing instead of a triangle, and no tail.

The next serious delta proponent was Germany's Professor Alexander M. Lippisch. He was a dabbler in rocketry and experimental airfoil design who operated an engineering and development institute in Vienna during the thirties, the period of Nazism's growth and bloom. His best known effort was the creation of a stubby World War II non-delta rocket fighter, the Me 163 Komet, designed when he had worked as a project engineer for Messerschmitt. Had it been developed earlier in the war, that fighter could have wreaked real havoc with the Allied bomber formations over Europe.

With the success of the Komet, Lippisch was ready for the next step, a supersonic fighter. For the new machine he chose the delta planform. A glider, labeled the Lippisch DM-1, was constructed as a test vehicle to evaluate the triangular wing shape—with a rocket-powered supersonic fighter plane to follow. The glider was constructed of wood, and the wing had a leading edge backward sweep of sixty degrees and a trailing edge forward sweep of fifteen degrees. The trailing edge contained the flight control surfaces, elevons. These consisted of ailerons outboard and elevators inboard. A large, triangular vertical tail sat atop the fuselage, its forward portion glazed. That served as the windshield and canopy for the pilot's head. The test glider was equipped with a tricycle landing gear. Expected flight performance characteristics included a top speed, in a dive, of 348 miles per hour, and a low landing speed of 46.6 miles per hour. The craft was somewhat diminutive, with a span of only 19.4 feet, a length of 21.6 feet and a height of 10.4 feet. Wing area was 216 square feet. Its loaded weight was 1,010 pounds, which included the pilot and test instrumentation. Empty, the little high-speed glider weighed 655 pounds. Its minimum sink rate was to be about 16.4 feet per second, about half the speed of a rock. The test glider was to ride to 24,600 feet mounted atop a Siebel Si204 light transport fuselage, à la the space shuttle piggybacking the Boeing 747. The delta glider was built and ready to test when the Allies won the war. It was soon captured and sent back to the United States, along with much other German supersonic flight technology.

Lippisch had planned at least five other delta aircraft to follow, if the glider tests were successful. There was the DM-2 to attain Mach 6 at 115,000 feet, the DM-3 to attain 6,210 miles per hour at 164,000 feet and the DM-4, which was to be hypersonic. These were all one-of-a-kind experimental project proposals. On the more practical military side, he

Mockup of XF-92A (Model 7002) as designed by Consolidated-Vultee (Convair). (USAF)

Port side view of XF-92A. Three were ordered, only one (46-682) was built. The vertical tail appears particularly large when viewed from this angle although designers thought it was needed to maintain directional stability at high angles of attack. XF-92A had cigarlike fuselage with stock P-80 installation of Allison J33-A-23 behind cockpit area. Engine produced 5,400 pounds maximum static thrust. (USAF)

had designed two ram-jet-powered delta-winged fighters, the LP-12 and LP-13. They were under development when the war ended. With these credentials, it was not long before the U.S. government grabbed him, immigrated him, and sent him off to Wright Field along with the other advanced aerodynamic information it found while sifting through the ruins of German scientific and engineering centers.

Dr. Lippisch was fifty-one in 1945 when he came to Wright-Patterson Air Force Base, where he was quickly put to work as a special projects consultant on high-speed aerodynamics. At this time, there were a few NACA reports dating from the early thirties concerning delta wings. NACA had learned through wind tunnel research that the delta configuration offered great promise for supersonic flight. Unfortunately, at the time there were no powerplants available, or even contemplated, that could take advantage of the high-speed possibilities of the radical wing concept. These few reports, along with Lippisch, comprised just about the whole body of knowledge about the radical delta planform, although Russia, Sweden and England were busily checking it out.

About the same time, Convair, famous for its intrepid B-24 Liberator bomber design, was to get in the ultrahigh-speed interceptor business at the request of the Army Air Force. Convair was the result of the March 18, 1943, merger of Consolidated Aircraft and Vultee Aircraft. Both parent companies were rich in aeronautical history. Consolidated had been founded by Major Reuben Fleet in 1923, and had grown through the acquisition of such historically significant American pioneer aircraft manufacturers as Gallaudet, Dayton-Wright, Thomas-Morse and Hall Aluminum Aircraft Corporation. Vultee, itself a major aeronautical company, also brought with it the historic name of Stinson. Convair's great wartime efforts with the B-24 and later the B-32 had earned it a good reputation with the Army Air Force, hence the request to embark on the ultra-high-speed fighter design.

In a conference at Wright-Patterson in 1945, between Convair engineers Frank Davis, Adolph Burstien and Ralph Shick (these three men were presented the aircraft design award by the American Institute of Aeronautics and Astronautics in 1981 for their work on the delta wing); the USAAF; and Dr. Lippisch the delta planform was decided upon as the shape for the new aircraft. Using the DM-1 glider as a starting point, the new experimental fighter design began to take shape. A wind tunnel model was constructed to prove the delta theory—at a cost of little more than $150! Tunnel results were impressive and the Air Force was now 100 percent behind the program. As for later delta models, they were subjected to over 5,000 hours in an unparalleled wind tunnel program as the secrets of delta design were unlocked.

The tests convinced even the most skeptical, and a go-ahead was given to construct a full-size delta aircraft. It was labeled Model 7002 ("seven-balls-two" to the insiders). One early scheme for the plane was based on its being ram-jet-powered with the

Looking down on XF-92A the 60° sweptback wing is evident as it forms an equilateral triangle. The span was a diminutive 31 feet 3 inches and the wing area was 230 square feet. (USAF)

cockpit mounted in a streamlined pod inside the ram-jet tube. To get up to speed for takeoff and ram-jet operation, it was to use a four-wheeled dolly that was rocket-powered!—shades of the Me 163 Komet. That somewhat bizarre initial start was soon dropped in favor of a turbojet and rocket design. In 1946, when jets were somewhat on the low thrust side, it was planned to use a Westinghouse J30 with 1,560 pounds of thrust, plus six 2,000-pound-thrust nitromethane rockets. That totaled over 13,000 pounds with enough fuel aboard for ten minutes of cruise and five minutes of combat. It might also be mentioned here that, while the aircraft was delta-winged, it also had a butterfly tail. It was to have been armed with four cannon.

To help along the design, Convair and USAAF personnel visited, in September 1947, the Wallops Island Flight Test Range, a NACA facility in Virginia, to discuss rocket model tests for the new delta design. Since there were no supersonic wind tunnels yet built, this was the only method of getting high-speed flight data in the transonic and above Mach 1 speed ranges. After being brought up to supersonic speed by solid propellant rockets, ⅛-scale models of the full-size plane would separate from the boosters and telemeter information back to the ground. In this way it was possible to obtain flight data relating to drag, stability and control characteristics through the transonic speed range—highly important data when dealing with such a new and radical wing shape as the delta.

Six model firings were planned; the first one occurred November 7, 1947. The model had a very short nose with a large inlet. Full scale, that would allow great quantities of air into the real aircraft's ram jet engine. (About this time, the USAF was beginning to doubt the advisability of reaching out so far with both ram jet propulsion *and* a delta wing. It decided to tackle the problems independently, and Convair was left with the delta wing—powered by a conventional turbojet.) The flight failed at once, due to longitudinal instability.

Nose to nose with a behemoth B-36 at Lindbergh Field, San Diego, the little XF-92A looks as if it could be stuffed in the bomber's cockpit. (USAF)

Three-quarter front view shows off tricycle landing gear, parts of which were adopted from existing aircraft. The nose gear strut came from a Bell P-63 King-cobra, mounted backward, and the main gear struts were lifted from a North American FJ-1 Fury though somewhat modified for use on the delta. (USAF)

The next model had the inlet faired with an ojival cone that also lengthened the nose. With the center of gravity now moved forward, longitudinal stability was achieved, and the next five models were launched successfully and did their job. Using eight-channel telemetry, longitudinal, lateral and normal acceleration data were sent back, along with control hinge moments, control position, angle of attack, total pressure and a reference static pressure. The angle of attack was measured by means of a floating vane mounted on the model's nose probe, a system developed at Langley. Compressed air provided the muscle to push the elevons up and down in 1.2-second cycles during the model's short flight. The data radioed back was enough to determine dynamic stability and trim.

The final NACA report to Convair and the Army Air Force indicated the delta configuration to be satisfactory. It was noted there were small changes in trim and some reduction in control effectiveness at transonic speeds. As the succession of models was tested, a nose inlet was once more added; however, now it was more closely sized to the inlet of the actual XP-92A (7002) test airplane that was under construction.

In outline, the XP-92A (soon changed to XF-92A) looked very similar to the DM-1, right down to the large triangular vertical fin and rudder atop the fuselage. The sixty-degree swept-back wing had a thickness chord ratio of 6.5 percent, with elevons on the trailing edge that were similar to the DM-1's; however, there was no fifteen-degree forward sweep to the trailing edge. Exhaustive scale-model wind tunnel tests were run and, finally, the full-size aircraft was sent to the giant NACA wind tunnel at Ames Laboratory at Moffett Field, California, in late November of 1947 for further preflight tweaking. After tunnel testing, the XF-92A went back to San Diego for engine installation.

While the original effort had started out as the XP-92-CO (Model 7) and was projected as a Mach 1.5 interceptor, it became a design study that was never built. However, the study did lay the groundwork for the later F-102 Delta Dagger design. The updated XF-92A, therefore, was intended to be only a one-of-a-kind to furnish further data from the actual flight test to aid in the F-102 interceptor design. To lessen the cost and speed up construction of the test vehicle, components of five different existing aircraft were used in its fabrication. The project was mostly company-funded when construction was started at the Downey, California, Convair plant. Many components were bought from secondhand or surplus dealers by individuals. They could obtain a lower purchase price than could the Convair company. Before the aircraft was completed, the Downey plant was shut down, and the machine was moved to San Diego for finishing. Three of the test XF-92A's were originally ordered, but two were soon canceled. The one actually built carried Air Force serial number 46-682, with the canceled aircraft having been assigned numbers 46-683 and 46-684.

The aircraft was interesting in design: a cigar-shaped fuselage housing the jet engine, with the cockpit located just in front of the powerplant. The engine air inlet was a circular hole in the nose similar to the Republic F-84 first-line fighter aircraft of that day. The delta wings sprouted from the sides of the fuselage to a span of thirty-one feet three inches with an area of 230 square feet. The aircraft sat on a rather intricate tricycle landing gear, the nose gear strut (from a P-63) retracted forward and the main gear (from an FJ-1) pivoted inward about halfway up its struts before the assembly retracted outward into the wings. The high, triangular tail brought the height to seventeen feet eight inches. Also atop the cylindrical fuselage was the canopy taken from the XP-81, as was the ejection seat.

Starting in May 1948, numerous high-speed taxi runs were made over the seven-mile-long dry lake bed at Muroc Air Base. Finally, shortly after dawn on September 18, 1948, the XF-92A made its first flight from the runways of Muroc, in the high Mojave Desert of California. The base later became Edwards Air Force Base. The flight marked a truly important event in the annals of aero development, for it was the first powered delta wing aircraft to fly.

The first flight was made with an Allison J33-A-23 jet engine, which had a stock P-80 installation in the interest of saving time. It developed 4,600 pounds of static thrust. The little research aircraft, after about eighty flights, was reengined with an Allison J33-A-29 with an afterburner. It provided 5,200 pounds of static thrust, which could be boosted to 7,500 pounds by injecting water and methanol into the fuel. The afterburner increased the aircraft's length to forty-two feet five inches. By 1952, the plane was able to go supersonic, in a dive. It would reach altitudes of 45,000 feet and 630 miles per hour (Mach .95) in level flight during its active research career between 1951 and 1953. Fully loaded with 295 gallons of fuel, the XF-92A weighed in at 15,000 pounds. Empty, it weighed 8,500 pounds.

E. D. (Sam) Shannon, at forty, with twenty years of flight test under his belt, was the test pilot of the XF-92A. Shannon had gone through a lot of airplanes in his day, including such diverse machines as the Martin B-10, the Martin Maryland, the Martin PBM, the Consolidated XP-81 with a turbo-prop in its nose and a turbojet in its tail, the Consolidated Model 39 (a B-24 developed into an airliner), the Consolidated B-32, the single-tailed PB4Y-2 Liberator, the 340 and 440 Convair airliners, the XB2Y-1 Coronado patrol bomber and the diminutive L-13 light observation ship, to name a few of many. With the new delta-winged aircraft for his next assignment, Shannon may have wondered a bit about his age in undertaking such a hot dog project.

One factor that didn't make the prospect any better was the extremely sensitive "no-lag" powered

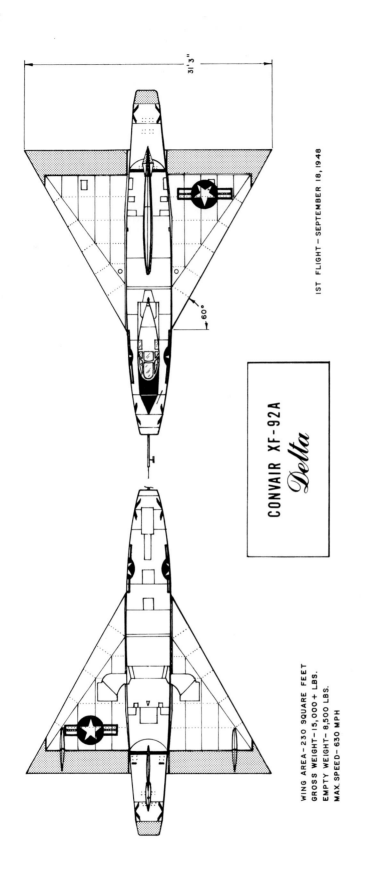

31' 3"

60°

1ST FLIGHT — SEPTEMBER 18, 1948

CONVAIR XF-92A
Delta

WING AREA—230 SQUARE FEET
GROSS WEIGHT—15,000+ LBS.
EMPTY WEIGHT— 8,500 LBS.
MAX. SPEED— 630 MPH

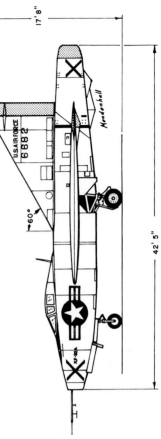

17' 8"

60°

42' 5"

U.S. AIRFORCE
6682

Montenhall

XF-92A

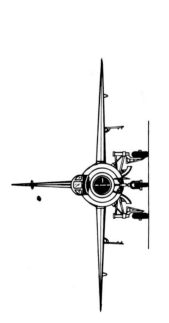

POWERPLANT — (1948) ALLISON J33-A-23 WITH 4,600 POUNDS STATIC THRUST OR 5,400 POUNDS
STATIC THRUST WITH WATER AND METHANOL INJECTION.
(1951) ALLISON J33-A-29 WITH 7,500 POUNDS STATIC THRUST. WITH AFTERBURNER IT PRODUCED
8,200 POUNDS STATIC THRUST.

control system that had been engineered into the aircraft to give instantaneous control response. Dual hydraulic control actuators had been provided without a manual backup. If one failed, the pilot was notified with a red light on the instrument panel. When *that* happened, it was a good time to land, as there was nothing of a safety factor left. The system was totally against Air Force practice, but Convair got away with it only because the XF-92A was a one-of-a-kind trial mock-up of a future fighter design. In the long run, however, Convair engineering was vindicated when the system proved successful enough to become standard on many aircraft. Shannon found the response to be sensitive, to say the least. It was, in fact, the most sensitive he had ever flown. After the system had been desensitized to some degree it was, while touchy, capable of giving the pilot exactly the responses he wanted. The hydraulic actuating system was totally irreversible so there was no need for mass balances on the control surfaces to prevent flutter.

Shannon found some interesting characteristics of delta wings during his testing. The delta would not stall out, per se, but if the airspeed got too low, it took on the flight characteristics of a bag of cement dropped off a roof. Shannon had flown the aircraft with airspeed as low as eighty miles per hour at altitude and had not stalled, but he had lost altitude at an extreme rate. To have any real control over rate of descent, the airspeed had to be kept in the range of 150–160 miles per hour. In an interview Shannon was quoted as saying, "You had to be certain you were ready to land before you put the gear down. If you were below 500 feet and below 150 miles per hour you *were* going to land whether you wanted to or not." One other item: Shannon disliked the ejection seat and had it disconnected—pretty gutsy when you consider the unknown flight envelopes he would encounter as he made flight after flight with the XF-92A, gathering data for the upcoming "hard ball" design, the F-102.

Months passed, and with them the XF-92A changed roles from a strictly Convair test project with Shannon flying it to one where numerous Air Force pilots were checked out in it. Two notables of this group were Major Charles E. (Chuck) Yeager, of supersonic pioneering fame, and Major Frank K. (Pete) Everest, another noted Air Force test pilot. Yeager said the delta "can out-turn practically any airplane at any altitude." The USAF pilots all learned the craft was extremely stable, but required a very high angle of attack (nose-high altitude) during landing, even though the landing speed was comparatively low.

Late in 1951, after the afterburner engine had been installed, the XF-92A was handed over to Air

The underside of the XF-92A reveals the streamlined housings for the elevon actuators as well as tail bumpers needed due to high angles of attack during landing. (USAF)

Force personnel at Edwards for advanced testing. By 1952, they had finished with it and NACA experts took it over—many years after that organization had pointed the way to delta design. By 1955 the XF-92A had outlived its usefulness as a test vehicle; so, mounted on a trailer, it began a tour with the Air Force of various air events. Today it sits in a refinishing area at the USAF Museum in Dayton, Ohio, awaiting a spot in the restoration lineup before going on permanent display as the world's first successful delta wing aircraft.

While Convair progressed rapidly in the direction of its design goal—a very-high-speed fighter in the delta configuration—some people in the industry were still not quite so sure about the delta wing. A good case in point was Clarence L. (Kelly) Johnson, chief engineer of Lockheed Aircraft Corporation. The NACA Wallops Island scientists were still testing and refining their delta rocket-powered models—as always, trying to work in the area of research that might most help the line manufacturers of advanced aircraft with their designs. They kept making the wing ever thinner—in thickness-to-chord ratio—and this was perfectly reasonable on real full-scale aircraft, due to the inherent short span and long fuselage-to-wing juncture allowed by the delta wing configuration. Finally, in late 1950 they got the friction coefficient down to the point where it was little more than would be expected of skin friction alone. The Air Force was greatly encouraged in its sponsor-

ship of the then developing F-102 and later projected F-106 aircraft. Johnson, however, was skeptical of the low drag results and cautioned NACA Headquarters that some "unscrupulous manufacturer" might propose and sell such an aircraft using the data as proof of credibility of design. At an SAE National Aeronautic Meeting in Los Angeles on October 2, 1953, he had some further, rather somber, comments on the desirability of the delta wing as a panacea of high-speed flight. The paper he gave was entitled *Airplane Configurations for High Speed Flight.* While much of it was of a technical nature outside the scope of this story, there were some interesting items brought out, which are quoted here.

"Recently there has been an extensive amount of publicity favoring delta-wing aircraft, both in this country and in England. With very little flight experience and, in some cases, very limited wind tunnel data, many companies (including Lockheed) started drawing and building delta-wing aircraft. Trade journals seized on the trend, and most aircraft advertising started to feature unstable, tailless deltas. Styles are bad things in engineering. If this discussion does nothing more than promote further critical evaluation of wing and tail planforms, its purpose is served.

"There has been very limited experience obtained with delta wing type aircraft. This design, which was pioneered in Germany by Mr. Lippisch, has several intriguing features . . . . Varied degrees of

The XF-92A had a niche all its own in aviation history—the world's first successful delta, as shown here cruising above fleecy cumulus clouds. (USAF)

success have been obtained with these airplanes, which have flown almost entirely in the subsonic speed range. No delta-wing airplane has obtained the high speeds reached by rocket powered straight or swept-wing research aircraft. In fact, few have reached speeds obtained by service aircraft. Within the next few years, this situation will, no doubt, be changed.

"The advantages of the delta-wing are primarily those having to do with structure. The high taper ratio tends to reduce the number of problems, although as one gets further into the designs, there are many important structural problems that still exist. The delta-wing airplane without a horizontal tail, must be predicted to fly at low angles of attack because of the high drag increase that comes about at high lifts. The longitudinal control is obtained by turning up elevons on the wing trailing edge, which decreases the lift considerably, in order to obtain pitching control. This feature, together with the high leading edge sweep, results in very low maximum lift coefficients for the delta configuration, which is the chief drawback of the type. Because the triangular wing section results automatically in low aspect ratio for any practical leading edge sweep, many of the structural advantages that go with low aspect ratio have been credited to the delta." Johnson then went on to compare the low aspect ratio straight wing, such as that found on the upcoming Lockheed F-104 Starfighter, with delta wings of a similar area.

"When the designer does this, it becomes immediately apparent the delta airplane has no patent on the structural advantages that go with low aspect ratio.

"The delta airplanes, in the main, have been the so-called tailless type. This is a very considerable misnomer because while they may not have horizontal tails, they make up for it by requiring terrific vertical tails. Also, while the comparison is very rough, the low wing loading of the delta types required to get reasonable takeoff and landing distances actually results in a higher surface area per pound of gross weight than with conventional types. For supersonic aircraft this is a very undesirable trend.

"To fly at supersonic speeds requires wing thicknesses that are so low that one of the primary advantages previously credited to the delta airplane has disappeared. This was the ability to put a great deal of equipment inside the wing. Actual delta designs are showing that the fuselage cross-section and length are as great for the delta type as for the conventional airplane. It is impossible to reduce the cross-section of the engine, the military equipment, the air ducts, or the pilot, by choice of wing planform, to any important degree. This means essentially that the aerodynamic drag of the delta type becomes greater than other types at supersonic speeds, because, while the fuselage drags are similar, the lower wing loading of the delta and its high vertical tail area increase its total drag. A major area in

Now painted a glistening white with red control surfaces the XF-92A sports a new Allison J33-A-29 turbojet with afterburner with 8,200 pounds of static thrust. (USAF)

16

evaluating the delta type is generally made in considering wing area without considering maximum lift and drag at high angles of attack. While the pounds per square foot sound good falling off the slide rule, the wing doesn't show up very well with its limited pitch control and low usable maximum lifts on takeoff and landing.

"Landing flare rates of descent required very long landing-gear shock-strut travel. The final value chosen for the Lockheed design, in order to get reasonable load factors, was 25 inches! While the basic wing structure started out to be quite light, two factors came into the picture which were very adverse. These were the high suction forces acting over large parts of the wing in pull-up maneuvers at low altitude and the use of numerous stressed cover plates to provide access to equipment in the wing, to make use of the space that was available.

Tufts of yarn are attached to right wing to study the airflow over the wing surface. The refurbished afterburner version was used for most of the formal flight test program. (Convair)

"When the actual weights were computed for the final design, the delta-wing type airplane weighed a few hundred pounds *more* than a competitive design utilizing a normal swept wing design with a tail.

"The maximum lift limitations of the delta wing aircraft without a horizontal trimmer, are due in large degree to the lack of a down turning trailing edge flap. In fact, the conventional trailing edge trimmer turns upward to reduce the maximum lift greatly. To date, little success has been obtained in trimming the delta wing with leading edge devices. Nor do most of them add much to the maximum lift. The maximum lift on the pure delta type is obtained at such a high angle of attack that it is unusable with practical ground angles and landing gear lengths."

When an SAE paper is published, particularly if the subject matter is controversial, a discussion (or rebuttal) generally is published at the end of the paper. It is usually written by someone who has expertise on the other side of the subject coin. In this case, it was Convair's Dr. Adolph Burstien.

Dr. Burstien wrote, in part, "We consider Mr. Johnson's paper both timely and provocative. However, we wish to discuss some of the points brought out by Mr. Johnson, within the limits of security.

"We certainly agree that styles in engineering are bad, nor do we wish to defend deltas featured in advertising, since we have been too busy to scrutinize these cartoons. Mr. Johnson is also correct in stating that no full scale rocket powered delta research aircraft has been flown at extreme speed and

The Convair XF-92A in the upper left corner of the photo now has wing fences as it is pushed further into development by NACA. Starting counter-clockwise, the other aircraft are the Douglas D558-1 Skystreak, Bell X-1A, Northrop X-4, Douglas D558-2 Skyrocket, and Bell X-5. Aircraft in center is the Douglas X-3. (USAF)

extreme altitudes. However, with the power and altitudes used, almost anything could be made to go fast. The recent speed record of the Douglas F-4D, may be more to the point of illustrating capabilities of a configuration that resembles a delta.

"This paper gives one the impression that Mr. Johnson's opinions are based primarily on data of 1947 vintage. We all know that very extensive study and tests of all configurations by NACA and others have taken place since that time.

"Looking at Mr. Johnson's illustration, we draw the opposite conclusion from the author as to structural advantages of deltas. If we consider bending at the side of a typical fuselage supported by these wings, it looks like only 40% to 50% of bending material would be required for the delta wing of the same percent thickness. The torsional stiffness of the delta would be about eight times that of the straight wing at the inboard end.

"Table one was used to show that deltas require very large vertical surfaces in terms of wing area. However, the British deltas listed have proportionately smaller vertical surfaces than the F-80 or F-86. We can only apologize for the large vertical fin of the F-92 and blame it on undue conservatism. We are not repeating this conservatism in our subsequent designs.

Maj. Charles Yeager, first pilot of the supersonic Bell X-1, makes ready to collect flight data for use on the upcoming F-102 delta. (USAF)

"Mr. Johnson points out correctly that modern fighter fuselages are tightly packed with engines and equipment. However, he is incorrect in saying that wing volume of a thin delta is unusable for fuel. One thing that puzzles us is, where does he carry his fuel and landing gear? The implication is that they are neither in the fuselage nor the wing.

"A big point has been made of the so-called low maximum coefficient of lift available in a delta airplane. As we all know, other factors besides landing speed, such as ceiling, maneuverability, and available volume, must be considered in choosing wing area. We have considered putting horizontal tails on our deltas (the first Convair study had a butterfly tail), but after evaluating all the factors, decided against them.

"A big issue is being made of the lift and drag penalties associated with trim of tailless deltas. One factor not generally realized, but pointed out by Mr. Johnson, is that fuselage lengths of comparative aircraft are about equal for all wing configurations. This means that geometric control lengths are in the same 'ball park.' This is particularly true for the supersonic case, which is the most critical. As a matter of fact, we have always considered the maneuverability of the delta as one of its important advantages.

Dr. Adolph Burstien, of Convair, mentioned he had been too busy to look at ads featuring delta wings. This was a typical one, from his own company, featured in *Air Progress* 1953–54. (Mendenhall)

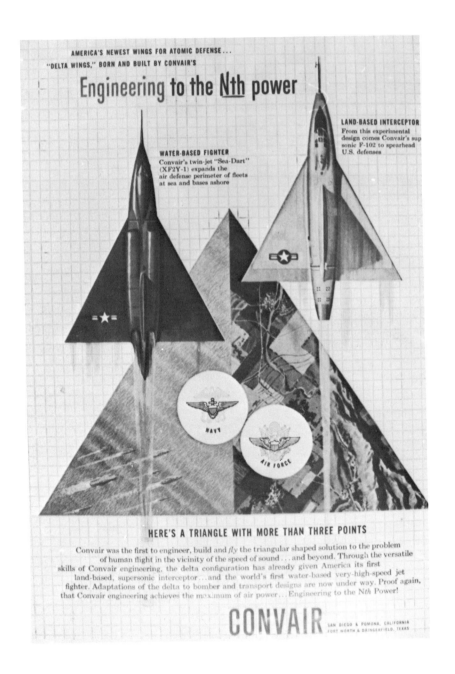

"Some very sad lift over drag coefficients have been quoted, evidently based on Lockheed's 1947 study. Unfortunately, security prevents us from discussing this subject fully. However, certain physical factors and tricks learned by NACA and ourselves paint a much more cheerful picture. As a matter of fact, the L/D quoted in the paper for the approach condition is actually at least twice as much, or similar to the F-80. Lockheed's study indicated that 25 inch shock-strut travel is required for landing. FJ-1 shock struts are used on the XF-92 airplane satisfactorily and represent conventional shock-strut travel.

"The statement that the tailless delta is very seriously restricted in allowable center of gravity, is incorrect. The usable CG range in inches has been very comparable to other configurations, and no unusual airplane layout problems have been encountered.

"In conclusion, these remarks are not intended to induce Lockheed to change to delta but to correct some of the statements made in the light of our experience. Convair does not claim that the delta wing is a panacea for all aircraft designs and problems. For some of our designs, delta came out to be the best solution."

A few weeks after these remarks were made by Burstien, the YF-102 would fly and, while in general his rebuttal to Johnson was right, the aircraft would have problems and be at first a disappointment to Convair.

This photo of XF-92A was taken in July 1980 at the USAF Museum as the craft awaited restoration. (Joseph Dodyk)

CHAPTER II
△ FROM DEBACLE TO DAGGER

△————————————————————————IT WAS KIND OF fat. The YF-102 had been scaled up from the XF-92A at a ratio of 1.22:1, so the delta lines were familiar. Of course, going from an X-type research plane to a first-line combat fighter required some deviation from the XF-92A's configuration. Perhaps the biggest change was in placing the pilot well forward in a pointed nose and moving the air intakes to a shoulder position on either side of the fuselage. This was what made the fuselage cross-section so large of girth.

It was October 24, 1953, on the high desert of southern California's Edwards Air Force Base, mecca for testing the new "century series" fighters and, of course, the fantastic X-planes. With a rumble, Convair's YF-102 hurtled off across the flats, rotated and lifted into the clear blue skies with Convair test pilot Richard L. Johnson at the controls. Johnson was a recently retired lieutenant colonel and chief of the Fighter Section, Flight Test Division USAF. He had left the service specifically to lead the F-102 flight test program. So far, so good. It was the first flight of the new ship that had been trucked over from San Diego a few weeks earlier. The design had gone through wind tunnel tests of small models that had predicted it would go supersonic in level flight, which was the new name of the game.

The aircraft, as it continued its climbout, was the result of an exotic mixture of aeronautical engineering, witchcraft and luck that went into those designs that were hoped to break the sound barrier and perform militarily in the region beyond.

The USAF had held a competition in 1950 for more than just a supersonic fighter plane—it wanted a complete interceptor fire control system. This meant one design source for the whole package, instead of trying to piece together the myriad components of many different manufacturers. Hughes Air-

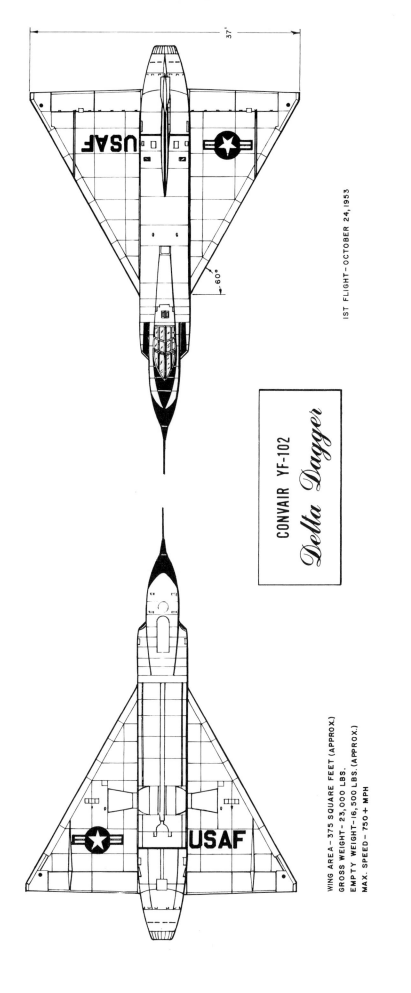

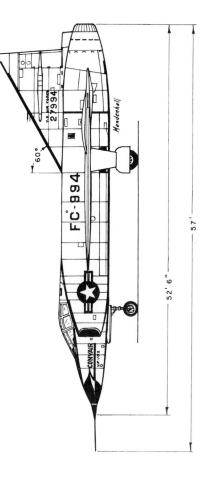

IST FLIGHT–OCTOBER 24, 1953

CONVAIR YF-102
Delta Dagger

WING AREA–375 SQUARE FEET (APPROX.)
GROSS WEIGHT–23,000 LBS.
EMPTY WEIGHT–16,500 LBS. (APPROX.)
MAX. SPEED–750+ MPH

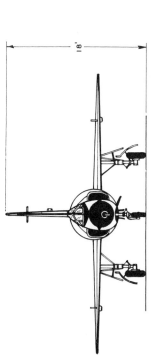

POWERPLANT–PRATT & WHITNEY J57-P-11 TURBOJET WITH 10,900 POUNDS STATIC THRUST. WITH AFTERBURNER IT PRODUCED 14,500 POUNDS STATIC THRUST.

craft won the contract with its F-98 Falcon (GAR-1), which had been started in 1947. Code named "Dragonfly," it was the first pilotless interceptor to be given an "F" designation. As powerfully explosive as an artillery shell, the Dragonfly was capable of accelerating at a rate of 48 g and traveling toward its target at Mach 2. Talk about a real zapper! (The only other nonpiloted vehicle to be treated likewise was the Boeing F-99 Bomarc [IM-99] interceptor missile.) The 120-pound, six-and-a-half-foot-long, light metal and plastic reinforced GAR-1 was ready for its first test within two years. Howard Hughes himself was interested in this one, so the project moved right along. The 6.4-inch-diameter missile housed a Thiokol solid-propellant rocket motor. The missile was radar-directed and flew on small twenty-inch-span delta wings, with movable guide vanes mounted near the exhaust nozzle. As the missile became more fully developed, the Air Force decided it was time to procure an aircraft to carry it. Several airframe manufacturers produced designs (and this included the massive eighty-two-foot-long stillborn Republic F-103), but Convair won out with a delta wing interceptor based on the now more or less proven XF-92A.

The powerplant of the new fighter was to be the country's most powerful, a Pratt & Whitney J57-P-11, with 10,200 pounds static thrust that could be raised to 14,500 pounds with afterburning. The engine was of the highest technology of the time, being of twin-spoon axial flow layout. That meant there were two rotors revolving on concentric shafts, with each rotor containing a compressor and turbine section. Eight burner cans, interconnected, were located in an annular configuration just in front of the turbine sections. Two of the new delta aircraft (52-7994 and 52-7995) were built having a span of thirty-seven feet and a length of fifty-two feet six inches. The large triangular vertical fin gave the plan an overall height of eighteen feet. The airfoil used was a thin modified NACA 0004 section.

Wind tunnel tests were heavily depended upon to establish the radical design. Since no supersonic tunnel existed to test full-scale models of real aircraft, smaller scale models were used. Unfortunately, there was some scale effect that was not fully understood when extrapolating model data to the full-scale mysteries of the new supersonic realm of flight. Across the country at Wallops Island, Virginia, NACA had once more been asked by the Air Force and Convair to evaluate the supersonic performance of the delta wing—this time with models of the YF-102. On July 24, 1953, an eight-channel telemetered rocket-boosted model was launched. Due to instrumentation problems during the test, the final data was a little murky. However, it did seem to indicate that the YF-102 would have a tough time of it accelerating past Mach 1.

The YF-102 continued its flight that October day and returned to the ground successfully without attempting any supersonic activity, and all seemed to be going according to plan. Several more flights were accomplished, and eight days later the first hint of trouble transpired: 52-7994 bellied-in a short dis-

"Numero uno" YF-102—this photo had to be taken quickly as the plane was only around on flying status for eight days before a belly landing ended the career of 994. (USAF)

tance off the end of the runway after takeoff, and Johnson was injured. One primary contributing cause was the lack of understanding of characteristics of the new twin-spool Pratt & Whitney J57. Prior to that engine, a pilot measured jet engine performance by rpm and exhaust temperature. With the J57, the pressure ratio gauge became the primary go/no-go engine instrument. In the case of the 52-7994, rpm and exhaust temperature were fine, but the pressure ratio was low. What this gauge actually showed was a comparison of pitot pressure (from the pitot-static system) and the engine turbine discharge pressure. Needless to say, after the crash, all J57 pilots became believers in the gauge.

Since there were two of the aircraft, the test program soon got underway again, and on January 11, 1954, the second delta (52-7995) was in the air. Another eight aircraft, identical to the first two, except for minor modifications, were coming along at the Convair San Diego plant for backup.

It wasn't long before it was confirmed that the wind tunnel data had mislead the Convair design team. The YF-102 was *not* going to go supersonic in level flight. The transonic drag exceeded the available thrust, the drag hump at sonic speed was more

than the aircraft was capable of. The Air Force threatened to cancel the program, disappointed in the new fighter's performance. Convair was not so easily dissuaded. It had a tremendous investment of time and effort in the design of delta wings and had projected its whole military contract future based on that wing type. To abandon it now would be a return to square one, where its offerings would be more conventional and probably behind those of McDonnell, North American, Lockheed and Republic—all arch competitors.

Fortunately, the National Advisory Committee for Aeronautics (NACA) had been putting the taxpayers' money to some good use as it pursued pure research in the still new area of supersonic flight. An NACA aeronautical scientist named Richard T. Whitcomb had worked up a new theory of what the correct airframe shape should be so that an aircraft might proceed through the sound barrier with relative ease, rather than blasting through with brute force alone (as had been done with the Bell X-1 and subsequent Mach 1-plus aircraft). Postulated in 1953, Whitcomb's theory became known as the area rule theory and resulted in what is often called the "Coke-bottle" fuselage. The theory stated that an air-

A low pass for the camera shows off the portly lines of the YF-102 that would prevent the design from gaining supersonic speeds. Basic design of the aircraft was clean, however, and smooth workmanship prevailed. (USAF)

craft designed to go supersonic should increase in total cross-sectional area from a long pointed nose, then the same maximum cross-section should be continued to the aircraft's aft end. The addition of any protuberance into the airstream, such as wings, canopy, tail or whatever, should be accompanied by a reduction of cross-section elsewhere. In 1954, Whitcomb, then thirty-three, was awarded the Collier Trophy, one of the nation's highest aviation awards, for his work. Since beginning work at Langley Aeronautical Laboratory (NACA) in 1943, Whitcomb had been working with the problem of transonic drag and now, after countless transonic

wind tunnel experiments, he had cut it down to size. The area rule had spoken.

Well, it was sure worth a try. Even though the theory had not been applied in actual practice, it seemed like one reasonable way out of the design mess Convair was facing with its fat-fuselaged fighter. For starters, while the designers worked up the YF-102A, they reworked the second of the existing YF-102 aircraft with lengthened nose and bulletlike bulges on the fuselage sides near the engine exhaust nozzle. It is still around today at the USAF Museum, witness to Convair's harried fire drill efforts. The performance was greatly improved,

The number two YF-102 flew in January 1954 and confirmed the fact that the design was not going to surpass Mach 1. Craft had a span of 37 feet and was scaled up from the XF-92A at a ratio of 1.22:1. Apparently the nose wheel was out for repair when this picture was taken. (USAF)

The same number two aircraft with Whitcomb area rule bulges on aft fuselage and lengthened nose. While better, the aircraft was still not supersonic but it pointed the way to the YF-102A redesign. (USAF)

but the highly modified aircraft was still not capable of exceeding Mach 1 in level flight. Meanwhile, some of the eight follow-up deltas were finished and handed over to Hughes for use in developing its fire control system.

One hundred seventeen working days later, Convair was back at Edwards Air Force Base with the newly revised YF-102A, 53-1787, and the test pilot was again Richard Johnson, who had recovered from his injuries in the first YF-102 crash. This time it had better work or Convair could kiss the delta concept goodbye. The designers had really done a job on it. The fuselage fineness ratio (fuselage length to diameter) had been increased. One of the first steps had been to redesign the canopy, substituting a sharp-nosed low silhouette for the more bulbous greenhouse framework design used originally, and this was placed farther forward on the fuselage. The fuselage itself was increased in length by fifteen feet nine inches, to a new overall length of sixty-eight feet three inches (most of the new length going in the forward fuselage, ahead of the wing). Over the wings, the fuselage was cinched in to give it a wasp-waisted appearance and to meet the area rule; and this was blended back into fairings at the rear to make the aft cross-section the same size as any parts in front of it.

The wing was also in for a redesign. It was made thinner, so thin that the actuating control elements had to be housed in external fairings. The span was increased slightly, one foot one inch to thirty-eight feet one inch. The wing area now stood at 661.5 square feet to lift a gross weight of 27,700 pounds. To finalize the design, wing fences were added to prevent a stall, due to an outward sliding boundary layer, from spreading along the wings. The delta-winged fighter was now ready to go for another shot at the supersonic golden ring. Now, at Edwards, everyone held their breaths. A lot was riding on the redesigned aircraft's performance. A first flight was made on December 20, 1954—a sort of up and down flight just to make sure everything worked. All seemed well, except for a minor landing gear glitch, so the next day Johnson, now eager to go, opened it up and easily sped through the magic Mach 1 *while in a climb!* All was forgiven and the Air Force once again reinstated the important contract.

In the interest of not wasting time, Convair was already producing YF-102A's on a production line at a slow rate. The idea was that any changes made through flight test discoveries with the initial planes could be introduced or retrofitted on subsequent planes coming down the line.

This was the case when later, on the sixty-sixth plane, the vertical tail surface was enlarged for greater directional stability to counteract a phenomenon known as "roll coupling." John M. Fitzpatrick, a former Convair test pilot on the YF-102 program, explained the phenomenon in layman's terms:

"The first real awareness of the phenomena came with the death of George Welsh, chief test pilot

for North American, in an F-100. While performing a high-speed roll the aircraft 'uncoupled,' or went divergent, in both yaw and pitch so that the structural limits were exceeded and the aircraft literally broke in two. Soon it became apparent that lots of aerodynamicists had reported on the phenomena for years.

"In fact, we had actually encountered it a few years before during F-86 roll tests at Wright Field. However, until the Century Series aircraft, we always had enough inherent stability that, although there would be some limited excursions in yaw and pitch during high speed rolls, they would always damp out. What made the difference was the increased length and weight of the fuselage of the newer aircraft. Realize that except in the rare case where the aircraft has a zero angle of attack, it does not roll about the horizontal axis of the aircraft; instead the nose of the aircraft rotates in a circle, the radius of which starts out a function of the angle of attack. Now consider the fuselage as consisting of two masses, one at each end. As the roll rate increases there is a flywheel effect that tends to make the nose of the aircraft diverge sequentially in yaw and pitch as it rolls. The early Century Series aircraft were designed with vertical tails that did not take this problem into account and eventually it was possible to attain a condition where the yaw effect caused by the roll-coupling exceeded the directional stability caused by vertical tail and the aircraft literally tried to turn sideways.

"During the F-102 program we used YF-102A #1787 to conduct roll tests in an effort to determine just how much more area we needed on the vertical tail. During one of these tests I became 'uncoupled.' It was fortunate that we were using #1787, which looked like an F-102A but had the basic heavy construction of the original YF-102's. During over sixty seconds of gyrations the aircraft alternately yawed and pitched to an estimated 48° of yaw (the instrumentation only went to 30°), plus 8 g's and minus 6 g's. The only damage was that the UHF antenna on the top of the vertical fin broke off and a canopy panel was broken, caused by my crash helmet hitting it."

"The basic heavy construction" of #1787 that Fitzpatrick referred to is of interest. The original YF-102 called for the Wright J67 engine and a planned maximum speed of Mach 2. The J67 was not developed so the next best engine was the Pratt & Whitney J57 that was powering the North American F-100. It produced only two-thirds the thrust of the planned J67. Therefore, the airframe for the modified #1787 YF-102A pulled from the production line was one of the heavy airframes designed for the powerful Wright J67 and the high temperatures anticipated in the Mach 2 speed range. It was recognized that *production* F-102A's would be several thousand pounds lighter than the predecessor designed for the J67. To make the weight and balance of YF-102A correspond to that of the lighter upcoming production machines, combat equipment such as rocket rails, fire control and navigational equipment were left out of #1787, since it was to be a test aircraft only. The bottom line was that the YF-102A #1787 was somewhat more sturdy than the subsequent production aircraft.

Along the lines of these special modifications it should also be mentioned that Pratt & Whitney gave permission to trim the existing early J57 for additional thrust (for a limited time only), which would more nearly represent Pratt & Whitney's upcoming J57 production engine for the F-102. To help matters along for this test aircraft, Convair redesigned the engine inlet and exhaust systems specifically for this engine.

Earlier F-102A models were retrofitted to the "larger-tail" standard. The tail area went up from sixty-eight to ninety-five square feet, a significant increase. In addition to the tail modifications, larger air brakes were fitted, and improved air intake ducts were added to cut down cockpit noise levels.

On somewhat later planes, 56-2336 and thereafter, the sixty-degree swept-back leading edge also came in for some up-to-date technology. A conical chamber that was most decided commenced at the wingtips, then lessened, conelike, as it tapered toward the fuselage. This was done to reduce inherent drag at high altitudes and to improve handling at the high angles of attack encountered during landings. This improvement was not retrofitted.

With a couple of the old "green house" canopied YF-102's for use as test beds the Hughes MG-10 weapons control system was developed fully. That mass of electronics gear shown weighed in at 1,425 pounds and used up 24.6 cubic feet of fuselage volume. (Hughes Aircraft Company)

Just to make sure the new model YF-102A had the power to go, it was fitted with a Pratt & Whitney J57-P-23, with a little more thrust than the previous engine.

The new aircraft was placed in production, and the first article reached the Air Force in June 1955. It was built in quantity and would eventually see service with the USAF, the ANG, and the Greek and Turkish Air Forces. It now finally looked like a dagger—and a very pretty, slim one, at that. Eight hundred seventy-three were built by the time the last one came off the assembly line in April 1958.

It was a hot airplane, and not just any Air Force pilot was capable of climbing in and flying it. Test pilots could, of course, and high-time pilots of some of the other "century fighters." But the younger, less experienced fighter jocks needed a way of gaining experience in the Dagger before soloing in it. Enter the TF-102A. It was a spitting image of the F-102A, except for the fuselage in front of the wings. Convair had built a side-by-side cockpit for the training version of its new fighter. Systemswise, it was capable of being fully operational, but more generally, it was used as a two-seat combat proficiency trainer. The main difference was that it could not go supersonic on the level, as the wide cockpit presented too much cross-sectional area to the airstream. When first built, there was a severe buffeting problem created

Another photo of the Hughes system shows it packed neatly into nose of YF-102. Components, and space for them, were developed jointly by Convair and Hughes so as to have the best possible mating of airplane and system. (Hughes Aircraft Company)

by the cockpit canopy, but it was soon solved by adding vortex generators to smooth the airflow in that area. Maximum speed for the trainer aircraft was now down to 646 miles per hour at 38,000 feet. Mach 1 could be exceeded however, in a slight dive. One hundred eleven of the training planes were placed on order, but only sixty-three were completed before their usefulness ran out.

As previously mentioned, at least two of the second batch of YF-102's went to Hughes Aircraft for installation of prototype MG-10 weapons control systems. One of the aircraft, 53-1779, was the first and was totally unmodified in any area rule standards. Hughes also worked on 52-7995 (with the lengthened nose and bulges along the side of the rear fuselage).

The Hughes MG-10 was an amazing electronic armament control system that had been specifically designed for the Delta Dagger. It was a *lot* of system. It weighed in at 1,425 pounds and swallowed up 24.6 cubic feet of the F-102's nose volume. That was indeed a heap of wires, vacuum tubes and transistors. Convair engineers, by working closely with Hughes, had made room for it though. The bottom line idea was that the F-102 could locate and destroy its target at supersonic speed, day or night, in any kind of weather.

The pilot was to be verbally directed by a Semi-Automatic Ground Environment (SAGE) ground controller, or else the initial intercept could be controlled by data link automatic target vectoring command signals transmitted by SAGE in digital form to the F-102. The MG-10, secure in its many black boxes in the fuselage nose, would then convert these signals to analog form for display on the pilot's radar scope on the instrument panel. Once the range was close enough that the target appeared on the scope, the pilot and MG-10 took over the intercept on their own, without ground radar assistance. The MG-10 computed the range and bearing of the target and pinpointed its position. After "lock-on," the Hughes system maintained the aircraft in a proper attack heading in spite of any evasive maneuvers the target might then be attempting. At a precisely calculated moment, the F-102's armament bay doors snapped open, and the Falcon (GAR) missiles were slung down on launching rails into the airstream and then were blasted toward the target with their rocket engines. Since the missiles were either radar-directed or infrared-sensing, the target was as good as dead at that point in time.

The Hughes GAR designation very soon gave way to the AIM designation for the various missiles. Using the new nomenclature, the armament used on the F-102/MG-10 weapons system soon contained the following grocery list of destruction. The primary system consisted typically of three AIM-4F infrared heat-seeking missiles and three AIM-4E

When all seemed at a low ebb for Convair its delta wing number 787 was taken from the line and really worked over to hop it up into the desired supersonic speed range. Lengthened fuselage nose, new canopy design, area rule bulges at the tail and huskier engine all helped to do just that. (USAF)

semiactive homing radar-guided missiles in the weapons bay, plus twenty-four 2.75-inch FFAR's (Folding-Fin-Air-Rockets), located in the weapons bay doors.

Since the F-102A/MG-10 weapons system could attack targets with automatic infrared or radar search, lock on a target, launch armament from any angle, and featured automatic flight control during radar attacks and during instrument landing approaches, it wasn't too far from what some of the Air Force brass had envisioned the ultimate F-102 to be—a totally unmanned interceptor! The idea of being able to defend against enemy bombers without risking the life of airmen was tantalizing, but, unfortunately, as this is written thirty years later, it proved not to be.

The designation AIM stands for Air Interceptor Missile. The primary use of the Falcon was its launch from one aircraft at another. The AIM missiles were self-steering by means of their own control surface movements and could readily maintain an accurate flight path toward the target. The Falcon (AIM) missiles came in two basic types, radar-guided and infrared-seeking. In the case of the radar-guided missiles, the Falcon homed in on the target in the reflected radar waves between the launching interceptor's radar system and the target aircraft. The infrared, or heat-seeking, Falcon was attracted to the

target by radiated heat energy, such as an afterburner plume, and was particularly effective in picking up targets at low altitudes. Used together, these two basic missile types were complementary, one being suited for situations that might have put the other at a disadvantage.

Every version of the Falcon was loaded with a warhead punch capable of knocking down any known aircraft. As mentioned earlier, the GAR-1, the first Falcon, was superseded by Hughes, and the new missiles soon became the primary weapons of the Air Defense Command. In addition to their use with the F-102A Delta Dagger, they were used on the McDonnell F-101B VooDoo and the later Convair F-106A Delta Dart, successor to the F-102. There were, and still are, a lot of variations of the original GAR-1. They include the AIM-4A, AIM-4B, AIM-4C, AIM-4D, AIM-4E, AIM-4F, AIM-4G, AIM-26A and AIM-26B. The range of these missiles varied from about five miles for the earlier versions up to seven miles for the later missiles. Speeds ranged from Mach 2.8 to Mach 4, as they were developed. Since they were such an intrinsic part of the F-102A, and later still active F-106A, a closer look at the missiles is in order.

The AIM-4A Falcon was the immediate successor of the GAR-1D and was equipped with a semiactive radar target seeker that homed in on the parent

Front three-quarter view shows off slick lines of the new YF-102A prototype. Overall length was 68 feet 3.3 inches, span was 38 feet 1.6 inches and height was 18 feet. (USAF)

interceptor's radar waves. After building about 4,000 GAR models, nearly 12,000 AIM-4A's were built for use with the F-102A.

Next came the AIM-4B, C and D Falcons, all of the infrared heat-seeking variety. The initial AIM-4B's were introduced in 1956, the AIM-4C following a year later with improvements to better withstand hot and cold temperature extremes. Both missiles had the same warhead, rocket engine and configuration as the AIM-4A, with the only difference being the nose cone. Hughes built about 1,600 AIM-4B's before switching over to the -4C's. The -4C's were also used with the VooDoo and Delta Dagger interceptors. The AIM-4D was the same as the earlier units, except it used a later model AIM-4G seeker head that was, at the time, a newly developed improvement that was able to lock on a smaller target at greater ranges than had been possible before. Over 1,300 of them were built. It was the final production Falcon in 1963.

As with many things that start out with a claim to fame, the next step was to come out with a "super" version; hence, the Super Falcon, the AIM-4E. The good things that made it super were a higher launching speed, longer range, greater combat ceiling and a more powerful warhead than that of its predecessors.

Just to make sure the "super" adjective stood up in court, it was also equipped with an improved guidance system, and the nose cone was fashioned with a new material that permitted use in a wider range of tactical environments. The AIM-4E was of the radar-guided variety, as was the earlier AIM-4A, with the same type of semiactive target seeker that depended on the launching interceptor for target illumination. It had the same diameter as its predecessors but was six inches longer and had an increased tail/guidance surface span. Hughes built about 400 of them before continuing on to the AIM-4F.

Came 1960, and also came the AIM-4F Super Falcon. The AIM-4F was improved in the area of its radar guidance system. It had greater accuracy and increased immunity to enemy decoy signals and countermeasures spewed out by the enemy target. Even the rocket motor was different, having a two-thrust-level capability. It was geared for a fast high-thrust launch followed by a lower level of push to sustain its initial velocity. It weighed in at about 150 pounds and its forward portion was covered by a white moisture-sealing sleeve. The F-106A got to use the AIM-4F; however, the F-102A didn't.

The next Super Falcon was the AIM-4G. It was the infrared missile whose heat-seeking sensor was

The YF-102A in flight over rugged terrain. This photo shows off well the wing fences used to prevent spanwise flow of the boundary layer of wing airflow at high angles of attack. (USAF)

used on the earlier F-102A-based AIM-4D. The AIM-4G itself was used with the F-106A, a topic to be discussed later.

In the spring of 1960 came the big boomers, the AIM-26A and -26B Falcons (one complete with atomic warhead)—a whole new generation of knock-down force. Actually, the -26A was the nuclear-tipped one. The -26B was the same, except it was armed with a conventional type of warhead. The AIM-26A was dutifully added to the arsenal of the F-102A, where it remained to the end of that fighter's active career. The missile's claim to fame was that it could ignore the enemy aircraft's countermeasures, and it was particularly effective in frontal attacks where pinpoint accuracy was most needed due to the small target area size. Hughes built nearly 2,000 of these, along with about 800 of the conventionally tipped weapons.

So it was with the Hughes missiles and their development. Convair kept pace to provide air-frames to carry this array of electronics and weaponry throughout the early fifties and into the sixties. Looking back, it was all the beginning of the successful hand-in-hand cooperation of high technology industrial complexes flexing their muscles on a training ground that, within the coming years, would result in sending a man to the moon and back using the same systems-oriented attack on the barricades of unknown technology.

In the late forties, the Air Force thought big. Then, the Russians in the early fifties—with first their atomic, then hydrogen bombs—really accelerated the pace of defense development in this country. It would no longer do to have individual fighter pilots take off on sorties hoping to scan the skies by eyeball and discover enemy bombers.

The cinched-in "Coke bottle" shape of the fuselage of the number 787 prototype is readily apparent in this photo. Also the redesigned knife-edge canopy shows up well. (Convair)

To the Air Force's way of thinking, what had to be done was to develop a system, or network, of defense that could assure that enemy bombers would never get through our defenses and strike at the heartland of the United States. To begin with, the shortest and most apparent direction from which the enemy would come was over the northern polar regions. The Russian Bison and Bear bombers, then coming into service, had the capability of delivering nuclear weapons over this route, and until they were nearly upon us, we would not detect them. They would be flying over the vast polar regions that were totally uninhabited by all but a scattering of Eskimos and perhaps a few trappers.

With radar now developed to a great degree, picket lines were built across the northern regions of the North American continent. The first to be completed was the Pine Tree Line, which consisted of twenty-four long-range radars set across Canada and manned by both United States and Canadian personnel. That would provide some initial warning that the continent was under aerial attack, but it was soon decided that a line should be built even farther north

to give the absolute maximum warning time in the event of an over-the-pole attack.

The Pine Tree Line had been completed in 1955, and any enemy targets it detected were subject to attack by F-86 and F-94 fighters. This had been a start in the right direction. However, the new line, much farther north, was to reach an unbelievable level of sophistication in aerial defense. It was called the DEW (Distant Early Warning) line, and it stretched for over 3,000 miles across the North American continent and Greenland. It was roughly located on the Arctic Circle, the seventy-degree north parallel. When it became functional in 1958, it was operated by both the United States and Canada. Gigantic radar sights, four main and seventeen auxiliary, were maintained by the Canadians, and thirty-one stations were manned by the United States.

At the time, bombers were the principal threat to North America, and with the far northern location of the DEW line, the early warning would allow sufficient time to get interceptors into the air to stop those bombers. The radar intercepts had to be relayed to a central clearinghouse, a place for the quick

These two photos of 53-1810 show the aircraft before and after modifications to larger vertical fin, larger speed brakes and redesigned engine air inlets. (John Vadas Collection)

34

evaluation of incoming information and decisions on how to act on it. This center was located at Colorado Springs, Colorado, deep within a bomb-proof shelter in a mountain. It was manned by a joint United States and Canadian organization. Its official title was North American Air Defense Command (NORAD).

The next step, on receipt of enemy contact, was to take the information and disseminate it quickly to the interceptor squadrons. That was accomplished with SAGE (Semi-Automatic Ground Environment), which had six locations, two of which were in Canada. SAGE came into operation in 1957. The linking with the NORAD computers was accomplished in early 1963. With SAGE and the Hughes weapons system, which constituted a very important part of it, it became possible to do almost science fiction wonders in the defense of the two countries against bombers.

Starting with the initial contact made with the oncoming enemy bombers, still hundreds of miles north of the DEW line, the information was soon transferred to the NORAD headquarters for evaluation. If the decision was made to launch a counterattack, it could be handled in moments by notifying the appropriate SAGE base to scramble its fighters. They were on alert for takeoff within minutes after a command to launch.

When production started on the improved modified F-102A Delta Dagger the Air Force was not completely satisfied with it. But the brass considered it an interim fighter design and felt the F-106 Delta Dart would be the more ultimate design. There had been so much changing of the Dagger that it was at best a competent contender for the present scene, but the F-106 would have the advantage of all the learning curve that had attended the F-102. *It* was not a warmed-over design, but instead a fresh start on a fresh sheet of paper, with all the experimentation that had gone before it as a starting point for the super interceptor they really desired. Still, they needed something at once, and the F-102 was it.

By April 1956, the Air Defense Command went operational, using the F-102A with the 327th Fighter Interceptor Squadron being equipped at Grange Air Force Base, California. This was followed in August 1956 with the equipping of the 11th Fighter Interceptor Squadron of the 343rd Fighter Interceptor Wing. The new fighters were attractive, being painted a glossy pale gray, with large buzz numbers on their flanks along with the red, white and blue star and bar insignias. In the case of the F-102, the buzz numbers all began with "F," which denoted fighter, and "C," which denoted an F-102. The last three digits of the buzz number were the last three digits of the aircraft's serial number.

Pilots of these aircraft had *two* sticks: one to control the aircraft with and the other for the left hand, to control the sweep of the MG-10 radar as well as its range gate. While doing this, the pilot kept his eyes closely on the viewing screen of the radar scope. When locked on a target, he had a veritable arsenal of weaponry at his command. The aircraft, with its weapons bay, carried the six Hughes Falcon

An early F-102A deploys its drag chute for demonstration during landing at Eglin Air Force Base, Florida, on May 8, 1956. (USAF)

missiles that were either infrared- or radar-guided. In addition, in the weapons bay doors there were twenty-four unguided Mighty Mouse rockets with the nomenclature of FFAR's. They fired two at a time in twelve rapid pulses.

As the full production quantity of 899 fighters was built during the next few years, they came to equip over twenty-five squadrons of the Air Defense Command's forces. As a result, their service was very widespread.

They soon wound up in Thule, Greenland, as part of the DEW line, the picket line set up to warn of attack and take countermeasures against any over-the-ice-cap raids on the United States or Canada that might occur. It was a cold and hostile environment, but the F-102's were constantly at the ready for their interceptor mission. This duty began in June 1958.

Alaska and Europe came next for the deployment of the F-102, and this was soon followed by the Pacific theater of operations. For almost ten years, the Daggers were a familiar sight in the skies of Europe and the Pacific, as they performed their daily rounds of target interception practice.

Some fun was had with one of the early aircraft, 53-792, which, after serving as a test aircraft, found its way to the 68th FIS based at Itazuke Air Base in Japan in the early sixties. Lt. Col. Park Waldrop recalls, "792 was an oddball, having been retained at the Convair factory for some time as the test bed aircraft for a number of modifications proposed for the fleet. The most significant difference betwen it and any other 'Deuce' was the location of the two switches used to open the missile bay doors. And said difference was good for a few laughs. Whereas all other 102's I know of had these switches in the left main wheel well, 792's were located behind a canvas flap in the nose wheel well. The standard routine was to make sure a new guy got assigned to fly 792, then have everybody watch his preflight inspection. He would get around to the left gear well, reach for the familiar switches, and find them not there! It was a riot to see a guy frantically glancing around looking for something that just had to be there but wasn't, meanwhile trying to maintain the basic fighter pilot nonchalance and cool. And I can vouch for the feeling of panic experienced by the victim—I had my 'turn in the barrel' along with all the rest! By coincidence, the guy who had originally picked this bird up at Convair when it was finally released to the Air Force was assigned to the 68th FIS at Itazuke during the time I was there, and he well remembered his own introduction to that machine and its 'missing' missile bay door switches.

"In case you may wonder why the missile bays were a part of every preflight inspection: We were required to have a minimum of, I think, twelve aircraft 'hot loaded' all the time. This meant that many of our daily training sorties were flown with 'hot' aircraft. That wouldn't be too critical except that we also flew occasionally with a test missile loaded on one missile launcher rail (the other five rails empty) to check out the weapon system. This test involved actuating all the arming switches during a practice intercept, and pressing the trigger. The system reacted just as it would in a live intercept situation— the doors would open, the missile rail would extend and a fire signal would be delivered to that launcher rail. The test, or Weapon System Evaluator Missile

This early F-102A, 53-1813, appears to have had its vertical fin enlarged without the larger speed brakes and improved engine air ducts being added. (John Vadas Collection)

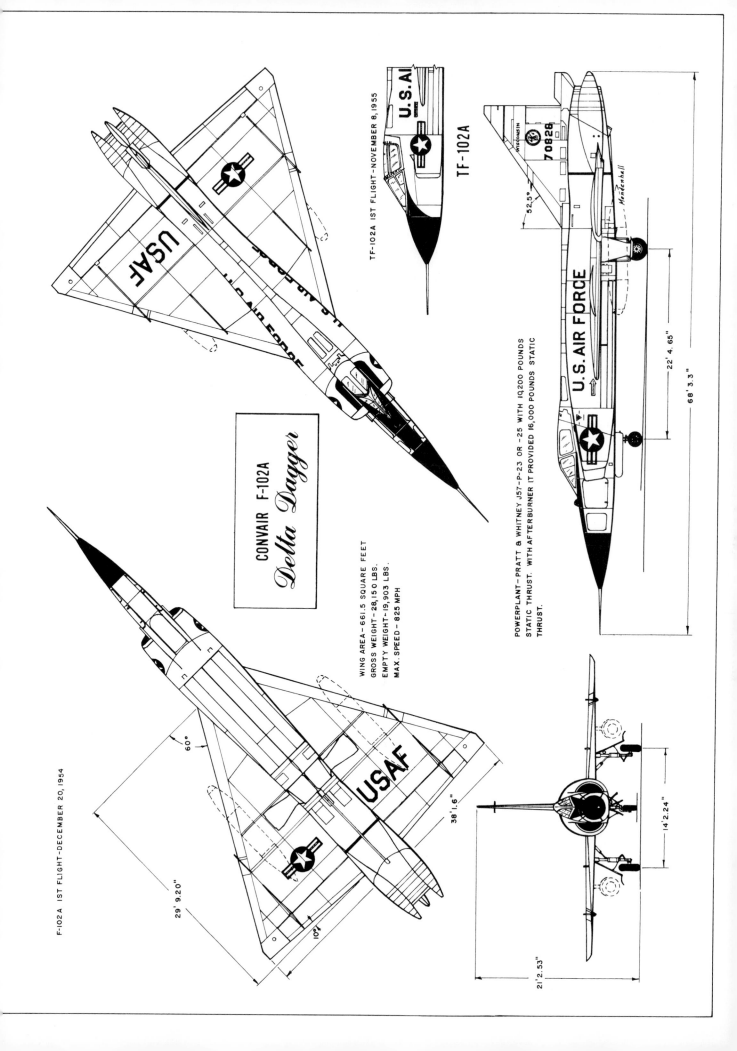

TF-102A 1ST FLIGHT—NOVEMBER 8, 1955

TF-102A

CONVAIR F-102A
Delta Dagger

WING AREA—661.5 SQUARE FEET
GROSS WEIGHT—28,150 LBS.
EMPTY WEIGHT—19,903 LBS.
MAX. SPEED—825 MPH

POWERPLANT—PRATT & WHITNEY J57-P-23 OR -25 WITH 10,200 POUNDS
STATIC THRUST. WITH AFTERBURNER IT PROVIDED 16,000 POUNDS STATIC
THRUST.

F-102A 1ST FLIGHT—DECEMBER 20, 1954

(WSEM), would record all the various signals sent to it by the system, including the reception of reflected radar energy off the target. Well, you can see the problem here. It would be a bit embarrassing to go through all this with a hot aircraft, thinking you had a test missile on board instead. So it was mandatory that the pilot confirm what kind of load he had by actual visual inspection before every flight. There were other precautions, too, having to do with 'safety wired' covers on the arming switches, but the visual check was the absolute confirmation that you had what you thought you had."

A real war was going on in Vietnam, however, and in March 1962, F-102's appeared for duty in that theater of operations. Here their job was to guard against the air forces of the communists in the north. Their job became so important that between 1967 and 1968 there was always a minimum force of at least fourteen F-102's on standby for immediate takeoff and the rest were on one hour call. As the big B-52's were ordered into the area, F-102's began to fly with them during their missions in the role of combat support. Their record was great from the

standpoint of safety and durability. During the entire campaign only fifteen F-102's were lost to all causes.

In December of 1969, however, they were all pulled out of Vietnam, as they were becoming a little on the old and tired side. By that time, the McDonnell F-4 Phantoms and the Republic F-105's were carrying the fight and, being later and more sophisticated warriors, were superior to the F-102 in most respects. However, it must be said that the brown and dark green camouflaged delta-winged fighter had fought the good fight without firing a shot in anger and left the theater with no hanging of its head.

Moving the F-102 around the world for various deployments was always interesting. True, in some cases they were simply placed aboard a carrier or other such vessel and deposited on a dock, by crane, at the destination. They were then transported by land to an airfield where they were checked over and test flown by a maintenance test pilot before being sent on to a line unit.

However, the long ferry flight type of aircraft movement was the more interesting. Lt. Col. Wilbur Wortham, Jr., took part in such a movement in Octo-

A nice three-quarter rear view of an early F-102A that is totally unmodified. Photo shows off deployed speed brakes, rear fuselage pods for area rule and large-area elevons. (Vic Seely)

ber 1969, when the F-102's were getting on in years. He was a pilot in the ANG, and the mission was to fly twenty-two F/TF-102A's from Bitburg Air Base in Germany to various ANG units in the United States. His story of the trip is typical of this type of high-density plane movement:

"On Saturday, 11 October 1969, Air National Guard pilots from several states began to assemble at Bradley International Airport, Connecticut. Captain Larry L. Leach and I flew in by commercial airline from Boise, Idaho.

"Sunday morning October 12 we assembled in the operations room at the Connecticut ANG facilities for briefing. Major Donald E. Joy, Jr., informed us that we would be flying twenty-two F/TF 102A aircraft from Bitburg, Germany, to various Air National Guard units in the United States. We would be under the operational control of the 2nd Aircraft Delivery Group at Langley AFB, Virginia, with the project titled *CORONET EAST 35.* We spent the entire day being mission briefed and outfitted with our survival equipment: basically a very uncomfortable water survival suit we referred to as our 'poopy suits.' The water survival briefings effectively convinced us that without the suits our survival time in the cold North Atlantic waters would be approximately six minutes, but with them we could hope to survive approximately 1/10 of an hour!

"I must say that the briefings had been well planned, effectively coordinated and professionally presented. I really felt fortunate to participate in the operation. I was a very small cog, but I could see the machinery was so well oiled and polished that it was a pleasure to be a part of it.

"Monday the thirteenth we loaded, along with our gear, on board a C-121 Super Constellation and flew to Otis AFB for supper and final checkout for international travel. We flew (what seemed like forever) to a middle-of-the-night landing at Lajes Field in the Azores Islands for fuel. We proceeded on up over the English Channel and entered Germany from the north and then back down to Bitburg Air Base. We arrived there very tired in the early afternoon on Tuesday the fourteenth. We were given a short in-briefing then released to get some rest. The weather was lovely and it was my first time in Europe, so I walked from the base into the small German town of Bitburg. I ate a fine meal in the local Hotel-Restaurant and walked back to the base after dark and got some real rest.

"Wednesday, the fifteenth, we reported to Operations and were given a complete briefing again on our flight route, emergency procedures, radio procedures, and we received the first chance to preflight our aircraft. I had been assigned 56-1077. It seemed strange to see an F-102 in camouflage paint. Our aircraft in the Idaho Guard were all painted in a gray paint with a fluorescent yellow trim. This machine looked more 'warlike.' Three of the twenty-two aircraft were to be delivered to the Idaho Air National Guard: 56-1057, 56-1076 and 56-1077. Captain Leach was assigned 56-1076 and we would be formation flying sister ships to Boise. We spent the day making sure everything was ready for the flight back to the States and were ready for a next morning departure.

"Thursday morning we woke up to fog, rain and low ceilings. We reported to Operations but the weather was below minimums so we received all our briefings from the day before again! We were all so 'briefed out' that we felt we knew everything we could be told. A weather delay is a most frustrating event for a pilot. We lounged around and waited and waited and waited . . . boring. Friday the seventeenth dawned the same way, but the weatherman forecasted better weather by noon. So we briefed and waited some more. Shortly after lunch the sun burned through a few holes and the ceilings lifted above minimums. We had time to launch half the fleet and get them on their way. Larry and I got airborne shortly after 1300 and were quickly above the clouds flying in beautiful sunshine. I was surprised by the 'accent' of the German air controllers, even though they spoke good English. I had never flown anywhere except in the States before and I really had to concentrate to understand all the radio transmissions.

"We proceeded almost straight north to the coast and out of Germany, then swung west over the North Sea to England. After we reached England we proceeded north. We were above a cloud deck the entire flight so we could not do much sightseeing. We were given a radar approach to Lossiemouth Air Base on the North Scottish coast. Having been above the clouds for the entire trip, I was not prepared for the beautiful sight that opened before me when we descended to land. I have never seen a land so brilliantly green—especially in October! Lossiemouth Air Base had beautifully manicured grass and flowers everywhere I looked. A lovely base with nice buildings and everything so spotless and well maintained.

"Our flight had taken 1.7 hours. We got our rooms and headed for the showers. Now came the second shock of the day. Their bath linens were just that—a small linen towel that was about as soft and absorbent as tent canvas! We all got dressed and went to the town of Elgin, Scotland, for the evening. We enjoyed the trip through the green Scottish countryside.

"Saturday, the eighteenth, we woke up to sunshine and beautiful VFR weather. We all headed to the flight line and prepared for our next leg of the journey. We were told the weather was good all the way to Keflavik, Iceland, but that we could expect some clouds and rain there. Just as our twelve planes were preparing to taxi for takeoff, the ten planes that had stayed at Bitburg the previous night were approaching to land. They would be behind us all day. We launched off and headed for Iceland. It was a beautiful trip with no problems. I was a little nervous over that much water in a single engine jet—but 077 was flying so well I soon settled down for a nice trip.

"We arrived 1.4 hours after takeoff and made a radar approach through light rain and thin clouds at Keflavik Airport, Iceland. While they were refueling our planes Larry and I went in to the Airport Terminal and bought some souvenirs and a fighter pilots lunch—two bags of peanuts and a Coke. We returned to our planes and were quickly headed west for Sondrestrom Air Base on the west coast of Greenland. This part of the trip was truly beautiful. The sky was clear and smooth, far below us the blue ocean was dotted with icebergs. Some of them must have been huge because from over 30,000 feet they looked like small islands. Crossing Iceland I was amazed at the tremendous expanse of ice. Ice fields as far as we could see in any direction. And at our altitude you could see a long way!

"I was grateful for the VFR weather for our arrival at Sondrestrom because the field is located in a fjord with steep mountains on either side and a fast rising ice field to the east. All approaches are from the west to the east and, once committed to land, there is little chance for a missed approach except in a very high performance aircraft.

"It had been a nice two-hour flight from Iceland. Even though the day was yet early because of the gain made in time zone changes we were all to remain overnight at Sondrestrom while the others caught up with us. I felt sorry for the pilots who had not been able to join us in Scotland last night, but we would all be together tonight in Greenland. The social life possibilities at Sondrestrom were limited at best! A sauna bath, some ping pong tables, a pool table and a small cafe! Boy, was I glad we would only be there overnight! All the rest of that day the aircraft continued to arrive. The sun sets early in October at Sondrestrom but the ramp was full of F/TF-102's that night. Everything was going very nicely.

"Sunday, the nineteenth, Larry and I were numbers seven and eight for takeoff bound for Goosebay, Labrador. This was the longest leg of our trip. We would be outside of navigational radio range for almost half of the flight. We would, however, be in communication with a C-130 Rescue Aircraft orbiting midway. The weather was not good at either Sondrestrom or Goosebay, but well above minimums at both bases and forecasted to remain so. Our flights were separated by twenty minutes, so one hour after the first two aircraft got airborne we were off and climbing above the clouds headed south. As we were flying we could hear the other flights in front of us talking to the C-130.

"It seemed that the weather at Goosebay was deteriorating. Just five minutes before Larry and I reached our point-of-no-return we were ordered to return to Sondrestrom because the aircraft landing at Goosebay had been caught in a blinding snow storm and the base was now closed because of the storm.

With drag chute out and speed brakes fully deployed, this Bitburg Base Deuce completes a landing rollout. (Daniel R. Kistler Collection)

We turned around and headed back to Sondrestrom. By now there were six more planes in front of us also returning to Sondrestrom, but they should be down before us, because Larry and I were the farthest away (and also the lowest on fuel). As luck would have it, the weather at Sondrestrom was also deteriorating and we would all have to make instrument approaches back into that narrow fjord! I did not like it—not one bit. We were going to be minimum fuel, in poor weather, making a strange field instrument approach to an airport that was not well situated. After a long, heart pumping, two-hour flight we were back at Sondrestrom, Greenland. The cold wind was blowing snow across the ramp and as we walked away from our planes that day we all wondered how long we would be weathered in at this hell hole! Why not back at Lossiemouth or even at Bitburg? Oh well, make the best of it and head for a sauna bath and hope for tomorrow.

"Tomorrow, the twentieth was no better, so we spent a dead Monday playing pinochle, ping pong and pool while it swirled snow all around our sleek jets parked outside.

A posed photo from the manufacturer shows off the clean lines of the Delta Dagger. That object resembling a wing fence on the vertical tail is actually the VHF antenna. (Convair)

"Tuesday the wind had stopped and the clouds raised above minimums again so the sixteen remaining airplanes were once more prepared for the long leg to Goosebay. This time Larry and I would be first off and we really hustled to get going. We had hopes of making three sorties that day and if all went well we would be at Pittsburgh, Pennsylvania, that night. Our flight to Goosebay went well, but when we got there we could see why we had been turned around on Sunday. Workers had plowed the snow away, but they must have had some storm because they sure had a lot of the soft white stuff piled everywhere!

"We quickly got fueled and headed for Bangor Field, Maine, where we were to clear customs. This was an uneventful process for me, but some of the pilots had stashed European wine and alcohol in every possible spot on the planes. One enterprising young pilot had rode all the way with his seat uncomfortably high because he had hidden wine under the seat! When questioned by customs he denied having anything to declare. How they suspected him I don't know, but they searched his plane and found over five cases of liquor. He paid a fine and had the excess confiscated—what he had planned to be a good investment had turned very sour!

"After clearing customs we were all free now to go our separate ways in the States. Larry and I wanted to reach Pittsburgh to spend the night. We headed south-west out of Bangor. Ten minutes later while still in the climb Larry called and declared an emergency. He had lost all his alternating current electrical power [vital to an F-102]. I got us clearances to the nearest military airport, Navy Bruns-

wick. We landed safely, but when we opened the bottom access panel to his generators a real nest of wire and broken parts fell to the ground. His AC generator had literally torn itself to bits and pieces. We made arrangements with the Maine Air National Guard to send a maintenance team and the needed parts to repair his plane. We had flown a total of 4.4 hours that day. How grateful we were that his emergency had occurred here rather than over the cold ocean waters when we were so far from emergency landing fields and maintenance assistance.

"Early Wednesday morning the Maine ANG maintenance men showed up with all needed equipment and really worked hard. Those boys really deserved our appreciation! They worked all day Wednesday and Thursday. It was ready for us that evening so we made a short forty-minute night flight over to Selfridge Air Force Base near Detroit.

"Friday the twenty-fourth Larry and I made three sorties, flying 5.2 hours, and arrived at our home station, Boise Air Terminal, Idaho.

"We had crossed the ocean and came half way around the world in eleven sorties and flown for 17.3 hours. 4.4 hours had been in IFR conditions and .6 hours and been nighttime. We were tired, pleased with our efforts and certainly willing to go again if the occasion should ever present itself."

One reason for the F-102's success was that all during its life it was subject to a constant update and modification program. Some of the progressive modification programs included such things as: newly introduced data link equipment, improved

Side view of an early production Deuce that has had the enlarged vertical fin, enlarged speed brakes and improved engine air inlets fitted during an update modification program. (John Vadas Collection)

42

MG-10 fire control, more advanced missiles, and newly installed infrared search and tracking systems.

As the Deuce got older some of them transferred to the Air National Guard. In the case of the Convair Delta Dagger, this was a good move. Not only were the aircraft a goodly supersonic step above the North American F-86 Sabres and such, they were also good training planes for the F-106 Delta Darts that were now beginning to appear on the scene in the regular Air Force. In the event the Guard was called up to active service during a conflict, its members would be nearly ready to assume command of the F-106's and to fly combat against the aggressor. Therefore, in 1961, the slow transition from USAF to ANG began, and the craft were to serve with the Guard until 1977, when they began to be phased out. The last were gone by the end of 1978.

Sometimes when the Air Force needs to get rid of semiobsolete equipment, the State Department comes to the rescue and, rather than scrapping the equipment, donates it to one of our less fortunate NATO allies. Turkey and Greece were selected to benefit from the reduction of the F-102 Dagger fleet.

Nineteen seventy-one saw the beginning of this transition from the USAF to NATO allies. Greece received twenty-four F-102A's and TF-102A's. The planes were operated by the 114 Wing of the 28th Tactical Air Command until 1977, when they were displaced by the newer Dassault Mirage F1CG's from France.

Turkey received thirty-five ex-USAF F-102A's and three TF-102A's, which went to two interceptor squadrons. Today, however, these aircraft are now struck from register.

Another use for semiobsolete fighter planes is their conversion to drones for use as targets for the new developments in the field of missile and air-to-air combat. So it was with the F-102's.

For every weapon there must be a target, and, as a corollary, to use every weapon effectively there must be the opportunity for target practice. What do you do for practice when the weapon's ultimate target is such sophisticated Mach 2 + aircraft as the Sukhoi SU-19, MiG-23 or MiG-25? The Communist countries, for sure, are not going to help out with the problem. Subscale targets such as the Firebee I and Firebee II are a start in the right direction, however, they are expensive, not too maneuverable and do not have the same type of radar signature as a fighter plane.

What was needed was a *real* fighter plane, albeit one without a pilot, so that practice warheads could explode into them and the whole war game would be completely realistic. Sperry Flight Systems had an answer. Sitting out in the desert boneyard at Davis-Monthan AFB were some F-102A's that were too tired for active duty but were flyable, supersonic and highly maneuverable. Sperry sold the idea of making target drones of the planes—radio-controlled target drones. Work began on the project in 1970, converting the F-102's into the Air Force's only full

External drop tanks each carrying 215 gallons of fuel are clearly defined during low-level flyby of a Deuce. (Daniel R. Kistler Collection)

scale, afterburning, supersonic highly maneuverable target. By January 10, 1974, they were ready for tests of a manned drone and by August 13, 1974, they had successfully flown an unmanned drone. As this is written, the PQM-102 has flown over 415 unmanned drone sorties, has made 1,123 hot armament firing presentations, has had 710 individual pieces of armament fired at it, and has sustained 122 hits, being "totally destroyed" seventy-seven times. The armament has been both in the form of air-to-air and ground-to-air missiles. In general, the air-to-air shooting has occurred at Tyndall AFB, Florida, and the ground-to-air practice at the White Sands Missile Range in New Mexico. The drones in New Mexico are actually operated out of Holloman AFB. They whistle over the missile range as low as 200 feet, presenting a target for the Army Stinger or Patriot ground-to-air missiles.

The conversion of an F-102A to a PQM-102 consists primarily of replacing the craft's ejection seat with an electronic control pallet, designed by Sperry, that slips into the existing seat rails. The official name for this unit is Flight Control Stabilization System (FCSS), and on man-rated drones (QF-102's), it is fitted into a compartment behind the cockpit.

The QF-102 aircraft system resembles the Mobile Ground Station and Fixed Ground Station control consoles and is used for controller training. The FCSS contains the following five major components: Flight Reference Computer, the basic flight control computational unit; Air Data Computer, computing Mach number, barometric altitude and calibrated airspeed; Interface Coupler, containing logic and control circuitry to engage and disengage modes and to take over in case of loss of ground control (to the point of aircraft self-destruct, if need be); High Altitude Maneuver Programmer, containing a backup autopilot and circuitry required to execute preselected commands; and Low Altitude Maneuver programmer, which is capable of performing three ground-settable command selected maneuvers at altitudes of a few hundred to 10,000 feet.

A Convair/Sperry PQM-102A is being prepared for a flight as a pilotless target drone. The drone presents about the same target size as the MiG-23 and -25 Russian fighter aircraft. (Sperry Flight Systems)

Other modifications to the aircraft to remake it into a QMF-102 are the addition of DIGIDOPS for a scoring system for near misses of missiles fired at the aircraft, a modified antiskid brake system and a twenty-eight-gallon oil tank to feed a smoke system for better target visibility.

Control of the PQM-102 is accomplished by two means. For takeoffs and landings a normal active runway is used, just as if a pilot were aboard. A double-decker Mobile Control Station is positioned alongside the runway so that the aircraft is in full view of the controller, very much like at the local radio control model flying field. After takeoff, the aircraft is handed off to a fixed ground control station that, with a two-man console team, then flies the aircraft through a carefully preplanned series of maneuvers by means of control panels containing normal flight instruments as well as radar. While the range of the mobile station is only about fifty miles, the more powerful ground station can reach out 200 miles. The normal mission length is from forty to fifty-five minutes, depending on altitudes and afterburner use. A typical mission might be as follows:

T − 2:15—Prepare target for launch.
T − :20—Target engine start.
T − :05—Prelaunch checks complete; chase plane airborne.
T − :00—Target launch under mobile control.
T + :05—Handover to Fixed Control Station on test range.
T + :10—Ready for presentations.
T + :30—Presentations complete.

T + :40—Handover to Mobile Control Station clear of test range.
T + :45—Recovery complete.

As for the people who man the consoles, many, if not most, are regular Air Force pilots with a wide range of experience. At Tyndall AFB, a typical example is Major Thomas M. Hammoms, who has flown the F-102 and F-106 since 1968, in overseas as well as continental FIS units.

Many wonder about the safety of having such a potent machine careening about the skies unmanned at speeds up to Mach 1.2 and altitudes between 200 and 56,000 feet, to say nothing of the unmanned craft's ability to sustain 8 g maneuvers without a pilot. Well, the designers thought about that one a lot. To have one of the QFM-102's out of ground control and, by fate, tangling with a manned aircraft, maybe even an airliner, would be the last word in being a klutz. Here's how they assure that such a disaster does not happen. First of all, a computer program is aboard that automatically assumes control of the aircraft if command signals from the ground are not forthcoming in 1.5 seconds. Backup is also built into the system, with a redundant auto-pilot, redundant command control and redundant automatic flight termination. (That last item means *it blows itself up* if all else fails.) After the aforementioned 1.5 seconds without ground signal, the aircraft automatically is directed to straight and level flight until the ground control signal is re-established or the flight is terminated.

This program is operated by independent backup electric and hydraulic power systems aboard the aircraft. If, for some reason, the ground signal is

Takeoff is made from a normal runway with the Mobile Control Station parked alongside. Once in the air the drone is handed off to the fixed control station whose pilots fly the aircraft through the target presentation phase of the flight. (Sperry Flight Systems)

not re-established after six minutes of this automatic operation, a fail-safe, fast-destruct mode is engaged aboard the aircraft, and after a preset interval of five to thirty seconds, the PQM-102 blows itself to bits. If, before all this transpires, the ground controller wants to wipe the plane out, he can—by means of an independent destruct command system on UHF, by a hardover control system command that flies the plane into the ground or by the normal redundant telemetry system used to control the aircraft. In any event, an uncontrolled PQM-102 will not go far before facing certain destruction, either by ground control or by its own suicide.

Requiem for the F-102? Of course. Back in her early design days in the late forties and early fifties, she had her problems. But didn't they all? The F-100 was fighting for its life as it took the daily tumbles through the blue stratosphere at Edwards, while scientists and engineers tried to unravel the secrets of the sound barrier on an operational basis. It was the same for the F-104 Starfighters and others fighting for contract continuance. The original data from the wind tunnel had been misleading, if not wrong. The engineering personnel of Convair had been misled, but they didn't stay down for long. They took a good look at the state of the art and came right back, using the area rule, and they built a good (in the words of the Air Force) interim fighter plane.

A sequence of photos showing the PQM-102A being approached, struck and destroyed by a missile. The graininess of the photos is due to their being taken from the ground at great distances from the target area. Air-to-air photography would be much too dangerous. (Sperry Flight Systems)

△ CHAPTER III
△ ETERNAL TRIANGLE MAKES GOOD

△——————————THE PREVIOUS CHAPTER COVered the F-102 from the standpoint of how it came to be and, roughly, its capabilities in the early sixties. This chapter is meant to deal more with the line fighter aircraft as it emerged, what it was as far as being a machine, and how it was operated.

A fine, but revolutionary aircraft it was indeed as it sat on the flight line. The long, slender needle nose faired into a fuselage that many thought reminiscent of the curvaceous Marilyn Monroe, movie goddess of the times. Others simply called it a "Coke-bottle" shape. To make it even more interesting, that wasp-waisted fuselage was carried aloft on pert, short delta wings unlike anything seen before in the annals of first line fighter planes. Along with the sleek dart-shaped wings was an equally sleek triangular vertical fin and a wedge-shaped cockpit. The craft sat there poised, almost ready to leap into the air from its wide-stance landing gear. If ever an aircraft reeked of speed, it was this one. Both Convair and the USAF were proud, for it represented a quantum jump forward in aero technology and stood as a real life embodiment of a successful breakthrough in aero design that most other nations and companies were afraid to touch with the proverbial ten-foot pole. It was *the* single-place, supersonic, all-weather interceptor, complete with radar fire control system, a powerful axial flow turbojet and a host of "first kid on the block" features.

Flying the critter, however, took some pretty fancy homework and a lot of flight training in lesser machines.

The complexity of an aircraft and its systems can usually be judged by the heft of the flight manual. The combined manual for the F-102A and TF-102A was about 400 pages, compared with about 120 pages for a North American P-51D Mustang of World War II or the pocketbook-size 45-page manual

47

for the de Havilland Mosquito. Never let it be said that the supersonic fighter jocks were behind the door when the smarts were passed out. To wade through and assimilate all the material in that manual, in addition to possessing a tremendous amount of flight experience before they even started to read it—well, they had to be right up there at the head of the class.

A romp through the manual, even for the casual aerophile, is an interesting experience—sort of what you always wanted to know about the Deuce but were afraid to ask. Starting from the ground up, the landing gear (yes, that mundane tricycle landing gear) had its share of interesting facets. To start with, those tires were not the soft superballoons on the family chariot. The nose-wheel tire got pumped up to 175 pounds per square inch, and the main gear tires went on up to 195 psi. Hard rubber would have served just as well, except for the heat dissipating qualities of the inflated ones. The tread of the main gear was a wide antiground loop, fourteen feet 2.25 inches, and the fore and aft distances (wheelbase to car buffs) between nose wheel and the main gear was twenty-two feet 4.65 inches.

The main gear retracted inward to the wing root and fuselage belly, while the nose wheel swung forward into the fuselage nose to a position just about under the pilot's feet. Retraction of the gear was accomplished by moving a wheel-shaped knob on the left front side of the cockpit to an up position. That movement was translated to an electrical switch that controlled hydraulic valving that moved the gear by hydraulic cylinders. The doors of the main gear were mechanically and hydraulically tied to the main gear struts and were automatically closed and opened when the gear went up and down. If, for some reason, the hydraulic system failed, the gear could be actuated by a backup pneumatic system.

Steering of the aircraft on the ground was accomplished by two methods, nose-wheel steering or differential braking. The latter method was usually not used, as it caused unnecessary tire and brake wear. By depressing a button on the control stick, the pilot could electrically activate hydraulic valving that controlled hydraulic cylinders on the nose-wheel strut to turn the wheel in either direction, up to about fifty degrees. The rudder pedals did the actual steering. Those cylinders also acted as shimmy dampers, without which the nose wheel would have shaken the plane to destruction during high-speed ground operation. The inboard side of the main wheels also contained the multiple-disc pneumatic brakes, which could be operated by a backup system should the main pneumatic system fail. Safety switches precluded the possibility of retraction of the gear with the aircraft on the ground.

In-the-air retraction took about four to six seconds, and it was accomplished before the aircraft reached 240 knots indicated airspeed on takeoff. A yellow radial on the airspeed indicator served as a reminder to the pilot that this was the maximum gear-down speed. The tires were rated for a maximum ground speed of 217 knots, so during an afterburner takeoff, the gear-up lever had to be moved to the retract position almost as soon as the aircraft broke ground so as not to exceed the gear-extended speed limit.

A wing-tank-equipped F-102A-90-CO sits on the ramp at Andrews AFB in May 1964. Note the "gum-ball machine"—the ball in front of the windshield. It is the housing for the infrared target acquisition seeker. It did not retract into the fuselage and aircraft fitted with it had been modified to carry the AIM-4C infrared homing missile. (AAHS Negative Library)

Lt. Col. Park Waldrop recalls that the early Deuces, up to about 53-1811, were "straight gear" F-102's, i.e., the main gear struts were essentially perpendicular to the wing from the side view. After that they were noticeably canted forward. Concerning this Waldrop said: "The significance of the gear configuration is that with the original straight strut the center of rotation was farther aft. This caused a bit of a problem in getting the nose up for takeoff. Skewing the strut forward shifted the center of rotation forward, of course, which had an effect the same as if the nose had been lightened. With the straight gear, one had to apply full aft stick to get the nose off the ground, and even then it wouldn't come up until almost liftoff speed of 140 knots. With the skewed gear, which was the only configuration treated in the

Two Idaho ANG Deuces in close formation—31087 is flown by (now) Lt. Col. Wilbur R. Wortham, Jr., KSANG. The other aircraft, 41397, was eventually used in a structural fatigue test to determine F-102 airframe life expectancy. The wings were literally broken off and the rest of the airframe destroyed in the test. (Lt. Col. Wilbur R. Wortham Collection)

Flight Manual, you were supposed to begin raising the nose at 125, and do so smoothly at a rate that would put you at the proper pitch attitude for takeoff just as you reached 140. We were graded on how smoothly we did this during our training in the 102 at Perrin AFB, where the Advanced Interceptor (F-102A) course was located in the 1961 time frame.

"It was important to brief a new pilot in the squadron at Itazuke on the quirks of the straight gear birds in order to avoid disconcerting surprises. When one is used to the nose coming up when he applies back stick pressure at 125 knots, then gets to that point in a takeoff and has absolutely no response when the back stick is applied, it is a bit worrisome! A couple of new folks aborted takeoffs when this happened to them. One naturally assumes that there's something wrong with the control system when an expected response doesn't happen!

"It was also important to remember you were flying a straight-gear bird at landing time. With the skewed gear, you would touch down at 125, hold the nose up for aerodynamic braking effect until about 100, then lower it smoothly. But with the straight gear, if you did this the nose would come crashing down on the runway due to 'heaviness' caused by the farther aft center of rotation about the main

This photo, taken January 23, 1958, shows an F-102A of the 317th FIS on its way to runway and takeoff on an alert mission. The snowy location is Elmendorf Air Force Base, Anchorage, Alaska. (USAF)

A Montana ANG F-102A ramp sits in the cold with its electronics bay and cockpit wrapped in a special protective blanket. (AAHS Negative Library)

50

wheels. Thus with these birds, you had to begin lowering the nose a bit earlier, when you had better control effectiveness, so that it could be done gently."

With respect to the gear doors being retracted in time, Waldrop recalls, "There was also a very noticeable difference in the ability of the fairing doors to withstand high airspeeds with the gear extended. With the straight-gear aircraft, you stood an excellent chance of losing the main gear fairings if you exceeded the 200 knot limit at all. In the two and a half years I was at Itazuke, I can recall three or four times that this happened. Evidently when the struts were re-engineered, the fairings were strengthened too, as the skewed-gear birds could be flown above the 'red line' speed with little chance of damage."

Another ground-related item that found its way onto the F-102A was the tail hook, similar to that on the Navy's carrier aircraft. With a tail hook, an aircraft with a blown main gear tire, a landing gear not down and locked, or even a landing gear that would not extend could be brought to a quick stop before the aircraft lost complete directional control and ran off the runway, inflicting damage to itself and probably to the pilot. The hooks were installed in the early sixties on some of the Century Series aircraft, such as the F-100, F-102 and F-104. The mating energy-absorbing-tape ground gear set up at the pilot's request on the approach end was called, in Air Force parlance, the BAK-9, BAK-12 or BAK-13. By extending the system tape across the runway, along with foaming the runway, the stricken aircraft's hook could engage the tape and it would be dragged to a hasty stop.

While this hook-type landing may have been completely routine for Navy carrier pilots, it certainly was not for the Air Force types. Sooner or later, though, the day had to come when some unfortunate fellow would have to use it for the first time. Since a tire blown at takeoff could be disastrous on landing (at the time the Air Defense Command had recorded about a one-in-four chance of wiping the plane out under those conditions), once the hooks were installed, it behooved the pilot to use the hook, no matter how many misgivings he had about the untried (for him) operation.

It was a warm, sunny July afternoon at the German Bitburg AFB when Capt. Leslie J. Pritchard, of the 525th FIS, released brakes and kicked in the afterburner of his F-102A to start his takeoff roll. He was flying right wing in a two-ship flight, both planes carrying full external drop tanks. At liftoff rotation and about 145 knots, Pritchard's left main tire blew, and his Dagger swerved toward his flight leader. While still on the ground, a midair collision appeared imminent. With a flurry of cockpit activity, Pritchard maneuvered right rudder, brake and aileron. He averted a collision, but was unable to abort the takeoff: The plane was airborne. The lead ship dropped back and looked the situation over. The tire was indeed blown. However, no other damage was

Another Montana ANG Deuce ramp sits in much better weather conditions. The "vision splitter," the black opaque wall that separates the triangular windshield into two distinct halves, is clearly shown. (AAHS Negative Library)

evident. The gear was retracted, and with two full drop tanks there was a spell to think the thing out. The Squadron Operations Officer soon decided it was time to test the new-fangled arrester hook on the disabled plane. Ground personnel radioed Pritchard the recommendation. Pritchard had never heard of such a landing being undertaken (in fact, the USAF hadn't performed one yet), but he had read an article that discussed the feasibility of such an undertaking. His first reaction was "no way." His actual reply was something along the lines of: "I don't know about that s__t . . . I haven't practiced it very often." However, after some cajoling from the ground and considering the benefits he would reap by using the arrester hook, Pritchard consented to give it a go.

All airborne aircraft were recalled to base, and a crash truck was positioned at the runway's approach end. Pritchard was told to jettison the wingdrop tanks, which he tried to do, but the cam-stop bolts were overtorqued and the tanks wouldn't blow. The tanks were by then empty, however, and that helped some. He let the hook down, he hoped, and made a low pass down the runway. Ground control assured him the hook was down, and the moment of truth arrived.

Pritchard locked his shoulder harness and set up for a five-mile, straight-in approach: gear down and speed brakes extended. He was now fairly light, so he flew a flat power-on final at about 170 knots, reducing speed to 160 knots over the overrun threshold, and set down on the overrun at about 140 knots. He popped the drag chute, lowered the nose and engaged the steering. The vibration from the blown tire was terrific; it rechannellized the radio, failed the wheel brakes and resulted in the loss of the drag chute just before reaching the BAK-9 cable. By this time the plane was angling toward the left side of the the runway. The hook caught the cable, and the F-102A came to a smooth halt after dragging out 720 feet of tape. Had the BAK not been used, the plane would have gone off the runway at 60 to 70 knots, probably wiping out the gear, or worse. The aircraft's engine was kept running until the rescue personnel stowed the hook. The hook had gotten pretty hot, dragging down the pavement, and there might have been a danger of fire from fuel discharge after engine shutdown. Pritchard headed for the officers club bar for a well-deserved drink and reflected on events of the day. He received a "well done" award and the tail hook itself, mounted on a

A Convair TF-102A of the 123rd FIS, Oregon ANG, sits ready for a sortie at the Portland Airport June 1970. This aircraft is different from the F-102A in that it had a special side-by-side cockpit for pilot training. Aircraft was supersonic only when in a slight dive. (AAHS Negative Library)

plaque with the inscription "Another first—without practice!"

Another ground-oriented device was the drag chute; the poor man's answer to reverse thrust, some say. The chute, of the ring-slot or ribbon type, was packed in a deployment bag and stored at the base of the rudder with the speed brakes serving as the chute compartment doors. It was designed to cut down the landing run and did so, with as much as eighty percent more stopping power on wet runways than if the brakes alone were used. It was to be deployed only after the main wheels were on the runway during a landing or on an aborted takeoff. The maximum deployment speed was 160 knots indicated air speed. Above that speed the chute just broke off, a safety feature that kept it from adding a tremendous

Two photos showing what can happen if a mechanic puts the J57 in afterburner without the plane being chained down. After a high-speed 360° spiral around the ramp, aircraft came to rest after bashing up a TF-102A and two other F-102A's plus an assortment of corrugated metal work sheds. Accident took place in Spain. Three of the aircraft were repaired. (Frank Merrill Collection)

Hickam AFB, Hawaii, was home for this TF-102A of the Hawaiian ANG in September 1968. (AAHS Negative Library)

A salvo of three Falcon missiles leave an F-102's launching rails and head for their target at Mach 3 speed. Range of rocket is about six miles. (Hughes Aircraft Company)

A photo taken at the William Tell Meet at Tyndall AFB, Florida, shows an F-102 letting go with a Hughes Falcon missile at a jet target drone. (USAF)

amount of drag while the aircraft was airborne, possibly causing a stall. Pneumatic pressure operated the deployment mechanism, and the shroud lines were covered with heat-protective strips to prevent their meltdown from the heat of the jet exhaust.

After landing, as long as the chute was deployed by forward movement of the aircraft, it was ok to carry it along. If it deflated due to rain, crosswinds, low forward speed or otherwise, and the aircraft was off the active runway, it was to be jettisoned. On downwind taxis, with a fifteen-knot tailwind, the chute had to be gotten rid of fast, as it could be blown into the hot engine exhaust and burned up. The means of activating the chute was by pulling a handle (shaped like a parachute for easy identification) on the left of the instrument panel.

Pulling the handle opened the speed brakes, regardless of the speed brake selector switch position, since the brakes were also the compartment doors for the chute. Put another way, the speed brakes could be deployed independent of the chute, but the chute could not operate without the speed brakes. Pushing the handle fully *in* jettisoned the chute after it had been deployed.

As long as the speed brakes are under discussion here, a few words about them are in order. Sometimes called "boards," they were hydraulically actuated but controlled by electric solenoid valves switched from the cockpit. Their use was, of course, to extend into the airstream and produce a significant increase in frontal cross-sectional area, thereby creating a lot of drag and a significant reduc-

An aircraft from the 525th FIS stationed at Bitburg A.B., Germany, is shown at San Pablo, Spain, in 1962. Maintenance test pilot Frank Merrill is about to take off. (Frank Merrill Collection)

tion in airspeed. The speed brakes were built strong and could be deployed at any speed the aircraft could reach. Their deployment changed the aerodynamic characteristics of the aircraft. The plane tended to pitch nose up upon brake extension and nose down when they were retracted. The brakes were controlled by a switch on the throttle lever that had three positions: in, out and neutral. The neutral position was used when the brakes were retracted, to take the hydraulic pressure out of the system and thus avoid at least one place where leaks might occur during operation of the aircraft. As with other hydraulically operated systems on the F-102, the backup was the high-pressure pneumatic system,

F-102A of 103rd Fighter Group, Connecticut ANG at Bradley Field, Connecticut, August 1969. (AAHS Negative Library)

The flight line at Boise sported this brown and green camouflaged F-102A in November 1971. Aircraft was from the 190th FIS of the Idaho ANG. (AAHS Negative Library)

which could extend the brakes if all else failed. Somewhere between the final approach speed of 170 knots and the touchdown speed of 130 knots, the brakes were put out for landing. They were important and effective enough that the area of the brakes was increased (on their upper side), as may be seen comparing photos of earlier and later F-102A models.

Still looking the aircraft over, while on the ground, the weapons bay was of interest. When closed you would never know it was there, for it appeared to be the skin of the lower midfuselage. When opened, however, the doors were in two folding sections that moved together, one on either side of the centerline of the aircraft, with a resultant three openings in the bottom of the fuselage. The outer two, one on either side of the fuselage, were for the Falcon missiles and their retractable launching rails.

On either side of the fuselage, narrow fairing doors were also opened to allow for the wide-open fuselage bottom openings required to lower the Falcon missiles into the airstream and launch them. The doors themselves were more than weapons bay coverings, as they contained twenty-four 2.75-inch folding fin unguided rockets, six in each of the four main door panels. There were three launching tubes in each of the doors, and each missile tube held two missiles, one in front of the other. Usually only one

missile was placed in each door tube, as there was the possibility of the rear missile being blocked in the passageway by debris left from the firing of the front missile. If that happened, the rear missile could explode on launching, for it could not leave the door, and it was then goodbye door . . . or worse. Therefore, only in the event of a hot war were all twenty-four missiles to be carried, and of course that never happened.

Other missile malfunctions could also occur with the Falcons, all worrisome; all serious. With the missile doors opened and the launching rails deployed, two types of missile malfunctions were possible: hang-fire and misfire. A misfire occurred if the missile was triggered but did not move on the launching rails. A hang-fire occurred if the armament moved on the rails without leaving them. Then the pilot, with a missile hanging out the open armament doors on its rail, had a problem. The intervalometer had instructed it to fire and the missile was still there. If, after a five minute interval the missile still had not ignited and left the aircraft, there was only a small chance it might go. Therefore, all switches were returned to a position to neutralize the missile firing. In the event of a hang-fire, retracting the missile was out of the question, unless some sort of real emergency existed, like needing to get the hell out of the area without being shot down by an

A Hughes Falcon missile is fired during the 1970 William Tell Meet by an F-102A of the 179th FIS Minnesota ANG. (USAF)

enemy. If lucky, it would only be a misfire and the missile could be retracted and the bay doors closed. If it was a hang-fire, the retraction would go only so far before an entanglement with the missile doors occurred and everything would be sort of bent up on the aircraft's bottom section, a dire situation at that point.

Aside from its war-making capabilities, the F-102's missile bay, on at least one occasion, came in for a much more bizarre use: the world's most expensive food freezer. After all, the aircraft *did* sell for $1,184,000 a copy. In July 1958, AF T/Sgt. Donald Loewen recalls that the Air Force went on worldwide alert because of a crisis in Lebanon. The 317th FIS deployed aircraft (F-102's) to Alaska from California. During that period the Alaskan king salmon were running, and the pilots and airmen, when not on duty, were hauling in fifty-pound examples of the magnificent fish. The fish were then frozen in the mess refrigerators for later consumption. Within four days the alert was called off, and the squadron made ready to head back to California. The big problem was how to get the fish back. Sharp Air Force minds soon solved the tactical problem, with the returning aircraft's armament bays carrying three radar-guided Falcons, three infrared Falcons and many assorted

salmon. It was never learned if a hang-fire could be encountered because of a massive fish getting in the way of a missile.

Except for abrupt rolling, there were no limitations on maneuvering the Deuce at any speed with the missile bay doors open. A look at photos of the aircraft with the doors open show them beefy enough to take the supersonic speeds in stride, without blowing off in the airstream.

Another, much smaller, opening on the lower starboard side of the F-102's underfuselage was the home of the RAT. This was not a rodent but a Ram Air Turbine, which could be moved out into the airstream, where a ten-bladed, variable pitch fan would drive a hydraulic pump should the two engine-driven hydraulic pumps cash-in due to engine failure or such. Under those conditions, a RAT was man's best friend, for it could provide enough hydraulic pressure to deploy the speed brakes, lower the landing gear and provide a reasonably responsive hydraulic flight control system during the landing phase of a flight. The only real limitations on using the RAT were its maximum speed deployment of 345 KIAS, above which it would overspeed and cause structural damage, and its minimum flight speed of 125 KIAS, below which the device became

F-102A of the 190th FIS, 124th FTR Group of the Idaho ANG taken at Boise October 11, 1971, trim colors were lime green and black. (AAHS Negative Library)

ineffective. Of course, at that low airspeed the whole aircraft became ineffective anyway, so it really didn't matter. It was time to punch out.

The pitot boom that stuck out several feet in front of the aircraft's nose cone looked like the stinger on some insect, except it was on the wrong end. Up close, it was not quite so slender, being almost three inches in diameter at the base and at least an inch in diameter at the tip. At its end was mounted the pitot tube head, a most important part of the aircraft's systems. This tube supplied static pressure to the airspeed indicator, the landing gear warning pressure switch (that was a system to prevent wheels-up landings), the engine pressure ratio gauge (so important to determine takeoff power) and the automatic fire control system (AFCS). Two other static pressure tubes that were a part of the system were mounted on the leading edge of the vertical fin. They supplied air pressure to the artificial feel device for the elevons and rudder. All three tubes had electric anti-ice systems, as it was important that they be clear and working under all conditions. It *was* an all-weather fighter, although some said this merely meant the plane did not melt in the sun or rain.

Directly behind the nose boom was the black, unpainted plastic nose cone or radome. It not only gave the fuselage nose a slick streamlined shape, but it also held the search radar dish and it had to be deiced under icing conditions. This was accomplished by forcing a glycol solution through a porous ring at the base of the nose boom. The airflow spread the deicing liquid over the nose cone. The glycol tank held two gallons of the liquid.

Behind the search radar dish were the radar transmission and receiving electronics, and to the rear of these were the racks for the preponderance of the MG-10 fire control system: all 1,425 pounds of its black boxes, although some components did overflow beside and beneath the pilot.

Starting on the outside of the plane and working in, the cockpit had a sharp triangular windshield followed by faired side windows. The flat windshield side pieces were held in heavy riveted metal frames, to withstand the high-speed airflow as well as to provide a knifelike low drag entry into the airstream for the cockpit. The windshield was divided into three areas by heavy electrical heating strips, which defrosted the two rear sections. The small front triangle was defogged with hot air. An opaque vision splitter ran from the windshield center frame to the top of the instrument panel to reduce cockpit reflections. This windshield worked out well for high-speed flight and was later adopted almost unchanged for the X-15.

The canopy itself was hinged at the rear when opened and rose high and out of the way for cockpit entry. It was a rather complex device compared to the old "just pull it ahead and latch it" bubbles found on previous piston-engine planes and early jet fighters. One interesting feature was the inflatable rubber molding that was installed around the canopy to seal the canopy, the fuselage, and the windshield frame. This seal maintained cabin pressure and was

A graceful sight—this Deuce—just before touchdown at Bitburg A.B., Germany. Airspeed during landing flare is about 135 knots. (Daniel R. Kistler Collection)

automatic when the canopy latch handle was pushed fully in. An initial pull of the latch handle dumped the pressure. A pneumatic cylinder counterbalance helped to raise or lower the canopy. It was located in front of the hinge point, to the rear of the pilot.

Other miscellaneous features of the canopy included a removable canopy ground support tool that fit between the canopy and its sill to hold the canopy open under all conditions. This prevented broken fingers, hands or arms should the heavy component fall inadvertently. A canopy knife could be used in case of entrapment in the cockpit after a forced landing. "Superman" could use it to break out through the glass in about two minutes; "So-so man" could do it in about ten minutes; and "no muscles" couldn't do it at all. All the more reason for the pilots to do their morning pushups!

The canopy was also an integral part of the ejection system. The ejection seat would not fire if the canopy was still in place. There was no value in bashing a pilot's skull as he rammed through the canopy at high speed due to the ejection seat cylinder moving him upward into the airstream. In the event an eject became imperative, the canopy could be jettisoned and, if that didn't work, it could be unlocked and thrust manually into the airstream, which would rip it off the aircraft. In any event, the canopy had to go before the pilot could eject. If the canopy was jettisoned below 125 knots, it would probably strike the vertical fin, but that usually did not result in loss of control.

An Air National Guard pilot, James A. Dykes, found out that the rip-off feature did not function below 150 knots. On a scramble out of Honolulu, Hawaii, he was passing through 1,000 feet when he noted the red canopy warning light on and the canopy handle sticking out. He attempted to jam the handle in. The cinch-down mechanism broke, and the canopy popped open. He found himself with all the dirt from the cockpit floor swirled into his face and unable to hear anything in his headset because of the airstream roar in the cockpit. By this time, the cockpit was wide open. He reduced speed and lowered the gear to determine whether the aircraft could be landed that way without stalling. That open cockpit made one hell of a speed brake. He found he could control the craft at landing speed and came in without further incident. The only damage was to the middle area of the rear of the canopy.

The ejection seat was a great idea. In the event of an emergency the seat, pilot and his parachute would be thrown automatically clear of the aircraft. At that point, the pilot would part company with the seat, his chute would open and he would float down unscathed. Certain publications even claimed that this was a viable procedure regardless of the aircraft's altitude and speed—including zero speed and

The business end of a Hughes Falcon infrared homing missile as it looks when extended on its firing rails. F-102A rail structure looks very sturdy when viewed up close. (J. Fetchko Collection)

zero altitude. Such a condition was really never tested on the F-102, or on anything else at that time. What Convair and the Air Force really recommended was that if a pilot was straight and level about 2,000 feet, he should pull the nose above the horizon, eject, and he would probably live to be a little old man. If the aircraft was really going crazy, 12,000 feet were needed to escape safely and attain the desired goal of little old man. In either case, it was much less of a routine circus act at low altitude than some of the public relations materials of that time might have had you believe. Ejection from anything under 2,000 feet became a gamble, with the chances decreasing as the height above ground became less. At zero-zero you could just about forget it.

Ejection, by the numbers, went something like this: stow all loose equipment; tighten strap of helmet and lower visor; set cabin air switch to RAM to prevent explosive decompression (if at high altitude); aim aircraft toward uninhabited area; set throttle to off position; sit erect with arms braced in armrests and tight against the body, head hard against the headrest and feet back against the seat; and—with a deep breath—it was time to leave the airplane.

The ejection procedure itself, and the sequence of events that followed, were: The hand grips on the seat sides were raised, jettisoning the canopy and exposing the ejection triggers, which were squeezed (either one could do the job). The seat was then catapulted from the aircraft at high speed to avoid the vertical fin and a lanyard played out between the aircraft and the seat for about sixteen feet, which tended to stabilize the seat. A further line began a snubbing action that started at twenty-four feet, completing its job at sixty feet above the cockpit. By this time the safety belt had been automaticaly released from the pilot, and the seat was snubbed to a stop with the airman and parachute continuing upward and the external pilot chutes deploying to pull the main parachute from its pack. At that point, the automatic chute opener deployed the main chute and a spreader gun fired to open the canopy. It all happened fast, but with just a little luck the pilot was on his way safely to the ground.

In the case of the TF-102A, with its side-by-side seating, it should be noted that either pilot could eject independently of the other without harm to the one remaining in the cockpit.

Being as sophisticated as they were, the cockpit interiors of the F-102A and TF-102A were quite complex with instrumentation. This instrumentation not only filled the conventional instrument panel at the front of the cockpit, but also covered consoles that ran along the sides of the cockpit on either side of the pilot, or pilots, in the case of the TF-102A. In the case of the latter, there were three consoles, one being located between the pilots. While *full* details of the cockpits are outside the scope of this book, a closer look at their makeup is in order.

In the case of the F-102A, the instrument panel in front of the pilot contained a large fire-control radar scope located at top center, with the flight attitude instruments located directly below it. These included an airspeed/Mach indicator, altimeter, radio magnetic direction indicator, MM-3 attitude indicator, vertical velocity indicator and compass (or course indicator). With those you knew how high you were, how fast you were going and in what di-

Nose-to-the-grindstone—except too much so. This 102A on Okinawa was getting old when the nose gear gave way. (Jim Monaco Collection)

rection. To the right of these were primarily the engine group, i.e., tachometer, fuel flow indicator, exhaust gas temperature, fuel quantity gauge, hydraulic pressure gauge, and the all-important engine pressure gauge. Located in the same area was the master warning light, with the individual warning lights panel located below the engine instruments. Also on this side were the canopy latch, AC voltmeter and assorted switches. On the left of the flight attitude instruments were such things as the drag chute release handle, landing gear controls and indicators, external tank controls and releases, clock, and arrest hook release handle. Across the bottom of the instrument panel was a narrow subpanel that held the utility switches, with a lighting control panel hanging down from the center of it.

In the left seat of the TF-102A, the instrument panel arrangement was much the same as in the F-102A; however, the instructor's panel for the right seat was primarily confined to flight instrumentation.

The consoles, right and left, were as complex as the instrument panel itself. The left console, starting at the aft end, contained switches, oxygen mask and anti-g suit controls, ciphony and fuel system control panels, the UHF command radio control panel, the throttle quadrant, the armament auxiliary control panel and the oxygen control panel. The right console, for things electrical and electronic, contained, starting at the aft end, the circuit breaker panel, chaff control panel, IFF/data link antenna selector panel, J-4 compass control panel, data link

The usual delta wing high angle of attack landing is demonstrated here by the prototype TF-102A. Shape of the TF-102A's engine air intake was very different from the F-102. First flight was November 8, 1955. (Collect Air)

An overhead view shows the difference between the TF-102A and the F-102A. The TF was a side-by-side cockpit pilot trainer and, to maintain the same CG, had a considerably shorter nose. (USAF)

control panel, IFF and ILS control panels, the instrument selector panel, TACAN and radar control panels and the electrical power control panel.

The left cockpit of the TF-102A had a console arrangement similar to that of the F-102A. The right seat, however, was somewhat different in that the center panel was similar to the F-102A's right panel, which put it on the left of the instructor pilot. The instructor pilot's right console contained his throttle quadrant interphone control panel, some oxygen controls and circuit breakers. One other item of interest was the optical sight that hung down in front of the pilot from the apex of the F-102A's triangular windshield frame.

Two cockpit items that will be covered in a bit more detail are the throttle quadrant and the control stick. The throttle quadrant contained the fuel control switch, ignition button, speed brake switch and microphone button. Also located in that small pedestal were the hydraulic emergency power handle and the rudder trim switch.

The control stick stuck upward between the pilot's legs like a heavy two-tined pitchfork. It was a masterpiece of packing all the functions a pilot might want in a hurry into a small space. The left tine, or control grip, contained such items as an anti-jam button, antenna elevation wheel, auto-search button and action trigger. With that control grip, the radar was managed and locked on the target. The right control grip was actually the pilot's stick, in conventional terms, with the nose-wheel steering engagement button, the microphone and elevon trim switches located at the top. The emergency damper disconnect switch was also located there. The armament trigger, which protruded outward from the control grip, was to be squeezed when and if the big moment arrived. Between the two grips was the optical sight switch, nose-tail switch and a left grip lock so that the two control grips moved as one.

With drag chute out, and early model small speed brakes deployed, TF-102A rolls out during landing. Vortex generators were added around cockpit to smooth the flight in the high transonic speed ranges. (Convair)

Directly behind the cockpit was the upper electronics compartment and, behind this, the powerful Pratt & Whitney J57-P-23A turbojet engine that provided the aircraft with 10,200 pounds of static thrust at sea level military power and 16,000 pounds with the afterburner lit. The J57 was of twin spool construction, with axial flow compressors. The term "twin spool" meant that the engine had two rotors revolving on concentric shafts. Each rotor consisted of a compressor and a turbine section. A characteristic of this arrangement was that the ratio of the turbine discharge pressure to the compressor inlet pressure was a more reliable indication of thrust than engine rpm. One percent variation in rpm resulted in about five percent variation in thrust at higher thrust settings. However, one percent variation in turbine discharge pressure resulted in only one and one-half percent variation in thrust.

The nine-stage low-pressure compressor was mounted on the solid inner concentric shaft of the engine and was driven by a two-stage turbine. The seven-stage high-pressure compressor was mounted on the hollow shaft that rotated around the solid, inner low-pressure system shaft, and it was driven by a single-stage turbine. Each compressor-turbine set rotated independently of the other. A compressor air-bleed system was used to direct part of the low-pressure compressor air overboard at low engine speeds to aid in fast engine acceleration. That was controlled automatically by a governor driven by the low-pressure rotor.

The combustion section of the engine consisted of eight burners that were interconnected in an annular configuration. The main engine accessory section was driven by the high-pressure rotor and provided reduction gearing and mounting pads for

Among the last F-102's built, this unusual photo shows the Falcon missiles deployed on their launching rails. (Collect Air)

Ground crewmen work in missile bay preparing this TF-102A for flight. The aircraft has been fitted with an infrared target acquisition seeker—the ball in front of the cockpit. (Ken Myers Collection)

the engine-driven accessories, such as fuel pumps and hydraulic pumps.

Two ingredients were needed to make the J57 come to life: fuel and air. Aside from the two 215-gallon external tip tanks that were sometimes carried, the aircraft's main fuel source was the internal tanks located in the wings. Each wing contained three tanks, and except for the space needed for landing gear retraction, these nearly took up the entire wing's interior volume. The number one tanks were near the wing tips and behind the spar that ran aft of the landing gear. They contained 141.5 gallons each. Inboard from them, and with the same width, were the number three tanks, containing 150 gallons each. In the triangular section forward of the spar, in front of the landing gear wells, were the number two tanks that contained 251 gallons each. This totalled 1,085 gallons, or 7,053 pounds of JP-4 carried internally in the aircraft. The addition of the external tip tanks brought fuel totals to 1,515 gallons, or 9,848 pounds. If you imagine a stack of twenty-eight fifty-five-gallon drums, it gives you some idea of the volume.

The fuel was pumped to the engine and afterburner nozzles by accessory-drive fuel pumps. Tanks were managed by the fuel system controls located on the left console, as mentioned before. Range and endurance of the F-102A depended as much on altitude and speed of the aircraft as it did on the quantity of fuel on board. Therefore, careful preflight planning was the rule of the day when undertaking a mission. Maximum allowable airspeed with the external tanks was Mach .95 or 435 KIAS, whichever came first. The tanks could be safely jettisoned at any speed below that. The pilot's manual also cautioned not to use full or abrupt rudder, as that could produce forces exceeding the design limitations of the aircraft. Of course, the actual fuel flow to the engine and afterburner was controlled by the throttle. The air required for the engine was admitted through the ducts located on either side of the fuselage near the cockpit. Hot engine bleed air was used to keep them deiced in cold weather operations.

That about concludes the fuselage rundown, except to mention that titanium alloy frames were used in the engine area to compensate for the heat. Most of the rest of the fuselage structure was aluminum.

The wings were built with five forged one-piece spars in each wing. They were covered with aluminum alloy skins that were machined to shape from blocks of aluminum. The elevons were of bonded honeycomb construction, which gave them lightness, rigidity and great strength. They were actuated by a dual hydraulic system that served as its own backup. The vertical fin structure was similar to that of the wing.

In the area of the aircraft's flight characteristics, there are many items of interest. Optimum performance was realized when the cg was maintained close to the aft limit, as less trim was required on the elevons, thus reducing trim drag. Control response was good at all speeds, even though there was a "snaking" motion in the transonic speed range, which could be damped by the yaw damper system. While

A posed company publicity photo shows Hughes test pilot Chris Smith looking over a Hughes AIM-26A Nuclear Falcon. The other missiles are an AIM-4A radar guided weapon on the left and an AIM-4C infrared guided Falcon on the right. (Hughes Aircraft Company)

this system trimmed out the yaw oscillations, a pitch damper performed the same duties in the pitch mode. However, that old devil roll, or inertia coupling, was still there, waiting to give a pilot the ride of his life if roll restrictions on the aircraft were not heeded. The primary restriction was that once he entered a roll, the pilot could not change the elevon setting. If elevator was inadvertently applied during the roll, the pilot could encounter excessive pitch and yaw which, if let continue, could become so great as to break up the aircraft as it tried to fly sideways. The answer was to neutralize the controls until stability was regained, and pray. Especially the rudder and elevator were to be neutralized, as they caused yaw and pitch reactions.

With the TF-102A, a harsh buffet was also felt between Mach .90 and .95, due to the disturbed airflow over the canopy. Vortex generators on the crest of the canopy diminished the condition somewhat, but it was still startling to the pilots when first encountered. As speed increased past Mach 1 the buffeting disappeared. The TF-102A could only accomplish supersonic flight in a slight dive. Also, on some TF's a loud bang could be heard as the craft passed through Mach .85. Nothing to worry about though, said the manual, it was only a cockpit panel below the left seat wrinkling, and it did not compromise the structural integrity of the aircraft. Try that explanation on an airliner and see how far you get!

Stalls. One thing about a delta is that it really did not stall. With low airspeed and the nose up, it did develop a healthy rate of sink, but the nose dropping of conventional aircraft was not present. Below 130 knots, control became almost zilch, even with

A great photo showing the underside of an F-102. Landing lights are visible on gear struts—even the RAT is out of its compartment. (Frank Merrill Collection)

the wings level and the nose at a high angle of attack. The sink rate was something else. Adding power and dropping the nose was the only way out, if the altitude was available. If not, prang!

Unleveling the wings with the ailerons could really get a delta aircraft in trouble at low airspeeds. A spin. This maneuver was prohibited in the F-102A, as recovery required an excessive loss of altitude as well as probably exceeding engine temperature limits. Spins, however, could be entered inadvertently due to poor recovery from snap-up attacks, aerobatics or anything else that combined low airspeed with high angles of attack.

If there was sufficient altitude available, one could recover from a spin by neutralizing the controls until the direction of the spin was definitely established, meanwhile retarding the throttle to idle. Next, if the gear was down, it was retracted and all external loads jettisoned. Failure to dump the drop tanks made a spin recovery almost impossible. At

A looking-pretty shot of the F-102A put out by Convair's publicity department. It's a nice pose and shows off a highly polished paint job—note reflection of FC number on wing surface. (Convair)

Unusual head-on views of an F-102A taken from the open rear doors of a Lockheed HC-130 Hercules. As the Deuce moves in closer its air brakes are extended to slow it down in the rough wake of the lumbering transport. (Maj. Gen. Wayne C. Gatlin Minn. ANG)

that point, one-half aileron was applied in the direction of the spin rotation. The spin would then stop shortly, and the ailerons could be neutralized. The aircraft would be in a dive condition. As soon as indicated airspeed built to over 130 knots, recovery from the dive could begin. The gospel word was that if you were not out of a spin by the time you were down to 12,000 feet, it was a good time to eject. Furthermore, the engine was in for a real going over after such a spin, if the aircraft was landed in one piece. In all probability, it had been overtemped.

Flying flat out, at maximum speed, pitch and yaw damper systems were to be engaged. As speed went into the supersonic region, the nose tended to tuck under slightly. The maximum aircraft speed permissible while still staying within the structural integrity envelope was Mach 1.5 or 665 KIAS, whichever came first. At low altitude care had to be taken not to exceed these limitations when in afterburner.

A typical takeoff, without getting too detailed, included a thorough walkaround of the aircraft, checking intake and boundary layer ducts, electronic bays, weapons bays, RAT compartment, doors, pitot and static ports, tire condition and gear struts, along with many other lesser checks. A formal checklist took care of the complex cockpit check once in the aircraft with the engine started, and the plane cleared to taxi to takeoff position at the end of the runway. At that time, the throttle was placed in full military power position, the engine instruments checked, the brakes released and, with aircraft movement, the nose-wheel steering checked. If all was still ok, the throttle was pushed into afterburner. The nose wheel did the steering until the rudder became effective at about 80 knots IAS. At 125 knots the nose wheel was lifted off, and with rotation of about fifteen degrees, the aircraft came unstuck and was airborne. With the afterburner booting the Dagger in an acceleration mode, the gear was retracted at once so as not to exceed its speed limits.

A normal landing consisted of entering the traffic pattern at between 300 and 325 knots, using the speed brakes if desired. A turn was made into the downwind leg with speed being reduced to 220 knots, the gear being dropped before turning onto the base leg. On base leg the airspeed was further reduced to 180 knots before turning onto final approach. With the descent now on final, the speed, with the help of the speed brakes, was further cut

down through 170 knots to a touchdown speed of 130 knots. Once down, the drag chute was deployed and brakes applied to complete the rollout. (Those speeds were revised if the aircraft was carrying armament or had more than the usual amount of fuel left from the mission. In such cases, the airspeeds were bumped up by about 20 knots for each part of the above landing.) Other phases of landing-type operations were the instrument approach, the go-around and the engine-out landing. Each had its own by-the-book airspeeds to maintain during the various parts of such maneuvers.

Well, the Daggers are all gone now, except for the unmanned ones flying out of Holloman and Tyndall, the sacrificial goats of advanced weapons systems. And that is as it should be. Why waste them in the smelters' pots? They never fired a shot in anger, nor were they ever fired on in anger. (There *was* one unverifiable episode in Southeast Asia when an F-102A was rumored to have let go with its missiles at an unseen helicopter or other aircraft. No hits were registered, and the story may be untrue. However, it did surface a couple of times during research for this book.) While Convair and the Air Force dubbed them Delta Daggers, most people who dealt with them called them Deuces, except for the TF-102A, which was often nicknamed "Tub," due to its wide, fat front end.

The Deuces were world travelers and certainly all-weather, if climate differences had anything to do with it. They had the best climates and the worst to serve in. They could be found in Hawaii, the Philippines, Spain, Florida, Southeast Asia, southern California and other tropic or semitropic paradises. They could also be found in such harsh places as Greenland, Alaska and Iceland. In between, they saw Germany and Central Europe, the northern United States and many other places too numerous to recount. Their reputation may have spared them from combat. After all, who in their right mind wanted to tangle with such an obviously potent adversary? For over twenty years they served well as first-line fighters until the plastic insulation of the wiring of their MG-10's grew hard and brittle and prone to short. . . ask any MG-10 technician working with the plane in its later years. It was almost a hardening of the arteries due to old age in the Deuce's case. There are still a few around at museums and on pedestals in front of Air Force bases. For a while, though, Deuces were wild. They could beat anything!

CHAPTER IV
THE HYDROSKI DARTS

△——————————IT WAS JULY 16, 1947, WHEN the dream started. The Saunders-Roe SR.A/1—an experimental jet fighter flying boat—had flown. With a span of forty-six feet and a length of fifty feet, the bulky hulled jet aircraft had attained a speed of 512 miles per hour, right in the speed range of then current jet-propelled land-based fighters. It was not swept-wing, and the scaled down hull was reminiscent of a World War II Short Sunderland, but it *was* fast and it *was* water-based. The U.S. Navy took good note and on October 1, 1948, decided to launch a water-borne fighter competition of its own.

That was right down Convair's alley. Immediately after World War II, when aircraft companies were scrambling for the bountiful new military business spurred by the jet age, Convair's engineering types had already commenced work on a water-based jet fighter concept. The rationale was sound. The Navy had, of course, looked at water-based fighters since the beginning of naval flight. After all, water warfare was their bag. The obvious first efforts were floats, a direct derivative of boats. Time after time, test results were the same. Boats were fine in water; however, when they were hung under an aircraft they induced drag and caused poor performance when compared to land-based aircraft. The Navy tried retracting the floats and even inflating and deflating them for compact storage, but those experiments all turned out to be halfway measures bearing no really useful results. The projects were, one after another, abandoned. Then the jet engine finally came on the design scene and renewed interest in a water-based fighter became apparent. The designers no longer had to worry about propeller clearances, spray and all the other things that had dogged the propeller-driven designs of times past.

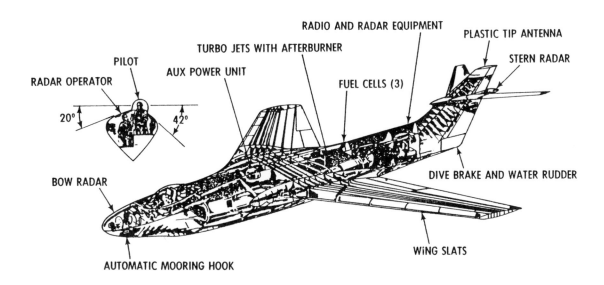

RADAR OPERATOR — PILOT — AUX POWER UNIT — TURBO JETS WITH AFTERBURNER — RADIO AND RADAR EQUIPMENT — FUEL CELLS (3) — PLASTIC TIP ANTENNA — STERN RADAR

20° 42°

BOW RADAR — DIVE BRAKE AND WATER RUDDER — WING SLATS — AUTOMATIC MOORING HOOK

SKATE

A model of Skate is towed behind a high-speed boat on San Diego Bay to investigate its hydrodynamic properties. (Convair)

Convair design people produced an interesting proposal. It had multisparred swept wings that blended mantalike into the fuselage. The swept vertical fin had a dihedral horizontal tail plane mounted about halfway up its height. The fuselage housed two afterburning jet engines, one in either wing root. The pilot and radar operator sat side by side (the radar operator was positioned at a somewhat lower level), and the bubble canopy accepted only the pilot's head. The aircraft was designed to float on watertight wings instead of on the usual floats. The fuselage was also watertight and fitted with a retractable step—at takeoff speed, the fuselage rose up on the step, clearing the wings from the water. The speed could then continue to build to takeoff velocity. Convair got as far as building powered radio-controlled models for testing on San Diego Bay, and the plane even picked up the name "Skate" along the way. Other models with varying hull and step shapes were towed by high-speed boats for further testing.

The National Advisory Committee for Aeronautics (NACA) had also been putting forth effort in the direction of hydroskis, instead of floats, for water operation of aircraft. It should be pointed out here that hydroskis ride on top of the water, just as a

The XF2Y-1 with hydroskis retracted was actually a small-hulled flying boat as shown in this photo of low-speed taxiing on San Diego Bay. Included angle of hull bottom was 110 degrees. (Convair)

water skier does. They are sometimes confused with hydrofoils, which have airfoil shapes and provide lift in a like manner to a wing while remaining submerged. An advantage of the more or less thin hydroskis was that they could easily retract into, or at least flush against, the fuselage. This would cut aerodynamic drag a quantum amount over floats. Another advantage touted by NACA was the expected lessening of pounding attendant to high-speed water operation with hulls during takeoffs and landings. The skis would be mounted on shock absorbers, just like the wheels of the contemporary jet fighters. With the oleo cushioning, it was expected that the airframe could be built lighter with subsequent higher airborne performance.

Convair was selected to make a comparative study of conventional hulls versus hydroskis. The company already had the job half done with the Skate design, so it had an inside track to get an experimental contract for this task. Engineers were also now well into the YF-102 design, which looked very promising, so why not design the new hydroski jet fighter as a delta? They did. The result was not quite a YF-102, but it was close enough to see the family resemblance. The concept looked as good to the Navy as it did to Convair's engineering department, and on January 19, 1951, the Navy Bureau of Aeronautics ordered two prototypes. The fact that the XF-92A had been flying regularly at Edwards Air Force Base probably did not hurt the Convair sales pitch much either.

Powered by two Westinghouse J34-WE-42 turbojets delivering 3,400 pounds of static thrust each, the most powerful engine available at the time, the

The XF2Y-1 had a span of 33 feet 8 inches and wing area of 563 square feet. Even with shock-absorbing struts, skis pounding on the water surface at high speed made for a rough ride at over 60 knots. Ship lifted off at about 125 knots. (Convair)

The intermediate, or beach, ski position shown here was used to accelerate from 10 to 125 knots during takeoff for least amount of hydrodynamic drag. (Convair)

XF2Y-1, as the type was designated, became the Navy's first delta wing fighter. The first one built was BuAer 137634, and it had to have the fanciest paint job of the year. It was dark blue with yellow stripes on the ailerons, rudder and around the engine air intakes atop the fuselage, to say nothing of the large areas of yellow on the top and botton wing surfaces. It was a handsome paint job for a handsome aircraft. However, the striping's true use was to provide attitude reference in instrumented photographs of the aircraft during taxi, takeoff and landing modes. The plane looked good, and on August 28, 1952, the Navy ordered more of them. The old design maxim came into play: If it looks good, it must be good. Convair dubbed the fighters Sea Darts.

The aircraft was small, about the size of an F-86 Sabrejet in the side profile. The wings had a short span of thirty-three feet eight inches because of the delta planform, but they were larger than the XF-92A that was now gathering delta wing flight experience at an ever increasing pace. Wing area was 563 square feet versus the XF-92A's 230 square feet. Fuselage length was fifty-two feet seven inches, with a height of sixteen feet two inches, hydroskis retracted. The empty weight was 12,625 pounds with an all-up gross of 16,527 pounds. On December 16, 1952, Con-

An early view of the XF2Y-1 Sea Dart shows off its dazzling yellow and navy-blue paint job. At this point its Westinghouse J34 engines were nonafterburning. (E. T. Hull Collection)

The first Sea Dart over San Diego Bay. Airfield at left is the North Island Naval Air Station. The hooked peninsula on the right enclosed the Municipal Yacht Harbor with Point Loma and the Pacific Ocean beyond. (E. T. Hull Collection)

vair launched the first Sea Dart on San Diego Bay to begin taxi tests. This was the beginning of XF2Y-1 test work that would run through most of 1957, when the program was finally closed.

To make beaching easier, the Sea Dart was able to taxi up a concrete ramp, out of the water, and back in again. There were small retractable wheels at the aft ends of the skis, as well as a partially concealed tail wheel in the fuselage rear. In the ground taxi mode (that is, with the skis extended), the high tilted attitude made the aircraft look like some giant prehistoric bird.

With hydroskis fully extended, XF2Y-1 settles its 52-foot 7-inch length onto the water past Ryan Aeronautical Company facilities in the background. (Convair)

E. D. Shannon, Convair's Chief of Engineering Flight Test, taxies the XF2Y-1 out of the water and up the ramp before shutting things down. Small wheels at aft end of skis and tail wheel on fuselage carried the craft's weight of between 12,652 pounds empty and 16,527 pounds gross. (Convair)

At almost the beginning of the water taxi tests, it became apparent that NACA had not quite worked all the bugs out of the hydroski concept. As speeds passed about sixty miles per hour on the water, the pounding of the twin skis against the waves not only gave the pilot a severe shaking, but provided a good beating to the airframe as well—and takeoff speed would be at least 140 miles per hour. The rougher the water, the greater the vibrations, amplified by the thin skis flexing between the front and rear main shock-absorbing oleos. With the front struts under the cockpit, the pounding reaction loads were to the point of being unbearable for the pilot, to say nothing of the equipment in the cockpit. The pounding was so serious that on some tests actual structural damage was done to the aircraft. The test pilot, Sam Shannon, of XF-92A note, even blacked out from the pounding on one occasion. A few weeks after launching, on January 14, 1953, the high-speed taxi tests turned into an unofficial first flight when the XF2Y-1 inadvertently bounded into the air and flew for almost a thousand feet before Shannon gingerly got it down again. However, the persistent efforts by Convair's engineers to reduce ski pounding finally resulted in an official first flight, without major ski changes, on August 9, 1953, with Shannon at the controls. Once in the air, he found the aircraft to be completely conventional during maneuvering. Given the area rule treatment that was soon to make the disappointing YF-102 live up to expectations, the Sea Dart could well have been one of the U.S. Navy's first-line fighters of the fifties and early six-

ties. That is, of course, if a solution could be found to solve the pounding problem during takeoffs and landings.

Another problem area encountered was salt water—bane of aluminum structures, hydraulics and electrical systems. Even with the best of piloting techniques, some of the voluminous takeoff and landing spray was bound to get ingested into the engine air intakes even though they were positioned high atop the fuselage. The resultant baked on salt deposits ruined the efficiency of the turbine compressor blades (and the engines were somewhat weak to begin with) and dropped the total engine static thrust or, worse yet, caused compressor stalls when going into the afterburner high-thrust condition. As a matter of fact, deposits could be built up just from being in the salt air. As a solution, a special twenty-gallon freshwater tank with appropriate spray apparatus was soon developed to wash the salt off the compressor rotor and stator blades, while still at idle power setting, just prior to takeoff. The system was added to Sea Darts one and three.

The V-shaped windshield was the classic precursor of the style used on the F-102A, the F-106A, and even the X-15 research aircraft. It had a few problems though. The field of view was poor because outside light was allowed to shine directly on the cockpit consoles and instrument panels, causing glare. The panes were not overly large either. The windshield and the structural canopy assembly swung open from the front and hinged at the rear, like the hood of a car. Though the aircraft had an

Typical construction of the Sea Dart's twin hydroskis are those of plane number 5 BuAer 135765 at Kissimmee, Florida. Weathered white paint scheme makes rivets and fitting details stand out well in photos. (R. L. Hogeman)

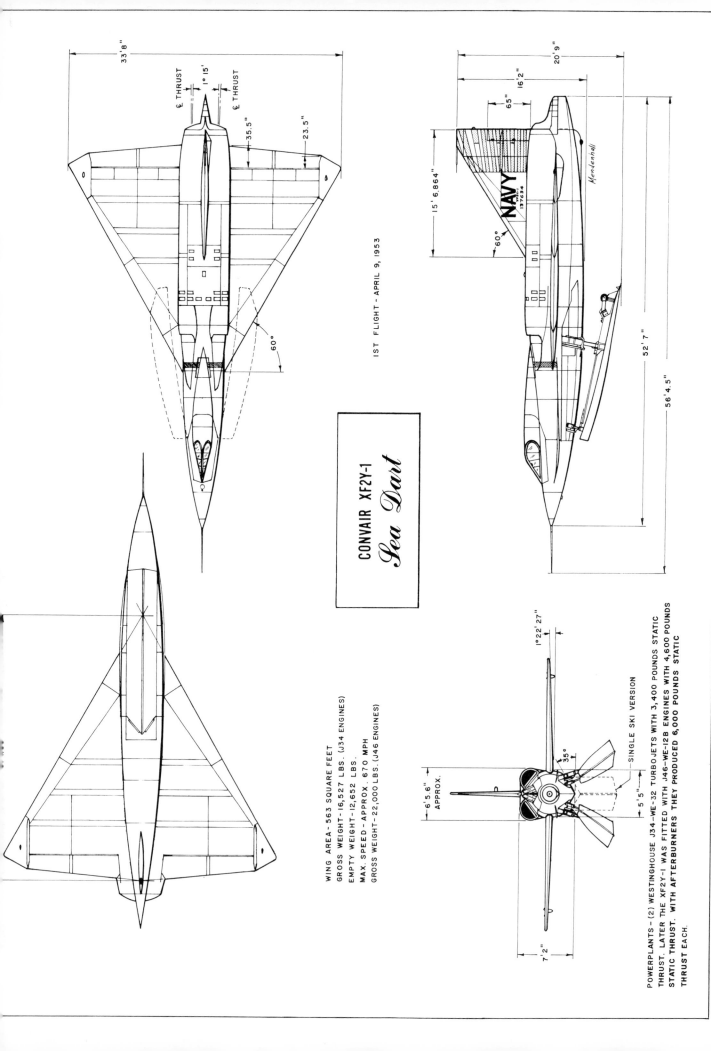

33'8"

1° 15'

℄ THRUST ℄ THRUST

35.5"

23.5"

60°

1ST FLIGHT – APRIL 9, 1953

20'9"

16'2"

65"

15' 6.864"

60°

52'7"

56'4.5"

NAVY
137634

Mendenhall

CONVAIR XF2Y-1
Sea Dart

WING AREA – 563 SQUARE FEET
GROSS WEIGHT – 16,527 LBS. (J34 ENGINES)
EMPTY WEIGHT – 12,652 LBS.
MAX. SPEED – APPROX. 670 MPH
GROSS WEIGHT – 22,000 LBS. (J46 ENGINES)

1°22'27"

6'5.6"
APPROX.

3.5°

5'5"

SINGLE SKI VERSION

7'2"

POWERPLANTS – (2) WESTINGHOUSE J34-WE-32 TURBOJETS WITH 3,400 POUNDS STATIC
THRUST. LATER THE XF2Y-1 WAS FITTED WITH J46-WE-12B ENGINES WITH 4,600 POUNDS
STATIC THRUST. WITH AFTERBURNERS THEY PRODUCED 6,000 POUNDS STATIC
THRUST EACH.

ejection seat, the chances of punching out successfully with that configuration were not too good. To have been a service-accepted fighter, it would have had to have been changed.

As would be expected, the cockpit was loaded with instrumentation. Aside from the conventional stick-and-rudder flight controls there were instruments, knobs, levers and circuit breakers—enough to make one's mind boggle. Actually, it broke down to a heavily instrumented front panel, a large left console and an equally large right instrument console. The extent of the instrumentation was in keeping with a high-performance test aircraft. It is interesting to note that while most of the instrumentation is similar to what one expected in a modern jet fighter of the fifties, there were a few rarities due to the configuration of the Sea Dart. On the left console, for instance, were such things as the struts extended warning light, left-hand and right-hand ski position indicators, skis up and down lever, ski position selector switch, ski position toggle linkage actuator, taxi wheels position indicator and the taxi wheels control switch. On the instrument panel itself was a water rudder indicator.

The small beaching wheels were not fitted with toe brakes on the rudder pedals. Instead brake controls consisted of two side-by-side handles on the right console. They could be pulled together for braking or separately for steering. Since taxi speed on land was so slow and awkward, the brakes did not pay their way in weight added to the aircraft.

To get off the concrete ramp and into the water, the hydroskis were placed in about a half-retracted, or beach, position. After the aircraft was floating on its own, the small wheels were hydraulically retracted through an arc of ninety degrees by actuating the electrical taxi wheels control switch on the left console. The skis were now ready for the first stage of the takeoff, still in the half-retracted (intermediate takeoff) position.

At engine idle, on the water, the aircraft's speed was two to three knots, or about 2.3 to 3.4 miles per hour. (Since most readers can relate to miles per hour better than knots, other performance figures will henceforth be given in miles per hour, even though it is a Navy craft.) By lowering the speed brakes on the underside of the afterbody and fully extending the skis, the speed could be reduced to

Flotation characteristics and waterline are evident in this rear three-quarter view of XF2Y-1 taxiing along at idle power. (E. T. Hull Collection)

about a mile and a half per hour—a slow walking speed. To steer at these low speeds, the speed brakes could be extended differentially combined with use of the rudder pedals. Power could also be used asymmetrically if desired. If an engine should flame out, however, directional control was not possible and taxiing could not be accomplished—except in a circle, of course. There were combination air brake/water brake/water rudder surfaces along the rear fuselage sides, but they were ineffective against the engine thrust.

To take off, now that the plane was in the water, the skis were fully extended and full military power, that is full power without afterburner, was applied. Under those conditions, the leading edges of the skis broke water at about ten miles per hour. At that point, the skis were immediately retracted to the intermediate position for hydrodynamic drag reduction, and the throttles were pushed past the detent into the afterburner position. The takeoff run began. The aircraft assumed a normal pitch attitude up to about fifty miles per hour. At 115 miles per

XF2Y-1 with single ski extended in landing or takeoff position prepares for an open sea landing. Beaching wheels are retracted. (E. T. Hull Collection)

Same aircraft configuration as previous photo except ski is semi-retracted for less drag at cruise speed. As high-speed flight was not an object of this test the ski did not have to retract completely. (E. T. Hull Collection)

hour, the best attitude was slightly nose up, two to five degrees. At 140 miles per hour, the ship was sharply rotated to about eighteen degrees for positive liftoff and water separation. At that point, the skis were retracted at once, just like in a standard land-based fighter, to let the airspeed build rapidly.

So much for getting the Sea Dart into the air. While up there, it was quite conventional, handling very much like any other high-performance jet fighter of its day.

Charles E. Richbourg, another Convair test pilot, soon joined Shannon in the high-speed taxi tests of the XF2Y-1. The aircraft had been refitted with afterburning Westinghouse J46-WE-12 engines. The twin skis were changed a little at a time to try to soften the high-speed taxi pounding and vibrations, especially in the cockpit. Tests of various modifications of the XF2Y-1's skis, over a hundred in all, continued to mid-1954.

A second Sea Dart, BuNo 135762, was completed in early 1954. The designation was now changed from XF2Y-1 to YF2Y-1, a sign of progress showing advancement from prototype to preproduction aircraft. The second craft was basically similar to the first copy, except for a small change on the afterbody. Richbourg now made the initial flights on the Y-model, exploring the high-speed performance,

control characteristics and aerodynamic performance. All tests thus far were from San Diego Bay. To really evaluate the Navy's jet fighter hopes as mentioned at the beginning of this chapter, it would be required to try the aircraft under actual conditions—on the open sea.

Several miles offshore, south of Point Loma, California, Shannon and Richbourg began testing the number two machine under those parameters. The test setup required standby rescue boats and auxiliary vessels that carried hydrodynamic instrumentation. Wave patterns encountered during landing were plotted after a flight from San Diego, coming to a full stop, then taxiing back to about the initial touchdown position before applying power once more for takeoff and a return flight to San Diego Bay. The test detachment also included a helicopter or two and a chase aircraft. In addition to their use from a safety standpoint, the aircraft were used for photo documentation for later evaluation of the flights by land-based personnel. Other testing involved a large landing ship dock used to find out what would be required in the way of open sea maintenance and support of the delta sea birds.

Richbourg, while continuing flight and twin ski tests in number two aircraft, finally went past Mach 1 on August 3, 1954, in a shallow dive out of

XF2Y-1 taxiing like a miniature flying boat. Hull immersed in the water lays down a heavy wake as it makes a U-turn. Note small bow wave and large quantities of spray thrown up by the jet exhaust. (E. T. Hull Collection)

34,000 feet. It wasn't the Mach 1.5 that was hoped for, but still the ship could be rated at Mach .99 in level flight. With a little larger engine and the area rule applied, the Navy could have had a winner on its hands.

The number one aircraft, the XF2Y-1, had now been modified to a single large hydroski instead of the initial twin-ski arrangement. The single ski was not fully retractable, but it didn't really matter, as the purpose of the single-ski test was to evaluate its hydrodynamic properties versus the twin-ski layout. Shannon and Richbourg quickly shook out the answers on this one in late fall of 1954. The single-ski machine was not as good as the model with twin skis, from standpoints of control characteristics or hydrodynamic stability. It was back to the drawing board and improving the twin-ski arrangement.

The second and third Sea Darts had beefed-up powerplants in the form of two 4,600-pound static thrust Westinghouse J46-WE-4's, giving the delta-winged fighters a swifter kick to high speed. The number one ship, as mentioned, was also retrofitted. The project appeared to have a lot of potential, and the Navy officially accepted the Sea Dart for evaluation of its own. The evaluation was conducted by Patuxent River (Pax River) Naval Air Test Center personnel; pilots CDR H. C. Weart, CDR V. L. Fretwell,

and LCDR E. R. Horrell; engineer LCDR R. N. deCallies; and BuAer observer LCDR P. E. Beck. The work was done at the Convair San Diego plant. Their findings in a June 1955 report summed up their work in this manner:

The YF2Y-1 twin-ski model was superior to the XF2Y-1 single-ski machine from a hydrodynamic standpoint—except for intolerable vibration during takeoff. Evaluators recommended, however, that the single-ski configuration be further investigated, along with suitable aircraft equipment and accessories for use in and around salt water. While many improvements had been made since the program began, the Navy felt the following items unacceptable:

1. Takeoff performance that required a one-mile run to reach takeoff speed.
2. High vertical forces as water speeds approached takeoff speeds, causing pilot difficulties and probable component failure with continued usage in that mode.
3. Marginal control on the water at over forty knots, in a five-knot cross wind. (i.e., the Sea Dart was directionally unstable on the water at high speeds.)

It is interesting to note that the "unacceptables" were all water-related. Airborne, the Sea Dart

XF2Y-1 up on its twin skis, throwing spray, at beginning of 5,500-foot takeoff run. (E. T. Hull Collection)

was a great little airplane and, with more powerful engines, even some of the "unacceptables" might have been fixed. This evaluation occurred even after one of the aircraft had come unglued.

On November 4, 1954, Richbourg was piloting the plane low over San Diego Bay during a public and press demonstration of the little speed merchant. He was in the number two YF2Y-1 and was clipping along at about 575 miles per hour when the airplane came apart in midair. The reason for the crash given by most engineering types is that the plane went into a longitudinal divergent pitch oscillation and disintegrated during the second nose-down pitch, a classic response to high-speed transonic effects at low altitude. Richbourg was, of course, killed. The early hydraulically powered flight control systems were such that they tended to help the situation along with pilot-induced oscillations. The other reasons sometimes heard were that salt water had taken its toll of the structure, that a fuel leak had caused the explosion or that the aircraft was being operated outside of its design envelope. Regardless of the accident's cause, the Navy suspended Sea Dart operations until a Navy accident board finished its investigation. When completed, all high-speed aero-

dynamic testing of the aircraft was canceled. Things were at a low ebb, what with the crash, the inability to live up to the expected performance figures speed-wise and the rough and tumble pounding from the hydroskis during takeoff and landing.

Convair pondered a way to remedy the situation. Perhaps a single-engine version with a more powerful tried and true powerplant could do the trick, say a 15,000-pound-thrust Pratt & Whitney J75 or a 12,000-pound-thrust Wright J67. Also, a more advanced single hydroski could be an improvement. This redesigned model was labeled F2Y-2 and was proposed to the U.S. Marine Corps. The new design was only on paper, however, and none were ever built. The Marines didn't buy it.

The Convair people were not about to give up on the program, and they were able to maintain continued, though lukewarm, support of the program from the Navy. The aerodynamic problems could be solved, to be sure, but the hydroski thing was still there. On December 19, 1954, Shannon was slated to resume taxi tests with the XF2Y-1, but a mild illness took him off the flight roster. Billy Jack (B.J.) Long, a Sea Dart chase pilot, as well as a knowledgeable seaplane pilot, was selected to pick up the program.

Number 3 Sea Dart BuAer 135763 poses with B. J. Long who made first flight in craft March 4, 1955. (E. T. Hull Collection)

This required the BuAer representative at Convair to give his ok, and this he quickly did to avoid further delays. As it turned out, Long was assigned to the program for almost two and a half years—until April 1957. During that period, he flew most of the first tests on ski configuration changes, made most of the important open sea evaluations (of which we will hear more later) and made the first flight with the number three YF2Y-1, BuAer 135763 on March 4, 1955.

The third aircraft was equipped with the optimum final twin-hydroski configuration. The skis had wheels that rotated about the tapered skis' afterbodies. The craft was to be used for final evaluation of the new twin-ski design demonstrating open sea operations. The testing with the number three machine continued thru April 28, 1955, the day of the last flight operation for that particular aircraft. One of the facets looked into was operations with JATO, rocket-assisted takeoff bottles, attached under the wings to reduce takeoff distances and, hence, at least the length of time the pilot and plane were subjected to the pounding. During a typical San Diego Bay takeoff, with wind-induced, two-foot waves, the pilot and cockpit area would experience plus or minus 5.5 g's at fifteen to seventeen cycles per second just before liftoff. To the pilot, it was sort of the way a rat must feel being shaken by a particularly energetic terrier. During the shaking the pilot had only "shotgun" vision, with nothing visible in the cockpit because of the severe vibration. About all he could do was to try to get the throttles into full afterburner and pull back on the stick for some sort of rotation.

Long also continued testing of the single-skied XF2Y-1, along with the twin-ski YF2Y-1. Single-ski qualities were being slowly but surely improved, especially on the open sea with touchdown speeds of about 138 miles per hour and liftoffs at about 144 miles per hour. Shannon, who was again doing some of the test work, felt the Sea Dart could take care of itself in the open seas, within reason of course. Success with the Sea Dart would have allowed the Navy great strategic capability in fighter deployment, for most any vessel could carry at least one of the aircraft.

Part of the test program was the high sink rate tests required by the Navy, up to nineteen feet per second, plopping down on San Diego Bay with no unacceptable impacts felt in the cockpit and, of course, no damage to the aircraft. Those front oleos could not be pumped up too much or the pilot could have his behind unacceptably driven through the bottom of the fuselage.

On January 16, 1956, the final open sea tests for the single-ski XF2Y-1 were performed. The purpose was to demonstrate the upper limits of rough sea operation. Long recalled those tests at a meeting of the Society of Experimental Test Pilots at Beverly Hills, California, in September 1976.

"The assorted helicopters, chase plane, rescue boats and auxiliary wave height monitoring boats were present." As Long tells it, "The waves varied from six to ten feet in height with a separation of fifty to one hundred feet. Small one- to two-foot waves were superimposed on the major wave patterns. A few waves measured twelve feet in height just prior to landing. This sea condition approached a rating of sea state 5. Landing and takeoffs were made parallel to the major wave pattern with the fifteen- to twenty-knot wind line about forty-five degrees to the right of the aircraft heading."

A YF2Y-1 at idle power on glassy bay moves along at a slow 2–3 miles per hour. Note spray rails near waterline below cockpit. (E. T. Hull Collection)

"Deceleration after a touchdown at 120 knots was rapid. Vertical and lateral motions experienced in the cockpit were severe. My hard hat struck the V windscreen with such impact in lateral motion that I suddenly tasted what I thought was blood. After forward motion was stopped, I removed my oxygen mask and realized that the impact had forced mucus from my sinuses into my mouth.

"Takeoff bordered on the catastrophic. I over-rotated prematurely because of heavy pitching motions, which made it appear that I might trip or dive into the heavy sea condition.

"This nose-high attitude kept me from simulating a torpedo, but it also delayed my acceleration so that I kept ricocheting off the tops of the waves. The resulting impacts experienced in the cockpit were intolerable. I was stunned. Aircraft test instrumentation recorded one vertical impact of 8.5 g's at a very high rate of acceleration under my seat.

"Finally, after the last separation from the water, Lou Hoffman, my friend and chase pilot in an AD-5, yelled for me to come out of afterburner so he could stay with me. The return flight and landing in San Diego Bay were routine."

That flight marked the last actual takeoff and landing of any Sea Dart. At the same time, it marked the end of the official single-ski test program. Both number one and number three aircraft were placed in storage until late 1956, when the BuAer people hauled number one out to test a small, rigidly mounted planing hydroski. The placement and rigid mounting of the ski precluded takeoff due to an incredible seventeen- to nineteen-degree nose-high attitude required for rotation. The configuration was tested by Long in April 1957. He never got it past sixty or seventy miles per hour, due to severe vibration and pounding loading in the cockpit. During the next eighteen days, three test operations occurred in that configuration before the program was concluded.

At this point in time, the Sea Darts had performed over 300 test operations with ship number one, the XF2Y-1, handling over 250 of them. The Navy had meanwhile given up on the program, canceling the whole thing in late 1956. It opted to continue with the conventional carrier-borne aircraft, but not entirely due to a lack of need for a water-borne aircraft. Tight funds for experimental projects were also a major factor in the Navy's decision.

Convair, now as a private venture, had one more ski configuration to look at. This was in the fall of 1957. It was a rigidly mounted ski, similar in design to its previous attempt, but twice as large.

With whitecaps showing here and there off San Diego, YF2Y-1 prepares for open sea landing from about 1,500 feet altitude. RATO bottles show clearly under wing—used to shorten takeoff distance and minimize bone-jarring vibrations. (E. T. Hull Collection)

The testing was conducted by Convair's chief engineering test pilot for the Navy, Donald P. Germeraad. His test work proved the ski to be not much good, just like the previous miniski. That ski is still mounted on the XF2Y-1 today. That *was* the end of the program.

Some writers have cast the Sea Dart in a poor light, being of poor design, a partial if not a total failure or just a wild experiment on the parts of Convair and the Navy that wasted the taxpayers' money.

The truth of the matter is, had the design been lavished with the engineering effort that was put in

Single-ski version of XF2Y-1 comes to a screeching halt during landing runout in rough water open sea test. (E. T. Hull Collection)

An open sea landing by a YF2Y-1 past a barge with crane, for salvage, in case it is needed. Smoke float and wave patterns show this to be a typical cross-wind landing as used by this type. (E. T. Hull Collection)

the F-102 and the later F-106, the results undoubtedly would have been a great deal different. It might have provided the Navy with a highly effective mobile base weapons system. While the big problem with the aircraft still remained the pounding hydroskis, Convair engineers had softened the takeoffs and landings to the point that flights could be made with skilled test pilots. The Sea Darts were, however, still too much of a go for ordinary service-pilots' use. It was pretty basic—water encountered at high speeds was far rougher than a cobblestone road.

The Sea Darts still survive, except for the number two plane that brought an end to itself and pilot Richbourg in San Diego.

As this is written, the XF2Y-1 (BuAer 137634), which was at the Naval Air Test and Evaluation Museum at Patuxent River, on loan from the National Air and Space Museum, is now located at the old Martin airfield at Baltimore. It had been displayed at Norfolk, Virginia. The number three aircraft sits upended in the "beach" position in the aircraft exhibit at Willow Grove, Pennsylvania, Naval Air Station. It is stripped inside and is painted gold and blue, rather than the authentic yellow and blue used during testing. Its BuAer number is 135763. Number four aircraft, BuAer number 135764, which was never fitted with engines, is currently in outdoor storage at Convair San Diego and has begun to get in a somewhat ratty condition. It is slated for eventual

restoration and display at the San Diego Aero-Space Museum. Number five, YF2Y-1 (BuAer number 135765, also never engined), is on display at the SST Museum at Kissimmee, Florida. That museum, which houses the mockup of the defunct Boeing SST, has repainted the number five Sea Dart in a manner more in keeping with the SST itself. It is all white with a red leading edge on the wing, a red nose probe, red outline around the engine air intakes, exhaust nozzles and, finally, a red, dart-shaped fin flash. With the blue and white star and bar insignias, it looks pretty sharp, even if nonregulation. It is owned and on loan from the Pacific Northwest Aviation Historical Foundation.

The Sea Dart was one of those really great ideas that should have been successful, but somehow just didn't pan out. Perhaps sometime in the future, now that powerful jet engines are commonplace and could reduce the takeoff distance, some aircraft manufacturer will again propose the concept to the Navy. Now, as then, the great flexibility of combat deployment could be a real advantage to a country equipped with such a versatile aircraft.

Big government sometimes has a communications problem. In the case of the Sea Dart, it is of interest that the aircraft's final designation was YF-7A. This was assigned almost six years after the program's cancellation!

Number 3 Sea Dart BuAer 135763 sits out at the outdoor aircraft exhibit at the Naval Air Station, Willow Grove, Pennsylvania. (E. T. Hull Collection)

CHAPTER V
△ STRAIGHT UP ON A POGOSTICK

△—————————"POGOSTICK" IS A STRANGE
name for an aircraft, but then it *was* a strange aircraft.
Sitting there on its tail with four oversized swivel
chair casters for a landing gear, it was certainly not
ordinary. Stubby delta wings, a short, fat fuselage,
and huge dorsal and ventral fins could have almost
completed the numerous surprises in this aircraft,
but there was yet another to come. Two large contrarotating propellers, their hubs encased in a massive black spinner, really topped off the design.

The object of the whole amazing contraption
was to go straight up from a standing, tail-sitting
starting position. There is no question that it was an
interesting idea. Straight up from almost any naval
vessel's deck, straight up from any cleared fifty-foot-
square area on land, all without any sort of runway at
all, thank you. Yes, it was an intriguing idea indeed
for the Navy brass in the early fifties, when the Cold
War was gathering a real head of steam. What had
made it all theoretically possible was the advent of
the turbojet, then the turboprop, which was powerful, light and reliable. To go straight up it was necessary to develop thrust greater than the aircraft's
weight. And the marvelous Allison turboprop engine
did just that.

The original idea for the tail-sitter goes back to
the Germans near the end of World War II. They
were obviously losing the battle for quantity of aircraft manufactured when compared to the by then
awakened industrial giant of the United States that
spewed out aircraft so fast there was no way the tide
could be stemmed. Therefore, the Germans looked to
advanced technology that might change the direction of the war. Rockets, jets, swept wings, delta
wings, swing wings and, yes, even a vertical takeoff
(VTO) fighter. The VTO design was the Focke-Wulfe
ram jet fighter, and it only got as far as a model and
some drawings before the war ended.

The projected machine was set on a cruciform tail very much like the Lockheed XFV-1 VTO, stablemate to the Convair Pogo. Around the middle of the aircraft's fuselage were mounted three large rotor blades with Lorin duct ram jets at their tips. The idea was to rotate the blades about the fuselage, helicopterlike, until the craft had attained altitude. The blades then stopped their rotation and, by changing pitch, became wings for conventional horizontal flight.

Allied Intelligence came across the curious design and, along with myriad other advanced technology, forwarded it to the United States for use by its by then highly sophisticated aircraft industry. As a result, and as early as 1947, the Air Force and the Navy initiated study contracts with several manufacturers for VTO designs and recommendations. The aircraft were primarily to be used as versatile convoy escort fighters, although land-based operation was not precluded. It was felt that turbojets were still too skitterish and underpowered for use on the proposed new planes, therefore lower airspeed, high-thrust turboprops were substituted.

Convair's answer to the Navy's request for a VTO fighter was the delta-wing turboprop XFY-1. Aircraft was relatively small with a span of 27 feet 7.75 inches and a length of 34 feet 11 inches. (Convair)

Lockheed and Convair were both able to come up with interesting proposals. Convair was awarded a contract by the Navy on March 31, 1951, for a VTO aircraft capable of taking off and landing on its tail. Three weeks later, Lockheed also received a contract for the same type of plane. These prototypes were to be capable of further development into fighters.

Curiously enough, both firms' aircraft were very similar in concept but quite different in appearance. Each used a twin Allison turboprop engine, with the pilot more or less sitting astride the engine's gearbox. Both had huge spinners and big contrarotating propellers to absorb the tremendous power, eliminate torque, and lift the aircraft vertically. For landing, the aircraft were to be simply backed down from a vertical prop-hanging attitude until the castered landing gear rested on the ground.

At this point, the similarity stopped. Lockheed decided to use the small straight wing it believed in and had proven on the XF-104 Starfighter, its high-speed interceptor. Convair, just as enamored with its delta-wing configuration, went that route. The delta wing made up two of the points for the four-point cruciform shape needed for the landing gear. A large vertical fin and an almost equally large ventral fin made up the other two points. In case of a level flight emergency landing, the ventral fin could be jettisoned.

There was some help for the pilot's "there I was, flat on my back" problem. The cockpit seat was gimballed, so that it could be swung forty-five degrees upright from the horizontal position during takeoffs and landings. This helped alleviate some of the problem of disorientation that occurred when compared to the standard aircraft layout. The instrument panel, stick and stirrupped control pedals also followed the position of the seat. It didn't help much in the backing-down-to-land mode, however.

The aircraft was fairly small due to weight requirements for vertical takeoff. The wing span was

Lockheed also obtained a contract for a VTO aircraft, the XFV-1. Powered by the same Allison YT40 turboprop engine as the Convair design, Lockheed chose the low aspect straight wing for its design—à la F-104. Span was 30 feet 11 inches, length was 37 feet 6 inches. (Lockheed)

An elaborate system of cables connected the XYF-1 to the 195-foot-high ceiling of a blimp hangar at Moffet Field, California. Test pilot J. F. (Skeets) Coleman made nearly 300 trips to the ceiling getting the feel of VTO before attempting an untethered liftoff. (Convair)

The XYF-1 program was really a system instead of just an aircraft. Shown here is a special trailer designed by Convair to haul the XFY-1 overland while towed by a Jeep. Trailer could also upend the aircraft and place it on the ground in a VTO position. (Convair)

Another accessory for the XFY-1 was the tepee maintenance hangar. Fashioned of wood, fiberglass and aluminum, the hangar contained lights and built-in ladders and platforms that allowed access to all parts of the XFY-1. (Convair)

twenty-seven feet 7.75 inches, and the wing area was 355 square feet. The vertical tail span was twenty-two feet eleven inches, obviously a very large vertical tail. The overall length of the aircraft was thirty-four feet 11.75 inches. The empty weight was 11,742 pounds and laden, it weighed in at a gross of 16,250 pounds. Another consideration was to keep the plane light for VTO, then, once airborne, go to air-to-air refueling to increase the aircraft's combat radius.

The powerplant to hoist this weight straight up was a 5,850-shaft horsepower Allison YT40-A-14.

The engine actually consisted of two Allison T-38 engines mounted together, and they delivered their shaft horsepower through a common gearbox. By means of twin power section controls, the engines could be operated separately or together. The three-bladed contrarotating propellers were steel-bladed Curtis-Wright Turboelectrics, and were sixteen feet in diameter. The massive spinner, which projected well forward of the propeller duct, was hollow and was used as a housing for a large parachute. This was also the case with the Lockheed XFV-1 as well. (Lockheed *had* invented it.)

To VTO it was necessary that the engine/propeller combination produce more forward thrust than the weight of the aircraft. The gross weight of Pogo was 16,250 pounds—11,742 pounds empty. During vertical flight the instrument panel and pilot's seat tilted forward at about a 45° angle to help maintain some of the normal feel of flying an aircraft. Once horizontal flight was obtained, seat and panel swung to a more normal upright position. (Convair)

The Pogostick was powered by an Allison Y740-A-14 that produced 5,850 eph. Propellers were steel-bladed contra-rotating 16-foot-diameter Curtis-Wright Turboelectrics. (Convair)

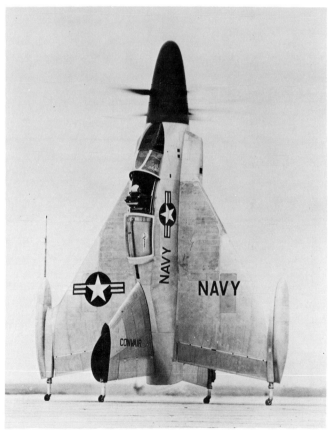

The chute was to be deployed in case of partial or full engine failure in the vertical mode and, to avoid the downward pull of air through the propellers, it had to be fired through the spinner and high enough above the aircraft to be in an upward airflow relative to the descending aircraft. The parachute canopy was weighted to help accomplish that, and spring strips around the canopy edges helped the chute to open quickly. It was predicted that use of the parachute would result in local damage to the aircraft's tail area, but that the pilot would escape unharmed. The system probably would have never been used, as the pilots generally spoke of ejecting themselves and coming down hanging on the shrouds of their personal chutes. The wing-tip caster housings, while initially filled with test instrumentation, were planned to later carry four, twenty-mm aircraft cannon, two in each housing, or forty-six 2.75-inch HVAR folding fin rockets for armament. In either case, the installation was simple, for it was not necessary to synchronize the firing with the multibladed propellers.

While the entire flight envelope of the XFY-1 was not examined before the project was eventually shut down, it was thought the aircraft could attain a maximum speed of 610 miles per hour at 15,000 feet and 592 miles per hour at 35,000 feet—not bad for a prop-driven aircraft.

The initial climb rate from low altitude, horizontal flight was a husky 10,500 feet per minute. Service ceiling was 43,700 feet.

By March of 1954, the XFY-1 Pogostick was at Moffet Field, California, where it was to be initially flight tested, fastened to an elaborate system of cables and pulleys strung from the ceiling of a blimp hangar. Unlike the Lockheed XFV-1, the Convair ship could not be fitted with a jury-rigged conventional landing gear because of its large ventral fin. The XFY-1 aircraft would have to fly from a tail-sitting position for every flight, including the first.

The engine testing had already transpired at San Diego, where the Pogostick was built. The test stand had consisted of a massive, four-legged steel structure onto which was mounted the Allison engine, contra-rotating propellers and a portion of the XFY-1 fuselage that included the cockpit. Under the test pilot's control, the simulator could rise five feet to give the inexperienced airman at least an initial feel for playing the throttle against up and down VTO aircraft movement. In the way of preliminary

For actual flight the ventral fin tip was removed (see earlier photos) and never replaced. Pods on wing tips held flight test instrumentation and would have been used for rockets or cannon if design had been developed into a fighter. (Convair)

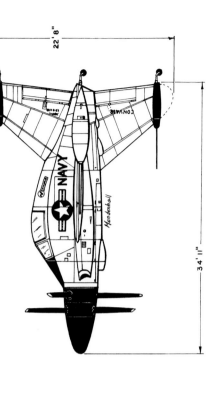

27' 7.75"

52°

22' 8"

34' 11"

1ST FLIGHT- (VTO) NOVEMBER 2, 1954

CONVAIR XFY-1
Pogostick

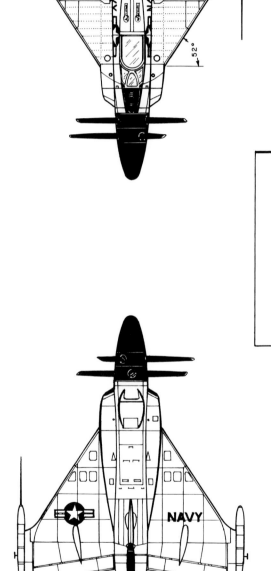

NAVY

WING AREA-355 SQUARE FEET
GROSS WEIGHT-16,250 LBS.
EMPTY WEIGHT-11,742 LBS.
MAX. SPEED - 610 MPH

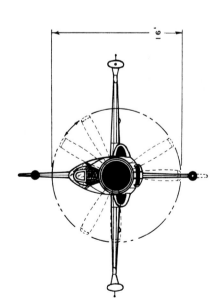

16'

POWERPLANT-ALLISON YT40-A-14 TURBOPROP PROVIDING 5,850 EHP.

testing, it should also be noted that a Pogo airframe was meanwhile undergoing static loading tests and proved out A-ok. Models of the XFY-1 were also tested in Langley Field's wind tunnel, as well as at Wallops Island.

At Moffet, the first attempts at hovering, but tethered hovering, flight began. The big Allison turboprop engine was the only copy rated at that time for sustained operation in the vertical position, its oil and fuel systems modified for this mode. It had been sent to Convair because the XFY-1 was not capable of taking off and landing horizontally, as was the Lockheed machine—a good deal for Convair, even if backed into.

The blimp hangar was 195 feet high, with the Pogo cables attached at a point 184 feet above the floor. This was enough to give the Convair test pilot,

J. F. (Skeets) Coleman, a good taste of what he would be facing when the ship was later moved outdoors for free flight. Coleman had been a Major in the U.S. Marines during World War II. In the 2nd Air Wing, he had flown ninety-one missions, many of them in the Solomon and Bougainville areas, flying both fighters and bombers. Along the way, he also picked up a seaplane rating. After the war, he had worked for an FBO before joining Convair with the XFY-1 project specifically in mind.

One good thing about those cables fastened from the nose to the ceiling of the hangar was that if the engine should falter or stop, there was little chance of damaging the aircraft or injuring the pilot. Safety of the pilot is always of paramount importance in a new project such as this one. Also important, of course, is the well-being of the prototype

Delta-winged Pogo had an ejection seat that fired horizontally but to be fully successful during an eject an altitude of at least 200 feet was required. (Convair)

aircraft, as many millions of dollars and thousands of man hours have been expended for its design and construction, all not easily replaceable. Therefore, the steps at testing time are usually small and almost timid, as the envelope of knowledge of the new machine is expanded and checked again and again before moving on to the next tentative step. Things still can go wrong, but at least everything possible has been done to assure success.

The test setup details are of interest. The aircraft was stripped of the massive propeller spinner, and the tips were removed from the ventral and dorsal tail members. Next, a steel tube ring was affixed to the aircraft above the propeller shaft. This acted as a guide for the aircraft-to-ceiling cable, so that in no case could the plane veer far from a vertical attitude during the test. While unlikely, the last thing anyone wanted was a *horizontal* XFY-1 bellowing about the interior of the blimp hangar. The cable from the aircraft's nose ran to a powered drum on the ceiling of the hangar and then to a counterweight, located over to one side. There was also a system of cable tension regulators and cables that attached to the Pogo's tail. Those allowed the plane to rise freely but also limited its lateral travel. Travel to the ceiling would be done in the range of three to four feet per second, and the pilot would also learn to make landings feather soft on the four oleo casters attached to the rear of the aircraft.

Nearly 300 familiarization flights were made to the top of the lofty hangar by Coleman during the summer of 1954. He grew more and more accustomed to the strange unnatural attitude of the aircraft. The Allison YT-40 engine, meanwhile, performed flawlessly, which in itself was unusual for so new a design. Finally, the time came when they could not hope to learn any more by flying to the ceiling of the blimp hangar and back.

On August 1, 1954, Convair moved the Pogostick outside the hangar to the apron. It was now one

This photo removes all doubt about the horizontal flight capabilities of the XFY-1 as it skims along a few hundred feet off the ground. (Convair)

of those moments of truth—would it or wouldn't it? It would! Coleman climbed the machine straight up, hanging on those big contrarotating props, the engine churning out well over 5,000 horsepower while everybody held their breath. Up and up to twenty feet, the Pogo hung there, then a gentle descent, backing down to the concrete. So far, so good. Try it again. This time Coleman held the throttles full open for a longer period and the unusual Convair creation climbed on up to 150 feet before the throttles were gently retarded and the Pogostick slowly eased itself back to the apron under the skilled test pilot's complete control.

"It's more maneuverable and responds faster than any plane I've ever flown. We'll do a little more maneuvering and try a few tricks as we go along," was the happy Coleman's report.

That was enough tinkering at the outpost airfield. It was time to bring the machine back to San Diego's Brown Field Naval Auxiliary Air Station, where the really serious work could start on investigating the flight envelope of the XFY-1. Once there, the instruments would be recalibrated for vertical and horizontal positions and a special rate-of-descent indicator would be installed.

The subject of moving the Convair VTO brings to mind an accessory vehicle Convair had developed in conjunction with the aircraft. It was a special four-wheel rig that could carry the XFY-1 in a horizontal position over the highway towed by a simple Jeep. The trailer was fitted with hydraulic cylinders that could lift the Pogo into an upright position, then deposit it sitting on its tail on the ground. It was all part of the early fifties system. Some in the military service were sure that VTO would be the ultimate conventional fighter plane. The aircraft solved very nicely the problems of runway availability and aircraft dispersion away from enemy attack.

Another accessory for the XFY-1 was the thirty-six-foot-high tepee-shaped hangar to keep the craft out of the weather and give ground crewmen protected platforms to work on any part of the aircraft. It was built of wood and steel framework, with fiberglass covering and was split into two wheel-mounted sections, which opened in clamshell fashion. The interior was illuminated to allow night

Passing overhead the XFY-1 Pogostick appears to be just like one of the other Convair delta designs, except of course for the propellers. (Convair)

maintenance work on the Pogo. It was actually used at the Brown Field test facility.

Meanwhile, at Edwards Air Force Base, the pilot of the Lockheed XFV-1, Herman (Fish) Salmon, was putting the XFV-1 through its paces on a regular basis. Due to the unavailability of a suitable vertical running Allison YT-40 (Convair had taken the only one), Salmon was making do with a jury-rigged conventional landing gear, but was still practicing the vertical flying mode at altitude. He would pull up, adding power as the Lockheed began to stall. At about eighty degrees he was able to complete the pullup to full vertical, with the ship settling down and hanging on its props. By backing off the throttle, he was able to descend rearward in the vertical mode at a slow rate, up to about eight miles per hour. At that point, the ship started to act up and become uncontrollable. A little more throttle and it returned to normal, and the pilot once more had full control. He also found that the maximum vertical forward speed was only about sixty miles per hour. To reach a higher climbing speed, the ship had to be laid over so that the lift of the wings could carry the plane's weight. Salmon personally passed these lessons, learned at altitude, on to Convair pilot Coleman. In the hairy business at hand, whatever one pilot learned was immediately shared with the other. There were no company secrets.

With the Pogo in San Diego and prepared for flight, Coleman once more began testing with tenta-

Yarn tufts applied to the vertical fin and fuselage sides help engineers chart the airflow around the fin-fuselage juncture. (Convair)

tive short VTO's. He took the Pogo to several hundred feet and even nosed it over to thirty degrees and flew the length of the runway. In all, he made about seventy free flights of this type. Then, on November 4, 1954, all was ready to go for broke. This time it would be a VTO takeoff, a climb to altitude and a transition to horizontal flight. After a short investigation of the conventional flight envelope, there would be a low swoop across the field followed by pulling the ship up vertically, avoiding a stall on the way up as it slowed by the quick addition of power. Then, hanging on the propellers, a slow controlled rearward descent would be accomplished. There was a lot for a pilot to do in a very short time. Any mistake would be the end of the ball game for, at the low altitude, no time would be available to get out. Sure, they had invented a new horizontal ejection seat with an ultrafast opening parachute to let the pilot escape, but who wanted to be the first guinea pig to try that? (In fact, the chute did work and became the basic design for the zero-altitude chute that came to be standard equipment in all military fighter aircraft.)

On the November 4, 1954, flight all went reasonably well. The engine performed faultlessly, the takeoff was as smooth as the previous ones, and the transition to level flight was not difficult; just pour on the power and fly on up and over. To make sure everything possible was learned from the flight, a Convair stenographer was assigned to transcribe every word said by Coleman during the flight. (Must be they didn't trust the voice recorders.) After about twenty minutes of flying as a conventional aircraft, Coleman passed low over the airfield and then pulled up to vertical. He carefully avoided a stall as he went past the magic eighty-degree stall point, then added power to hang on the props. He was somewhat uptight at this point and, though it looked like a textbook VTO landing to some spectators, it was not so with Coleman. Flying backward was for the birds . . . no, that's not right, even the birds wouldn't do it. It was a very disorienting feeling with no sense of speed. The descent had to be very slow and gentle for the pilot to maintain control. The flight was finally terminated on a fifty-foot square, and this, of course, left the door open for *more* flights, even though the back-down was distasteful. More flights soon took place. Over San Diego Bay, this same day, Sea Dart number two met its end.

For the first successful VTO flight in history, Coleman was awarded the Harmon Trophy. He also was the subject of one of the Dupont Company's *Cavalcade of America* television series in 1955, titled, "Take Off Zero." The next day a public demonstration was made and, in the following weeks, more flights were made, amassing a total of about forty hours of flight. The full flight envelope was never explored, however. Charles E. Myers, Jr., also came on stream as a test pilot. He later became director of Air Warfare for the Defense Department, before becoming a consultant.

The Ryan X-13 Vertijet was a pure jet VTO design for the USAF. It made its first full transition flight April 11, 1957. The back-down landing problem was still there and the project was dropped. (Collect Air)

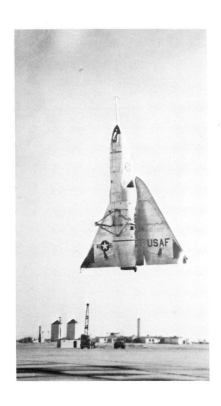

As the Pogo program moved along, Coleman was interviewed in a 1955 *Popular Science Monthly* article and laconically reported that taking off was like "driving your car over the crest of a hill," while landing was like "backing your car into the garage with only inches to spare along the walls." Coleman allowed, "The first 150 feet were the toughest both going up and coming down. That's the line above which I can explode myself out of the cockpit and land safely by parachute, and below which the odds aren't so good.

"When flying vertically, the plane literally hangs on the props. After 200 feet I'm ready for the transition into horizontal flight, when the wings will take over. I push the stick forward, nosing Pogo over. At the same time, I ease the swinging seat backwards so I'll be sitting up comfortably instead of leaning forward.

"Landing is different. Slowly I pull Pogo into a nose up attitude. Over my shoulder I see the concrete appear. For a moment I hang motionless. I move the throttle a fraction and begin to back down. It's a gentle precise maneuver. Where airlines settle for a landing at 500 feet per minute, Pogo descends at only 300—nice and comfortable."

Other aviation experts viewing films of the landings were not so sure it was all that easy. To them the ailerons and vertical control surfaces seemed to be moving almost violently during landing and at one point, about twenty feet from the ground, the XFY-1 appeared about to tip backward. It was also difficult for them to see what could be done about sideways drift in a strong wind.

Yes, they could do it. Planes could take off from a tail-sitting position, change to level flight and fly about like a conventional aircraft. They could even return to base and make a reasonably good landing, tail first. Coleman called Pogo "both the world's slowest and fastest propellered airplane." That was the mission, and both the Convair XFY-1 and Lockheed XFV-1 had shown that it was possible. Unfortunately though, the aircraft would require pilots of the caliber of Coleman and Salmon to fly them, and there were not many of them around. Certainly the young graduates of Pensacola Navy flight training were not going to be up to it, nor probably

The Pogo's end. Sitting VTO style behind a neatly trimmed hedge at Norfolk Naval Air Station—the plane's propellers have a wooden clamp to prevent their rotation in the wind. Perhaps being a monument, of sorts, is not such a bad end. (National Airchives)

would most of their elders in the ranks above. That backing down bit was mind boggling, and even the two expert test pilots had trouble with it.

Then too, to some it was not clear why it should be necessary to land tail first. The VTO idea was OK, but why not use the great power of the turbojets to lift and lower the plane while it remained in a more orthodox straight and level attitude?

With the program still under way, development of pilot aids continued, two of which were of great help to the XFY-1 pilots. One was special headgear, which had a snug-fitting eye shield to keep dust and propeller blast out of the pilot's eyes during takeoff and landings. The helmet was also of a special sound-deadening design that required a new oxygen mask fitting. An electronic rate-of-climb meter was the other aid, essentially a CW doppler radar that used the ground below the aircraft as a reflecting surface. The installation was in the left wing pod, where colored lights could be viewed by the pilot as he looked over his left shoulder at the ground. Each light represented a desired velocity range. Furthermore, an actual rate-of-climb/descent meter was wall-mounted in the cockpit and also in the pilot's line of vision to the ground. The system was extensively tested in a helicopter before being applied to the aircraft. Its useful range was between zero and 200 feet altitude.

A drawback that became apparent, however, was the overall performance of the planes, even if the transition problems of landing could be overcome. They were prop-driven and even at the very best could not be expected to go past Mach .8. When work had first begun in the late forties, that was pretty much all right. All the then-new jet fighters were going about that speed. However, with the military putting the heat on to speed them up, the sec-

ond-generation jets were easily passing the speed of sound, and some were going on to the Mach 2 region. That type of fighter was completely out of the class of the Lockheed and Convair VTO's. Therefore, as fighters, they were obsolete even before their development programs were completed. However, it was an avenue of aeronautical design that cried out to be pursued, and it was. Unfortunately in the end, it was a dry hole. An announcement was made in January 1956 that the development programs for both the Convair and Lockheed VTO aircraft were terminated. Findings of the two would be filed for future use.

The Ryan Aeronautical Company thought it might be able to save the idea, and so did the USAF, which offered a contract. Ryan designed and built the X13 Vertijet, which did the same thing as the earlier Lockheed and Convair designs, except with a jet engine. The first full transition flight was made April 11, 1957. The backing down problem was still there, however, and after initial success as far as flying goes, the project was dropped.

The VTO idea did not die, just the tail-sitting arrangement was discarded. The fleet Harrier fighters used by the USMC and the British Royal Navy show that the concept is still alive and well and even in production on a fully certified-for-combat operations basis. The planes operate by means of thrust-directing nozzles that allow the pilot to retain his natural right-side-up orientation. With that, pilots have their share of problems accidentwise, as the Harriers are still somewhat touchy to fly when compared with standard performance aircraft. Had the Convair and Lockheed VTO's been put in production, the Harrier's accident record would have probably paled in comparison.

CHAPTER VI
△ HUSTLER, THE DELTA QUEEN

△————————————THE ULTIMATE DAZZLER—
that was the B-58 Hustler. Looking back, its name, even in today's parlance, wasn't all that far off base. Just like in a B movie, the Hustler was born beautiful, led a fast life (Mach 2) and died young. Only ten years encompassed all its active service. That's pretty short when compared to the venerable B-52's, A4D Skyhawks, and C-130's, all veterans of first-line service for almost thirty years. The problem sure wasn't lack of performance. If high speed, high altitude and high destructive capability had anything to do with it, the Hustler was a winner in every respect.

With a span of fifty-six feet ten inches and a length of ninety-six feet nine inches, it was not a large aircraft when compared to the giant B-36 Peacemaker or the B-52 Stratofortress. Its fuselage size, however, was not all that small. It was only a couple of feet shorter than the B-29, which was considered to be a rather large aircraft in 1944. The short span, of course, was due to the delta wing planform. With an area of 1,542 square feet, it had more lifting surface than the Boeing B-47. Its real problem, and not its fault, lay with the military's transition from manned to unmanned bombers. The intercontinental ballistic missiles were coming along, and most of the eggs were put in that basket.

The nine-foot-high landing gear gave the aircraft a storklike appearance, particularly when the weapons or fuel pods were not slung underneath the fuselage. The long spindly gear allowed clearance for the pods to be wheeled underneath the fuselage for attachment. Each main gear consisted of eight wheels, four in a row, that gave a sufficient footprint on the runway so as not to break up the concrete. Runways regularly used by B-58's, however, still had their problems. At Bunker Hill AFB (now Grissom), the bomber's touchdown at 180 miles per hour tended to break up the concrete by the shearing action of the tires when they hit. Parts of the surface concrete broke away in shallow pieces about ¼-inch thick. The cure lay in coating the runways in the touchdown area with a mixture of epoxy and sand.

The Hustler's tires were only twenty-two inches in diameter and were inflated to a pressure of 240 pounds per square inch, or about eight times that of the family car. The tires were mounted on nonfrangible steel wheels that would continue to roll even if all the tires blew out at once during a hard landing. The main gear retracted rearward hydraulically, with each of the gear's two sets of four wheels rotating about the end of the strut to lay one set ahead of the other in the wing. Since the wing was

only about eighteen inches thick at that point, it was necessary to position the wheels in the center of the airfoil cross-section and add bumps, or fairings, to both the top and bottom surfaces of the wing. These bumps were then smoothly faired forward to streamlined points.

Brakes were hydraulically actuated, as were the gear doors. In case of a hydraulic system failure, and this probably would never happen as there were two complete and independent hydraulic systems, compressed air bottles were provided to lower the gear and apply brakes for one landing only. The nose gear consisted of two wheels that were slightly smaller than the main gear wheels and those were also nonfrangible. The nose gear was hydraulically steerable. The strut "broke-in-the-middle," with the

Head-on photo of B-58A shows a truly lean and mean machine. Area ruled fuselage is clearly evident as is the streamlined shapes on each wing that make up the housings for the retracted main gear. These "bumps" were required because the wings were thinner than the main-gear tire diameters. (General Dynamics)

nose wheels retracting forward into the wheel well as the upper portion of the strut retracted rearward into the well. The twin, nose wheel doors were closed hydraulically after the gear was in place.

The wing was constructed in a manner that was certainly different than the usual rib, spars and stressed-skin construction. There were no ribs used to provide the airfoil shape, unlike the usual method for this sort of thing. Instead, thin corrugated aluminum spars ran from one wing margin through the fuselage to the other wing's margin. The spars were closely spaced, from eleven to fifteen inches apart. Their height determined the airfoil shape. The only

longitudinal members in the wing were structural in nature and used to support and attach engine nacelles, elevons, and the main landing gear struts and doors.

The covering on the wing structure (i.e., the multiplicity of lateral spars), was a honeycomb sandwich material, whose composition varied with its location on the wing. The major portion consisted of two .040-inch-thick aluminum sheets with phenolic-fiberglass honeycomb heat-bonded between them. The structure was very strong, rigid and light. It was also, due to being a poor heat conductor, able to stand the 250°F temperatures generated on the air-

Interesting view of the Convair solution to getting a completed B-58 airframe from Ft. Worth, Texas, to Wright Field at Dayton, Ohio, for structural testing. The two inboard propellers of the B-36 were removed and the landing gear was left extended for the duration of the nonstop flight. Reason for the trip was that Convair did not have equipment with a capacity to test such a large airframe as the B-58. (General Dynamics)

craft's skin surfaces due to extended flying at Mach 2 airspeeds. Some of the panels, where more strength was required, were made of the same aluminum sheets, but the filler was thin aluminum in honeycomb form, with the whole assembly brazed together. On the lower wing surface behind the inboard engines, even this was not strong enough. In that area, and on the elevon undersurfaces that were exposed to the jet blast, brazed stainless steel honeycomb and outer sheeting was used. At a point twenty-five feet behind an engine, running with full afterburner, the temperature could reach 700°F, so the stainless steel panels were definitely required.

Convair, to prove the durability of the wing panels in the engine exhaust area, actually ran a ten-hour test with inboard engines in full afterburner and sound at 171 decibels.

The honeycomb was not formable once the bonding had taken place; therefore, the sheets were held in jigs of the contour desired during the brazing operation. They were cured at 350°F and 175 pounds per square inch, in the case of the phenolic honeycomb parts, and, of course, at much higher temperatures in the case of the all-metal brazed sandwiches. The finished individual skin sections were then attached to the spars with titanium screws. With the

Convair's B-58 production line was nearly a mile long—hence the many bicycles in this photo. Photo was taken in 1960. (General Dynamics)

type of construction used, it was possible to build an extremely light (though strong) airframe. The dry structural weight of the B-58 was only fourteen percent of its gross weight! One problem though, from a maintenance standpoint, was that whenever a honeycomb panel was removed from the airframe, the structure of the aircraft had to be jigged, and the airplane could not be moved until the panel was once more screwed in place. The honeycomb panels covered about ninety percent of the wings and seventy percent of the fuselage. The screws were treated with a gasketing material, since most of the wing's interior was used for fuel tankage, as was most of the fuselage interior. This was possible since the weapons were carried exterior to the aircraft in the underslung pods.

The JP-4 jet fuel was carried in four tanks aboard the aircraft, with room for additional fuel in the weapons pod when it was used. The largest tank took up most of the aft part of the wing and could hold 39,794 pounds of fuel, with the forward wing tank holding 20,648 pounds and a reserve tank above the wing in the fuselage holding 4,163 pounds. In addition to these three, there was a tail tank in the fuselage about the level of the elevons that held 8,195 pounds, and it was used to balance the aircraft, that is, keep the center of gravity in the correct place

at the various speed and altitude combinations the aircraft encountered. The center of gravity was monitored by a crew member (the defense system operator); however, the actual work of pumping fuel fore and aft as required was computer-controlled. It is interesting to note that a similar system is still used today on the Concorde supersonic transport.

The area-ruled fuselage was constructed similarly to the wing, with the through-wing spars forming bulkheads and providing the cross-sectional contours. Again, the honeycomb panels provided the strong, light, stressed-skin covering. The fuselage panels were constructed similarly to the wing panels, except they were strengthened with additional beaded inner skins bonded to the aluminum skin of the sandwich. This was done to improve heat dissipation from the fuselage interior.

Starting at the nose, it was apparent that the fuselage was designed for speed, for it was long, slender, and rocketlike. The pitot tube extended several feet in front of the pointed plastic nose, out ahead of any disturbance to the airflow. The pointed nose itself was made of dilectric plastic to house the radar dish. Moving rearward, the crew cockpits were then encountered: the pilot, the bombadier/navigator and the defense systems operator, one behind the other and in distinct, separate compartments.

For a time Convair had the best of both worlds, the B-58A Hustler supersonic bomber and the Atlas SM-65 ICBM, shown here side by side. Missile is 85 feet 6 inches long versus the B-58's 96 feet 9 inches. (General Dynamics)

The pilot had a view out the pointed, six-piece windshield. In addition, there was even a couple of small eyebrow windows for viewing above for such times as during refueling. The other two crew members were exposed to claustrophobia, as all the touch they had with the outside world was a diminutive four-by six-inch window on either side of their respective cockpits. Each cockpit was fitted with an individual canopy that could be jettisoned for ejecting in case of an emergency.

In 1962, as the B-58 was developed, an enclosed escape capsule was installed (or retrofitted) for each crew member, so that at high altitude and supersonic speed they could still escape a stricken aircraft. The capsule would descend safely beneath a forty-one-foot-diameter parachute and could float if it came down on water. It contained a radio, a rifle, a change of clothes, food and water for a week, a desalinization unit, and other survival gear. The capsule was fitted with clamshell doors that slammed

The XB-58-CF, 55-660, first flew on November 11, 1956. Nose, vertical fin and wingtip had colorful red and white paint schemes. (General Dynamics)

Prototype Hustler, shown here with weapons and fuel pod slung underneath fuselage, was powered by four General Electric J79-GE-1 turbojets with afterburners. Each produced 10,500 pounds static thrust, 15,600 pounds with afterburner lite-off. (General Dynamics)

Snuggled up under a KC-135 at about 375 miles per hour and 25,000 feet, fuel is transferred to the bomber at up to 5,500 pounds per minute. (General Dynamics)

A view of a B-58A from the KC-135 "boomers" position. Small winglets on boom are used to "fly" the refueling probe into a *connect* position joining the two aircraft. (General Dynamics)

shut just before ejection. This really meant that crew members could not be too large of stature and still fit in the capsule. Which also meant some prospective B-58 crewmen were rejected. However, "If you didn't quite fit the capsule during qualification, you certainly would after the doors slammed shut." It must be said that everything was done that anyone could think of to make the safety and security of the crew members as great as possible. Harsh circumstances were anticipated for the B-58's, because of the speed and altitude required of them, as well as the unhospitable destinations of their missions and the enemy's weapons potential.

Aside from the emergency precautions and the cramped crew space, an effort was made to provide a bit of creature comfort for the crewmen. Two air-conditioning systems, each with an eighteen-ton refrigeration capacity, prevented the cockpits from getting unbearably hot due to the supersonic skin friction and controlled the heavy heat load of the electronics the craft carried. The air conditioners also took care of dehumidification and windshield rain removal. However, if the temperature of the electronics began to creep up above a safe level, the systems automatically switched all the cooling air to the black boxes and away from the crew. You could

The number two XB-58-CF, with drag chute still full, taxies past after a test flight. Normal landing rollout was about 2,600 feet using chute and brakes. Chute was popped at about 160 knots. (USAF)

The B-58 was handled by a 3-man crew: pilot, navigator/bombardier and defense systems operator. Latter two had only a 4-by-6-inch window on either side of their cockpit to see what was going on outside. (USAF)

continue to fly and fight with a sweating crew, but not with inoperative electronics. One last point on crew comfort: high altitude breathing. The aircraft was fitted with bottled liquid oxygen fed through diluter-demand regulators to the pressure-breathing face masks worn by the crew members. A pressure regulator was placed in the cockpit exhaust vent and kept the pressure differential up to 7.45 pounds per square inch.

In the pilot's cockpit, the seat and instrument panel were located to the left of the aircraft's centerline. The usual stick and rudder pedals were used for flying the aircraft, when it was not on autopilot. A trigger on the control stick allowed the pilot to deactivate the autopilot's pitch control during landing flare without taking his hand off the stick. Of course, with the high speeds involved, as well as the general size of the plane, all the pedals and stick did, through an intricate linkage of cables, was control valves for the hydraulic actuators that moved the control surfaces. There was artificial feedback to the pilot, however, that gave him "feel" much like a conventional small aircraft. The autopilot was also always at work to prevent the pilot from making any control movements that might take the aircraft outside the safe structural or stability envelopes. At

The spidery, storkish landing gear of the Hustler was required to provide ground clearance when the single, or double, weapons and fuel pods were slung under the fuselage. For all its complexity it was fast acting. (General Dynamics)

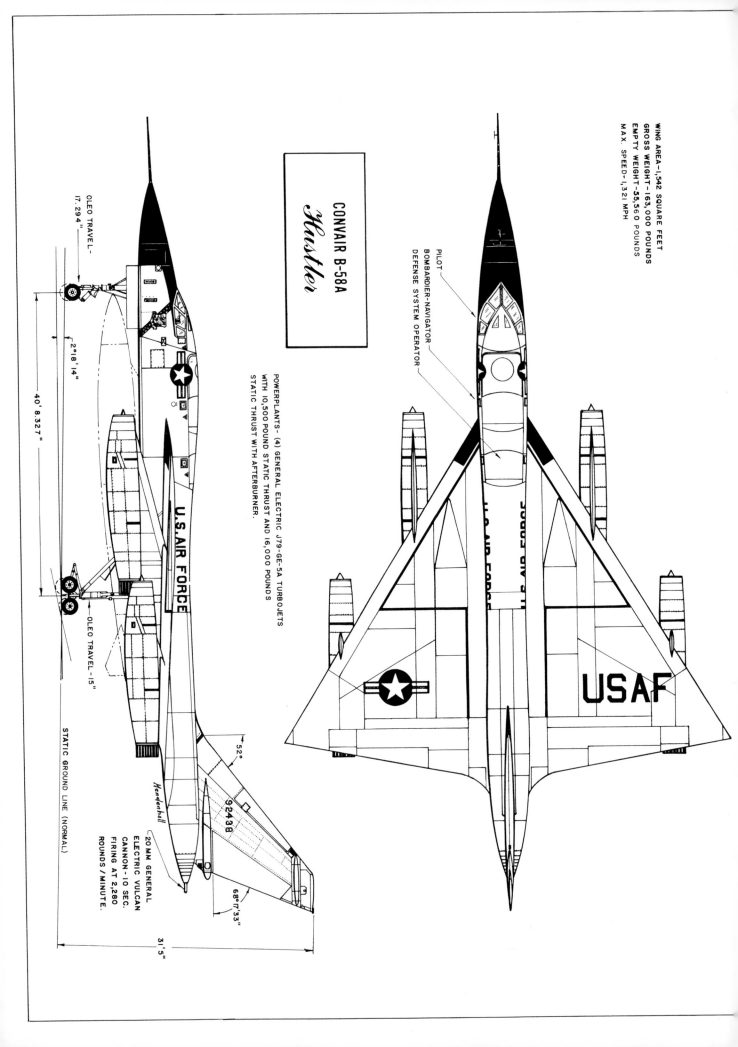

WING AREA—1,542 SQUARE FEET
GROSS WEIGHT—163,000 POUNDS
EMPTY WEIGHT—55,560 POUNDS
MAX. SPEED—1,321 MPH

PILOT
BOMBARDIER-NAVIGATOR
DEFENSE SYSTEM OPERATOR

CONVAIR B-58A
Hustler

POWERPLANTS— (4) GENERAL ELECTRIC J79-GE-5A TURBOJETS
WITH 10,500 POUND STATIC THRUST AND 16,000 POUNDS
STATIC THRUST WITH AFTERBURNER.

OLEO TRAVEL—
17.294"

2°8'14"

40' 8.327"

OLEO TRAVEL—15"

STATIC GROUND LINE (NORMAL)

52°

Mendenhall

92438

68°17'33"

31'5"

20 MM GENERAL
ELECTRIC VULCAN
CANNON-10 SEC.
FIRING AT 2,280
ROUNDS / MINUTE.

U.S. AIR FORCE

USAF

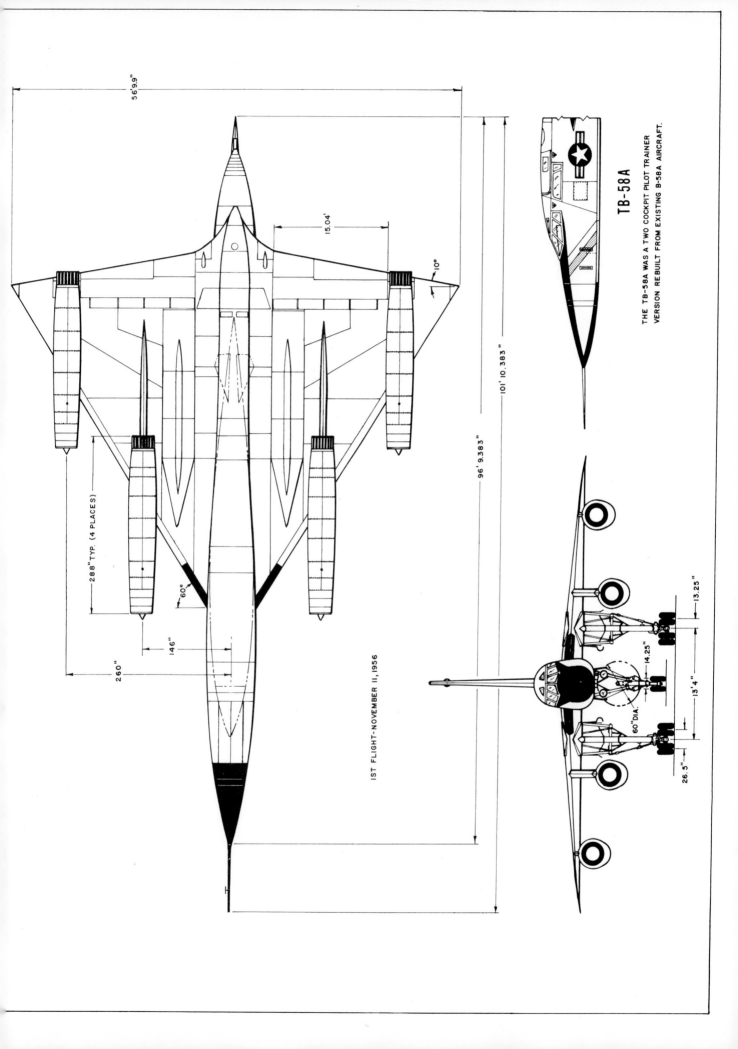

56'9.9"

15.04'

10°

101' 10.383"

96' 9.383"

288" TYP. (4 PLACES)

60°

146"

260"

1ST FLIGHT-NOVEMBER 11, 1956

TB-58A

THE TB-58A WAS A TWO COCKPIT PILOT TRAINER
VERSION REBUILT FROM EXISTING B-58A AIRCRAFT.

13.25"

14.25"

13' 4"

60"DIA.

26.5"

supersonic speed, this was necessary, as pilot response time would be too slow and coarse to be effective under such conditions. The flight instrumentation was on the panel's left side, and the engine information was on the right. A large knob on the panel's left side was for actuation of the landing gear.

Some instruments were peculiar to the delta bomber. One was the elevon-position indicator. In order to trim the plane up for level zero-g flight, the elevons were always up to some degree, the slower the speed and lower the altitude the more they were automatically raised. At low airspeed particularly, the pilot needed to know how much unused elevon travel he had left for maneuvering. Automatic flight controls were also part of the equipment used to help the pilot fly the Hustler. These aids responded to the input of the autopilot amplifier, which received its information from the air data computer and included air temperature, Mach number and altitude. The gross weight computer also provided input to the autopilot amplifier, as well as the tracking and flight controller units, which provided pitch and roll corrections. Too, there was the primary navigational system putting out pitch, roll and heading data and the accelerometer and rate gyros. With those inputs,

the autopilot could sense and dampen the rates of roll, pitch and yaw to prevent airframe damage caused by too sudden a change in direction. The system could even control the engine output in accomplishing that task.

To keep track of the "state of the aircraft," two warning systems, one visual and one auditory, signaled the pilot of any malfunction as soon as it occurred. The signals were a red light on the pilot's instrument panel right side illuminating the words Master Warning and a yellow light reading Master Caution. The pilot, in the event either of these lights went on, looked to the warning and caution panels on the cockpit's right side for a detailed warning in the form of a smaller light beside appropriate nomenclature. For more immediate attention getting, a soft, feminine recorded voice, with twenty stored messages, would tell the pilot he had an engine fire or other such interesting dilemmas. It was a good attention-getter, and many pilots wondered if the woman behind the voice looked as good as she sounded.

The second cockpit back housed the bombardier/navigator, who also had some rather sophisticated electronic equipment in the form of

The 60° sweptback delta wing provided 1,542 square feet of wing surface with a span of only 56 feet 10 inches. Wing had no ribs, only multitudinous spars that ran from edge to edge while also acting as formers for fuselage. (General Dynamics)

the Sperry AN/ASQ-42 bombing and navigation system. The heart of this system was a 1,200-pound analog computer. By today's standards, that massive collection of electronic tubes and transistors is pretty archaic. The F-16's twenty-pound digital computer can do the same job! By directing the aircraft's autopilot, the Hustler's system could guide it at a constant Mach number to *any* point on the globe, which covers a lot of territory to say the least. The navigator located his current position in latitude and longitude coordinates, then dialed in the same information concerning where he wanted to go. The computer, supported by sensors of various kinds, did the rest.

There was also much other equipment available to the bombardier/navigator. There were inertial navigation systems, one primary and the other on standby. A doppler radar transmitter and receiver mounted in the tail constantly measured the aircraft's true ground speed. There was also a star tracker unit mounted in a slightly domed area above the fuselage, which could be locked onto the sun or any major visible star and could then provide constantly updated heading information. In addition, a remote compass was located up in the fin, and high resolution search radar in the nose also provided a display on the radar scope of features on the ground. The air data system, mentioned earlier, also provided the navigator with true airspeed, pressure altitude and air temperature for the navigator's computer. An inflight printer also recorded such things as time, position, speed and altitude on punched paper tape.

When the time came for the navigator to turn his hat around and become bombardier, there was an electronic black box to take care of that, too. During the run-in over the target, he could track the progress of the bomb run on his scope, which was marked with predetermined check points to indicate how closely the release point for a burst over the target was going to be met. He had a control stick in his right hand that would allow him to make small corrections through the autopilot if that was required. During SAC practice runs, he also had a radio tone he could turn on as a run began, with its tone stopping abruptly when the bomb was released. On the ground, monitoring crews could determine how accurate the mission would have been had it been the real thing.

Back in cockpit number three was the defense systems operator. Until such time as the mission got entangled with enemy defenses, he did not have a great deal to do, defensewise. He, therefore, helped the pilot by reading off checklists for the various stages of the flight and by monitoring the fuel consumption, optimum flight altitudes and the all-important location of center of gravity based on speed and altitude. However, this all became secondary when the enemy was finally joined. He then operated the track-breaking radar (or electronic countermeasures equipment) that confused the enemy ground-to-air missle systems. He also directed and fired the 20 mm M-61 six-barrel cannon that was mounted in a barbette in the tail. It was

This photo taken at Edwards AFB October 12, 1961, shows aircraft number 59 used for sonic boom studies. (USAF)

trained on an attacking intruder by means of radar. The intruder, displayed on a scope, was tracked automatically, figuring elevation and windage. The system even notified the third cockpit crew member when to fire the weapon.

With respect to the B-58's electronic countermeasures (ECM), staff weather officer of the 43rd Bomb Wing, Joseph M. Kovac, Jr., recalls that they were pretty potent:

"The electronics countermeasures system was well advanced over those being used operationally.

An automatic reaction had been built into the electronic wizardry to ease the workload on the DSO at critical moments. Similar to a modern day CB scanner, it would cycle through preselected blocks of frequencies, stopping to analyze those signals transmitted toward the aircraft. If the variation of the signal strength or character indicated that a 'lock-on' was being attempted, the system would automatically respond to 'cancel' the detection system.

"In the weather station we had to be careful with our weather radar when interrogating sus-

The wide array of B-58 armament was spectacular. To the left is the component pod (B-2-4) and weapons section (B-3-6) that nestles into it. Four tactical nuclear weapons that could be mounted on underwing hard spots are next. A mockup of the Vulcan 20 mm tail cannon, and its many rounds of ammunition complete the weaponry of the Hustler. (General Dynamics)

pected thunderstorms or shower cells of rapid and intense development. If a B-58 was in the corridor making a training run at the same time we were sector scanning or manually measuring a cloud buildup in the same direction, we would find our weather radar suddenly blooming with an overload of regenerated energy. Protective relays would cut off power within the system. The time required to build back up to operating power would often put us off the air for half an hour or more; the price we paid because we had accidentally scanned across a B-58 more often than the aircraft's ECM equipment 'thought' was necessary."

The powerplants on the B-58's were in themselves as important in the building of the supersonic bomber as the bizarre-shaped airframe. They were built by General Electric and were J79-5A's or -5B's. They were axial flow turbojets with afterburners capable of belting out a whopping 10,000 pounds of static thrust each and moved right on up to 15,600 pounds with maximum afterburner. That was a total for the four engines of 62,400 pounds of push for some real zappy performance, and even today they

power the F-4 Phantom II fighters. Some notion of the engine's power can be noted from the fact that suction from the intakes could pull a man into the engine from as far in front of the engine as twenty-five feet. At the aft end of the nacelles, the danger area extended to 250 feet. At fifty feet the 700°F exhaust lashed out at over 400 miles per hour—faster than the howling winds of a tornado! The powerplants were built from the start for the supersonic regime.

The engines were equipped with a variable position inlet spike that hydraulically moved inward and outward to keep the conical supersonic shock wave outside the engine air inlet during supersonic operation. Variable position stator vanes were located in the first six stages of the compressor. Their pitch was automatically adjusted, based on engine speed and inlet temperature, to direct the incoming air against the rotating compressor vanes at an angle that would help prevent compressor stall.

Primary and secondary tailpipe outlet nozzle areas, by means of convergent/divergent slotted vanes, also provided optimum thrust and specific

The open cockpits of the Hustler reveal the supersonically rated escape capsules that closed around the crew members just before ejection. The "wastebaskets" over the engine inlets were to prevent ingestion of foreign objects during the many taxi tests. (General Dynamics)

fuel consumption under a variety of engine operating conditions. They were automatically opened and closed along with the throttles. The throttles had six settings: off, idle, military, minimum afterburner, maximum afterburner and overspeed. The latter requires a little explanation. It would permit 103.5 percent of rated thrust for a short period where maximum performance was absolutely needed. It could also be run at 105 to 107 percent for a maximum of five seconds or less without damage to the engines. Anything over 107 percent required the engines be removed, inspected and probably overhauled.

Generators were driven by engines one, two and three to provide 115- to 200-volt alternating current to the fuel pumps, instruments and most radar and navigational equipment. Some of the AC current was rectified to direct current and voltages between 28 and 250 VDC to operate the autopilot, caution and warning lights and some radar and navigation equipment. There was also a small, 28-volt battery for emergency use if the other systems failed.

While on the subject of the electrical systems, it might be added that the defense system operator's cockpit also had the circuit breaker and fuse boards located in it for his monitoring. A blown breaker or fuse could be located by touch, as they were marked with buttons that protruded about an eighth of an inch from the panel when they blew. These interconnected electrical systems did have a shortcoming in that, while they saved weight and space, they could also cause trouble, for an electrical malfunction in one area could cause multiple malfunctions in other parts of the electrical system.

The gear comes up quickly during takeoff-climbout. The large weapons/fuel pod is slung underneath. There were 28 different pod combinations tested and 40 different bomb configurations. (General Dynamics)

The aircraft's hydraulic pressure was provided by a dual system, each component having two, 3,000 psi engine-driven pumps. Either could be used to move the control surfaces and so on in the event of one of them failing. However, should both fail, an immediate bailout was required; as there was no further backup and the aircraft could not be controlled. The high pressure was used to save weight; however, it also caused many problems with leaks in the system.

The streamlined pods hung underneath the B-58 generally carried fuel and a nuclear weapon. There were two systems used. The first, the single pod system, used the type MB pod, which was fifty-seven feet long and contained mostly fuel. Pod diameter was sixty inches maximum. The second system used two pods, with the upper pod nestled inside a concave hollowed-out portion of the lower pod. This system was called the TC pod. The upper

pod, attached to the fuselage, carried a warhead and 2,450 pounds of JP-4. The length was thirty-five feet. The larger lower pod, which wrapped partly around the upper pod, carried only fuel and was dropped before the run-in on the target. It was fifty-four feet long.

The pod systems, in either case, were designed to conform with the Whitcomb area rule in combination with the parent airplane. During testing of these two configurations, twenty-eight different pod combinations and forty different bomb configurations were tried. Uses for the pods included missile and bomb carriers, photo reconnaissance platforms, passenger compartments, gun bays, research facilities and, of course, fuel. The system was so flexible that almost any combination of these items was possible.

From the description of the Hustler, it can readily be seen that it was *some* airplane, even by today's sophisticated standards. Due to the pods, it

A drop test of the large fuel pod leaves the smaller fuel and weapons pod still intact on the Hustler's belly. This would be the configuration for target run-in after a long flight using the fuel in the larger pod. (USAF)

was one aircraft that could weigh more in the air than on the ground. Normal maximum takeoff weight was 163,000 pounds, due to landing gear structural limitations. However, once in the air, with aerial refueling, the Hustler could weigh 176,890 pounds, with over fifty-seven percent of this weight being 101,627 pounds of JP-4.

Every design has its beginning, and in the case of the B-58, 1949 marked the year of the Convair proposal to build a supersonic bomber for the USAF. The company had worked on advanced design studies for bombers since the end of World War II and when, in 1948, the Air Force asked for a bomber able to deliver a nuclear weapon at supersonic speeds, it wasn't long before Convair answered with the same. On June 6, 1951, the USAF presented Convair with a contract to work on GEBO II, a continuation of GEBO, a design study already underway for a GEneralized BOmber.

After initial weighing of the possibilities, including pure jet versus turboprop engines, Convair (already immersed in delta wing design) produced a design for a delta-winged bomber with a jet engine in

the tail, one under each wing, and a dropable payload pod with a jet engine in it. The pod at that time (January 1950) was called a parasite. The pod design caused some consternation with the Wright Field people. The pod extended the full length of the bomber's fuselage, and since the craft was of tricycle gear design, two nose wheels were required: one attached to the pod and dropped at takeoff, the other retracted in the nose of the fuselage for extension when landing. With nose wheels dropping on the populace during takeoff—and pods doing likewise before landing—it did pose a small problem to say the least. The solution, of course, was to shorten the pod so a conventional nose wheel might be used.

The composite unit did not have the 3,000–4,500-mile range required, so it was suggested the whole thing be carried by a B-36 to within striking distance, wherein the dropped minibomber would continue to the target at about Mach 1.6, drop the pod and the wing engines, and return at a high unladen speed with the tail engine to the B-36 mother ship. The concept then evolved through several basic designs before eventually reaching the B-58

The *Firefly* set a New York to Paris speed record May 26, 1961, covering the distance in 3 hours 19 minutes and 51 seconds. The flight also set a Washington-to-Paris speed record of 3 hours and 39 minutes. Both the Mackay and Harmon Trophies were awarded for this. (AAHS Negative Library)

area-ruled, four-jet bomber with conical cambered wings and a lower pod carrying the bomb. It was September 1953.

Boeing was also at work on a supersonic design called the B-59, which was in direct competition with the Convair B-58. On October 9, 1952, both Boeing and Convair presented their designs to the USAF Air Research and Development Command for evaluation. The Air Force soon chose the B-58 as being more capable of the supersonic nuclear missions it envisaged. About the only change from the mock-up to the final design in August 1954 was the separation of the jet engines into four separate pods, instead of the two twin-engine pods as submitted, and the elimination of wing-tip tanks, a move that wind tunnel tests and Wallops Island rocket model tests showed to be desirable.

By August 31, 1956, the first article had been rolled out, and it was without doubt the most advanced aircraft in the world. After much tweaking, engine runups and all the other final chores required to completely finish a new and complex airplane, it was finally ready for taxi tests by October 29. These tests did not involve just traveling down the runway to see if the nose-wheel steering and brakes worked. Some runs were as fast as 250 miles per hour, with the craft being rotated to takeoff position before cutting back the power and braking.

Finally, all was considered ready for the first flight. The Fort Worth day was clear on November 11, 1956, when the B-58 lifted off at 2:41 p.m. for a thirty-eight-minute flight followed by a more or less uneventful landing. The crew was Convair's chief of B-58 flight test Beryl A. Erickson, 2nd Station operator J. D. McBachern and flight test engineer C. P. Harrison in the third station. Upon landing and rollout, these gentlemen were in for a long and detailed debriefing. The test flight made the headlines, as the press had been invited to watch the whole show. This was pretty gutsy, for what if the flight had failed?

The two different types of weapons pods used were the 57-foot-long MB pod and the dual system TC pod consisting of a 54-foot-long lower element containing fuel and a 35-foot upper pod containing the nuclear weapon and fuel. (General Dynamics)

Thirteen prototypes had been ordered, 55-660 being the first. The next two years were spent in preparing the aircraft for operational use by the USAF. With confidence, the Air Force now ordered an additional seventeen machines. A fleet of thirty test aircraft represented an unusual number, but then the B-58 was an unusual airplane. Being so far advanced, there was much to be learned about its operation before it could become operational. Of the first thirteen, three were lost in fatal accidents, as the mysteries of the supersonic bombers were unraveled. Like most previous breakthroughs in the field of aviation, the price in lives was paid.

There are predicted flight envelopes that come from the engineer's sliderules (at that time—computers now), and then there is the real world flight envelopes that come from painstaking test flights that investigate every conceivable flight characteristic of the new plane, plotting data point after data point progressively from the easy and known to the very outside edge of the aircraft's capacity to perform. When these tests are completed, and only then, the handbooks and instruction manuals that will keep the operational pilots in line organizations out of trouble can be written.

During these test programs things sometimes go wrong, causing accidents because not enough is known to forestall such an occurrence happening. An engine could flame out and cause severe yawing at high supersonic speed, throwing the aircraft into a sharp turn and massively overloading and breaking off the vertical fin. The computer for maintaining the center of gravity by means of fuel transfer could go whacky, placing the aircraft into an unflyable condition; or freezing of the elevon ratio changers could occur. Sure, there were fixes for all these things, but they were not much help at Mach 1.8 at 50,000 feet! To be sure, it was "punch out" time—as soon as possible.

Kid glove handling, even by master test pilots, was not always enough. To make the craft go fast, lightness of construction was required, which was ok as long as the structural stresses were applied to the airframe in the directions they were designed for; but there could be sheer disaster if applied otherwise. The Hustler, for example, was stressed for a maximum of $+3$ g's and a minimum of -2 g's. At supersonic speeds it didn't take much heavy-handedness on the controls to exceed those limits and experience catastrophic—and generally unsurvivable—failure.

The absence of extreme performance conditions, however, did not mean the pilot was home free. One accident occurred when overheated tires exploded after retraction into the wheel wells, rupturing fuel and hydraulic lines, with a subsequent wipeout of the airplane. This is a good example of how these events during testing time contribute operational data to put in the manuals. Graphs produced from such data points, for instance, showed that at 80°F and 165,000 pounds at sea level gross weight, the B-58 could be taxied less than 20,000 feet

The heat waves are intense behind this B-58A as it takes off. Liftoff was about 190 knots with a 17,000-foot-per-minute rate of climb with a full load. (General Dynamics)

without the tires overheating. With inflation of 240 psi cold, the pressures became astronomical when subjected to the heat of rolling.

Angle of attack of the delta wing was probaby the most important difference between that planform and a conventional-winged aircraft. The delta would not stall as the nose is brought up, but the rate of sink increased at a gallop.

If the angle of attack exceeded more than seventeen degrees, the aircraft was apt to pitch up sharply and then spin, a totally different reaction than the nose dropping after a stall in a conventional aircraft. Such a spin, below 15,000 feet, could not be stopped in time to avoid disaster. Above 15,000 feet, recovery could be made by cutting the throttles, applying full ailerons in the spin direction and dropping the nose. Therefore, this part of the flight envelope and the development of the data into chart form was of great significance to the B-58 pilot, so as not to get himself into deep trouble. Other examples of this were such things as the takeoff rotation angles requirement: It must be fourteen degrees, no more, no less. With more you killed off forward speed and

destroyed lift; with less you were not taking full advantage of the available lift at takeoff airspeed. Another place the angle of attack became important to fly-by-the-book was on landing. Twelve and a half degrees, plus or minus one degree, was the approach angle, with a nose-high altitude of fifteen degrees when the drag chute was popped. Without the chute the angle could be increased to seventeen degrees to slow the aircraft.

The high landing angle of attack comes into focus more when it is realized that below 200 feet the pilot could no longer see the runway and had only his peripheral vision and instruments to guide him. Considering that the 75,000-pound aircraft was coming over the fence at 190 knots, there was little chance to correct for a landing too short, too long or not quite lined up with the runway. Under those conditions—and they occurred in all kinds of weather—the Hustler acquired nicknames like "The Flying Manhole Cover" and "The Lead Sled." One thing that added to the craft's landing weight was the requirement that it have at least 12,000 pounds of fuel remaining in case a go-around was required.

This photo is interesting because of the three-man crew running toward their plane during a scramble; also for the clarity with which it shows the drooped wing tips due to the conical cambered leading edges. And the Vulcan cannon and tail radar show up well. (USAF)

Those numbers were only part of the angle of attack data of great importance. Even during level flight, the angle changed with speed, load and altitude. Data points for each of those conditions had to be taken in actual practice—from the patently safe areas to those most extreme—to determine what the safe operational flight envelope should be. Interestingly, it was found that the angle of attack could be as much as 9.4 degrees at Mach .5 at sea level to maintain level flight. Yes, thirty test aircraft were none too many when the amount of work in unknown flight areas had to be determined to make the Hustler operational. Finally, however, the work was complete, the required changes made, the manuals written and the aircraft delivered to the USAF. The Air Force took over 55-655 on February 15, 1958, to begin the service testing required to determine its characteristics as a purely military machine instead of an experimental aircraft. Even before this, General Albert Boyd had become the first USAF member to fly the aircraft on January 22, 1957.

On December 1, 1959, the first truly operational production aircraft was delivered to the Strategic Air Command's Carswell Air Force Base and became the first supersonic strategic bomber anywhere in the world. On March 15, 1960, the 43rd Bomb Wing was designated to be the first operational USAF unit. Those who applied for Hustler duty already had logged a lot of jet flight time and had "the right stuff," as Tom Wolfe called it. The training was rigorous before the candidate was admitted to the "Mach 2 Club," but more than eighty percent of the SAC selectees surrendered spot promotions just to become Hustler crew members.

As with any select group, the esprit was high and, in fact, a little offensive to other military aviators. To show their stuff, a 43rd crew flew the Hustler on a simulated mission covering over 11,000 miles at an average of 620 miles per hour—the longest Hustler mission ever achieved, but it proved the point. Here was a bomber that was ready for the Cold War of the sixties. A year later, a second bomb wing of B-58's was formed, the 305th. The 43rd was soon moved to Little Rock AFB and the 305th was stationed at Bunker Hill AFB (now Grissom), near Peru, Indiana. There they stayed until the Department of Defense determined that the B-58 fleet would be dismantled, the announcement being made October 29, 1969. It was effective by January 31, 1970.

Between December 1, 1959, and January 31, 1970, however, the B-58 Hustler pulled off some amazing things for the record books. A sampling follows:

1-12-61: A USAF B-58 set three international speed and payload records flying at 1,061 miles per hour over a closed 2,000-kilometer course (that's 1,242 miles).

1-14-61: The Thompson Trophy was won by flying 1,284.73 miles per hour around a 1,000-kilometer course.

5-10-61: A B-58 averaged 1,302.07 miles per hour for more than thirty minutes winning the Bleriot Trophy.

5-26-61: The New York-to-Paris Speed Record fell to the B-58 when it flew the distance in three hours nineteen minutes and fifty-one seconds. At the same time it set the Washington-to-Paris record by

This Hustler, aircraft 59-2435, was nicknamed "Shackbuster." Pod dropping was its specialty with 17 small component pod drops, 11 large component pod drops and 40 bomb drops. (AAHS Negative Library)

flying that distance in three hours thirty-nine minutes. The flight won the Mackay Trophy and the Harmon Trophy. However, tragedy marred this performance, for on June 3 the aircraft was totally destroyed during a flying display at the Paris International Air Show. Its first flight in Europe, the dramatic Hustler was one of the highlights of the Paris show, particularly after the steaming performance across the Atlantic only a few days earlier. During a demo flight for the crowds, Maj. Elmer E. Murphy, USAF of the 43rd Bomb Wing, made a low pass at a speed of about 630 miles per hour in front of the spectators, then began a shallow climb with afterburners on. He then cut the afterburners and began a roll just below the 4,000-foot cloud deck. Apparently, an engine was lost, the dreaded high speed yaw was encountered, and the plane broke up and was destroyed. Four years later, in 1965, a second B-58 was lost during the Paris show, killing its pilot.

3-5-62: A nonstop Los Angeles-New York-Los Angeles flight was performed in four hours forty-one minutes 11.3 seconds at an average speed of 1,044.96 miles per hour, winning both the Mackay and Bendix trophies.

9-18-62: The Hustler set two altitude and payload records with a flight to 84,360.84 feet, carrying a 5,000-kg payload. The Harmon Trophy was awarded to the crew.

10-16-63: A flight by a 305th Bomb Wing Hustler set five world speed records during a nonstop supersonic flight from Tokyo to London. Its average speed was 935 miles per hour, which included five subsonic in-flight refuelings. All the records were certified by the NAA and FAI. It was called "Operation Greased Lightning." And it sure was! To get the aircrews to the level of proficiency noted here required training to the nth degree.

There were a few moments of levity in the program, however, straightlaced and businesslike as it was. One that weather officer Joseph M. Kovac recalls is as follows:

"During one of the first winters after the 43rd Bomb Wing had a full complement of aircraft, Carswell AFB and the Fort Worth area were covered by a thick layer of ice deposited by freezing rain. Very few people moved about. The important crew training program, already behind due to multiple causes, faced a few more days delay unless something could be done to clear the parking ramps, taxiways and runway.

"Someone with sufficiently high authority to put the plan into effect decided that the exhaust of the B-58's would be used to melt the ice. Just by standing on the ramp looking at the aircraft, a disinterested observer could note that the aft ends of the engines were higher than the front, leading one to suspect that the flame from the exhaust might not point at the ground. The decision was made to proceed with melting the ice. Only two of the four engines had been started on the first B-58 when it be-

came obvious to many people that the plan just might not work. The aircraft jumped its wheel chocks and began moving across the ramp. Attempts to stop, to turn, to do anything other than slide on the ice were futile. The short but exciting trip was brought to an abrupt conclusion as the pitot tube impaled the aircraft in a hangar door. The parking ramp over which the plane slid showed no evidence of melting from the hot air vented upward by the engines."

Originally, the pilot of a B-58 was subjected to his first solo in the craft and his check ride all at the same time. There just was no other single-cockpit large aircraft that performed the way the Hustler did. The B-58 did handle similarly to the somewhat smaller F-102, however, and some high performance delta experience could be obtained by flying it. There was also a ground-based simulator—much less sophisticated than those today—that could also help prepare pilot and crew for actual flight. The real answer, however, was a two-place variant of the B-58 that could provide two cockpits in tandem for training purposes.

Convair had proposed such an aircraft early in the program, but the Air Force was not willing to give it the priority needed until the B-58 proper had proved itself. Why build a fancy trainer for a plane that might not make it? As the B-58 became an apparent winner, that all changed, and the USAF wanted something right away, since it was going operational.

The initial TB-58 was a reworked survivor of the first thirty test aircraft. Actually, eight TB-58's were finally built after sifting through what was left of the thirty and finding those aircraft with the least wear and tear on them. The first of these conversions, 55-670, made its initial flight on May 10, 1960. While at it, Convair upgraded another two of the original test planes to the standards of the production models—the test planes were too expensive to be left to sit and rot. In his January 1959 State of the Union Message, President Dwight Eisenhower mentioned, with a bit of anger considering he was trying to balance the budget, that the B-58's "cost their weight in gold." That was literally true, with gold fixed at $35 a troy ounce.

The TB-58A had the instructor-pilot cockpit located in the second cockpit normally used by the navigator/bombardier. It weighed 3,000 pounds less than the parent aircraft and had extra glass fitted for sideward and upward visibility. Other changes included the deletion of the autopilot, bombing and electronic countermeasures system, and active defense system. This was to be strictly a pilot's training plane, and there really was no need for the weapons system.

The second station canopy was enlarged, and the cockpit was fitted with throttles, a control stick, duplicate brakes, and a nose-wheel steering switch. Of course, the complete instrument panel was also a duplicate of the one in the pilot's compartment.

These aircraft worked out just fine, and during the career of ten years of B-58 active service they were booked up solid most of the time as new crews were trained.

In the early sixties, all was well. The B-58 had been developed and made operational, there were training aircraft available for the type, and records had been set right and left. So why weren't more of them built, and why aren't they still around? On October 16, 1962, the Air Force accepted the 116th, and last, B-58 to be built. From 1963 to the end of the road in 1969, the B-58 units were considered to be one of the first-line deterrents to enemy action, right up there along with the B-52 fleet and the ICBM missiles. The aircraft became very reliable as the crews

became ever more proficient; however, the type was always treated with a great deal of respect, for it was a demanding son of a gun to fly.

A fine account of a typical Hustler mission was written by R. Cargill Hall, deputy command historian, HQ/MAC, Scott AFB, in his paper, *The B-58 Bomber: Aeronautical Innovation for Supersonic Flight*. It is quoted here:

"Power . . . maximum A/B; Tower, Jack Three Zero, rolling; instruments checked; 100 knots . . . airspeed checked; S1 ready now . . . looking good; 170 knots . . . rotation; 185 knots . . . airborne. Before reaching 200 feet the brakes are applied to stop wheel rotation and the landing gear handle is moved to the 'up' position. The Hustler is throttled back and

Now residing, for display, at the Air Force Museum. B-58 59-2458 was the Thompson Trophy winner from the 43rd Bomb Wing while based at Carswell AFB. Crew was Maj. Harold E. Confer, Maj. Richard Weir, and Capt. Howard S. Bialas—pilot, navigator and DSO respectively. (Collect Air)

A photo of 59-2458 when it was on normal active duty (not setting records) and was known as the "Cow Town Hustler." (USAF)

climbs out at 425 knots indicated airspeed. Above 30,000 feet the flight control dampers and the center of gravity is checked, and the controls for the engine inlet spikes are placed in 'automatic.' The power is advanced to minimum afterburner. With all burners lit, the pilot again selects maximum afterburner and then advances the throttles into 'overspeed.' He pulls the nose up in a shallow climb. The aircraft is allowed to accelerate until the Mach meter reads 2.0 and, at about 50,000 feet, he levels off and immediately reduces power to maintain engine ram air temperature below a certain limit. Supersonic flight might continue for two hours, the time allowed for safe afterburner operation at that altitude, but fuel capacity will limit sustained flight at this speed to about 45 minutes maximum. Suffice it to say that our Hustler crew can log more time at Mach 2 on one mission than the average fighter pilot will know in an entire career. Outside, one can see the zone of increased air density that marks the standing shock wave undulating before the pitot boom and engine spikes. All sound is left behind except the 'white noise' of the air flowing past the crew compartment. Inside, the windshield is hot to the touch. Moving at 20 miles per minute in a cloudless sky, 10 miles above the midwest, the sensation of speed is fantastic; the one-mile section lines below go by like the slats of a picket-fence. This is an experience long-remembered by the professional aviator."

A reason for withdrawal of the Hustler was the aircraft's safety record. Fully twenty percent of all B-58's ever built crashed, many during its service career. It was a fairly dangerous aircraft to fly. The fatality rate was the highest in the Air Force, and when some of the crews let it be known that they were actually afraid of flying the airplane, it became obvious: Perhaps this one was a little too advanced in the state of the art. After all, the crew members, just to be let near a B-58, had to be first class—a cut or so above the average—so their opinion certainly counted.

The old mission had been high-altitude, high-speed penetration of enemy airspace. Now with the advent of ground-to-air missiles and long range radar in the enemy's hands, those days were gone forever. Now it was ground-hugging, low-level missions under the enemy's radar and to the target and past, before missiles could be trained on the intruding aircraft. The Francis Gary Powers U-2 episode pointed up the futility of high-altitude attacks once and for all and the B-58 was not built for low-altitude ground-hugging missions.

The B-58 was also a demanding aircraft to service, what with its ultrasophisticated electronics system. It was a little questionable whether the aircraft could be kept safely flying in the heat of a war. The complex avionics system required many specialized instruments and pieces of equipment to keep them tuned and operable (some forty pieces being needed just for the bombardier/navigator systems). The high-density aircraft was made for compactness, sort of like the proverbial ten pounds in a five-pound bag, but this in turn caused problems. For example, an often-serviced part of the nose radar could be reached only by hoisting the pilot's ejection capsule out of the cockpit. After working on the radar, the capsule had to once more be installed before applying power to the radar to check out the unit. If all still was not right, out had to come the capsule again. It was sort of like having to remove the engine from the car to change spark plugs.

Another little maintenance gem was the 3,000-pound weight that had to be hung from the Hustler's nose when the weapons pod was defueled and dropped in order to load a weapon in the upper pod. If this weight was overlooked, the bomber would rear up and sit on its tail.

Of course, the new long range ICBM's, the Atlas and Titan, and upcoming Minutemen, were also there to heap dirt on the B-58's grave. Why risk air crews when a missile could do the job probably even more effectively? It might be added that the North American XB-70, another real step ahead in aeroscience, also bit the dust for generally the same reasons; however, well before it had gotten past the prototype stage.

Had the status quo remained, Convair was ready to continue the B-58 development, for it had a supersonic transport based on the Hustler on the way as well as a titanium version that would do 2,000 miles per hour. As this is written, it was the last strategic bomber to reach production in the United States. Hustler . . . It was a fantastic airplane.

CHAPTER VII
△ DART BY DESIGN

△—————————————THE CONVAIR DELTA DART brought the company's faith in the delta-type aircraft to its zenith. The slick airframe is, however, only one part of a complex weapons system, the rest being sophisticated armament in the form of infrared- and radar-guided missiles and a carload of amazing black boxes that electronically controls the whole smash. The pilot needs only to take off on a target intercept, then the automatic guidance controls can take over, establishing heading and climb toward an unseen invader that has been picked up by the all-seeing eyes of the sophisticated ground radar system. Through any kind of weather, the aircraft can be ground-controlled and locked on its target until intercept—the pilot is only there for the ride. On approaching the target, it is quite possible, especially in heavy weather, that the pilot will not even see it! The sleek Falcon or Genie missiles are fired automatically, and the F-106 banks around for the return flight to home base. Only during landing flare is the pilot obliged to retake the controls and complete the touchdown and rollout. It's almost Buck Rogers stuff.

Initially, the F-106 had been developed in two ways: first by virtue of the improved F-102A Dagger and, soon after, by the *greatly* improved F-102B, which was to maximize the cleanup of the design. As the Air Force put it, the earlier A model was an interim fighter, and the B model was to be the ultimate fighter. But the changes that were necessary for the B model, it soon became apparent, so far outstripped the original F-102 that it became appropriate that a new number be given the aircraft—now named Delta Dart. The J57 engine was a hard and fast part of the F-102 design, and the new model was to be equipped with first the J67 and eventually the J75. These basic differences in engines made the fuselage parts and pieces of the old and new design airframes far from interchangeable, not only physically, but from a performance standpoint. The original F-102 airframe had a speed limitation of Mach 1.5. The new, more powerful Pratt & Whitney J75 could hurl the B model through the skies at speeds considerably surpassing that.

Therefore, in 1956 the F-102B was finally redesignated the F-106A, as that was the next available number in the line of continuity. Actually, the F-106 designation had already been used for a short time to designate the XF-106 Republic turboprop version of the F-84, until that project reverted back to the XF-84H. Yes, the F-106A was a completely new aircraft when compared with the F-102A.

In December of 1956, the new delta first flew from Edwards Air Force Base and approached the Air Force requirements of a top speed of Mach 1.9 and an altitude of 57,000 feet.

As a stopgap between the F-102 and the F-106, Convair (always agile and alert for new and increased business) proposed an F-102C as an interim design between the end of production of the 102 and the beginning of production of the 106. It would have embodied all the improvements made on the F-102A, but also would have included the more powerful, J57-P-47 and the newer MG-14 fire control system for the MB-1 rocket and Falcon missiles. The USAF, with its eyes on the upcoming F-106, wasn't buying any more interim aircraft, so the project was dropped.

The Air Force was glad it waited. When the new F-106A Dart became available it presented several major differences to the eye of the aircraft

The first flight of the Convair F-106A-CO took place on December 26, 1956, at Edwards AFB. Design had begun as the F-102B. However, so many changes were made a new classification number was issued. Speed brakes, drag chute and nose-high attitude mark this landing. (USAF)

Another touchdown at Edwards of the first F-106A just before the drag chute is popped. Aircraft incorporated the Whitcomb area rule right from the beginning and the result was a much slimmer fuselage than the F-102A. (USAF)

127

watcher. It was about the same size as the F-102A and, while without doubt a derivation of same, it was much sleeker to look at. The engine nacelle openings were placed much farther back from the cockpit, almost at the leading edge of the wings. The vertical fin, before high and triangular, was now truncated. Twin nose wheels were now in place instead of the original single wheel. However, the foremost difference was the fuselage. It was now slimmer, even though it housed a much more powerful engine. The big reason, of course, was that the airframe was now designed from the very beginning to abide by Whitcomb's area rule rather than making do with the original fat fuselage of the F-102. It showed. The aircraft was definitely much sleeker and more capable of high Mach numbers than the earlier model F-102A.

The first F-106A squadrons became operational in May 1959. As of January 1981, the Defense Department Strategic Forces planned to retain seven F-106A squadrons on active USAF duty through 1981, with a reduction to five squadrons in 1982. In addition, the Air National Guard fielded five F-106A squadrons, to remain at that strength through 1982. That's twenty-three years of active duty and still going strong, as this is written.

Testing a new aircraft is always of great interest, particularly to the layman. It brings forth visions of the airframes being wrung out while pushing to the maximum boundaries of the performance envelope. The pilots are usually thought to be either in the employ of the plane builder or the Air Force or Navy. However, the engine builders had test pilots, too. Robert Denn and Walter Allen were the F-106 test pilots for Pratt & Whitney. Some of their work was peculiar to the engine manufacturer's needs rather than having much to do with the airframe itself.

Allen recalled several incidents of this nature. He was checked out in the F-106 early on in its development. In fact, he received his Mach 2 Club membership, number 22, on January 20, 1959. Instrumentation for studying the engine's flight characteristics took up the space that normally would be used for the Hughes fire control system. That arrangement, as might be expected, brought about a few unforeseen problems and unique solutions to them. As part of the afterburner development work, a lot of zoom climbs to high altitude were made. It was soon found that the electronic engine monitoring equipment, located in the unpressurized section, was arcing due to the low atmospheric pressure at altitude. A novel solution to the problem was

A Convair publicity photo of the initial Delta Dart. At this point the aircraft had wing fences carried over from the F-102A. After a few models were built they gave way to "saw-cuts" in the wing's leading edge that did the same job but with reduced drag. (Convair)

quickly arrived at by putting a block of dry ice in the equipment bay just before a test flight. The dry ice not only provided cooling for the instrumentation but, as it sublimated, it pressurized the compartment as well. Should the pressure build too high, the compartment was vented through a relief valve installed for that purpose.

Other problems could happen only to an engine test pilot. The engine manufacturers go to great lengths to make their product relatively automatic in operation. So it was with the afterburner nozzle normally automatically opened and closed with respect to throttle position. This was not so with the Pratt & Whitney test engine installed in the F-106. It was left disconnected so that the test pilot could manually vary it with respect to the throttle for his experimental work.

Allen was taking off down the 15,000-foot Edwards runway. It took him 13,000 feet to get airborne, and by the time he figured out why it took so

The number two test F-106A had its name emblazoned on its nose and is odd in that the radome is painted over rather than being the usual black. Photo taken June 20, 1958, at the Air Force Flight Test Center, Edwards AFB. (USAF)

The same number two aircraft, now with a black radome, poses with its high-gloss polyurethane gray paint used for Mach 2 heat protection of the aluminum. Aircraft was soon found to be capable of 1,525 miles per hour (Mach 2.31) at 40,000 feet. (USAF)

long and what had happened, he was committed to takeoff. He had had a wisdom tooth removed that same day and, distracted by pain, had forgotten to close down the nozzle manually.

Other all-in-a-day's work events encountered by Allen included running out of oil due to a loose nut in the oil system plumbing and operating at zero oil pressure for ten minutes while he got the plane back onto the runway. He took care of the company product though, immediately reducing power and making a simulated dead stick landing at Edwards. Teardown of the engine revealed no sign of emergency distress. It was luck and a gentle touch. A few months later an Air Force pilot didn't do so well when he ran out of oil on a low, high-speed pass. The bearings froze and caused the high-speed turbine shaft to fail.

Of course, a compressor stall, as Allen mentioned, was the thrill of a lifetime. It caused the air-

Now a full-fledged test aircraft for the USAF, the number three plane had a red nose, tail tip and wing tips. Span was 38 feet 3.5 inches versus 38 feet 1.6 inches for the F-102A—about the same. Note the small rudder area. (USAF)

Ground servicing is always required before any flight, as in this photo of the 3rd F-106A—once again with the radome painted over. Note also that the wing fences still exist. (USAF)

craft to yaw so much it threw the pilot to the side of the cockpit. This was caused by the air coming in one inlet and being forced out the other. It was usually encountered as he investigated compressor surge line and inlet ramp schedule optimization. His most exciting flight came about as a result of this phenomena. It followed a zoom climb to 75,000 feet that resulted in a compressor stall and turbine failure. This early model engine had an air turbine motor (ATM) for electrical power generation, instead of the constant speed drive found on later production models. When the compressor stall occurred, the ATM had insufficient pressure to operate, so the primary electrical bus dropped off the line. Unfortunately, the secondary bus did not supply power to the automatic flight control system. Since the aircraft was flying in the unstable transonic speed range, it became somewhat violently involved in an exaggerated Dutch roll. It was a wild ride before the aircraft slowed down and control was regained. It was only a *simple* matter then of setting down on the dry lake bed—the first set-down with a failed turbine.

One would think that with the testing of the airframe, engine and fire control systems by their respective manufacturers, along with the official Air Force acceptance tests, that might be the end of it. Not so. A good example is the test work performed by retired Lt. Col. W. H. (Bill) Lawton, now chief of flight test engineering at Piper Aircraft Corporation. The aircraft he flew was the F-106B, 57-2507, the first of the line. This was after it had been around for a while. During the mid-sixties, he flew several ejection seat test projects, including the escape systems for the Lockheed SR-71/YF-12 and the NASA Gemini spacecraft, all in the F-106B.

Both projects required very high dynamic pressures, which in turn required high altitudes and Mach numbers. The craft he was using had the early inlet ducts and would not quite get out of Mach 2, which the newer F-106B's did easily. The best he could get was about Mach 1.8, as he recalls, at 48,000 feet. He was required to get a pressure suit for some planned 65,000-foot drops that were canceled when it appeared the aircraft's performance was not enough to accomplish them without great difficulty.

The aircraft was, however, an excellent item of equipment for parachute test work. It was fitted with two cockpit canopies: a standard one and an ejection seat test item that had a hatch over the rear seat that departed the aircraft just prior to an ejection seat firing. The front seat was separated with a pressure bulkhead fitted with a window, so Lawton could observe the seat firings. His cockpit remained pressurized, but even with the oxygen on 100 percent, he could still smell black powder and sulfur odors when the rear seat was ejected.

The craft was adaptable, for when not engaged in test seat firings, a standard canopy was fitted and the rear seat reinstalled. In that configuration it was used as a chase aircraft, to observe other aircraft involved in the ejection seat test programs. Lawton recalls that the SR-71 program was very secret and that while he didn't know what the ultimate use of the data he was creating was, he knew it must have been important, as spare parts to keep the F-106B flying were always immediately available when needed.

This Delta Dart front view shows the large air scoops needed to feed the big Pratt & Whitney J75 engine, the razor-sharp cockpit canopy and, finally, how *short* delta wings look when compared to the fuselage cross-section. (USAF)

At other times the government tended to be a little more on the stingy side. During the Gemini program, Lawton was grounded with a broken ankle. From what else? A parachute jump! Since the tests required were for the first Gemini launch, NASA explored hiring a civilian pilot to take his place. The several they contacted required rather large bonuses, so NASA elected to wait for Lawton's ankle to heal.

While being an active Air Force officer, he received no bonus for his work. He did get an Air Medal for his subsequent drops, however, and Gemini launched on time.

Another facet of test work is the subsequent postproduction testing required as an aircraft, such as the Six, is updated. In this case, there was always an effort on the part of the Air Defense Command to

Two interesting photos of the south end of an F-106A pointing north. As can be readily seen, the deployment of the speed brakes greatly increased the cross-sectional area of the plane. This caused drag when it was desired to slow down fast. (USAF)

keep the interceptor up-to-date and raring to go, as they have done for over twenty-five years. From 1967 through 1969, G. R. Hennigan was the ADC project officer/test pilot for the modifications to the F-106A aircraft. Included during this time frame were such improvements as air refueling, supersonic drop tanks, clear top canopy and the installation of the M61 20 mm Gatling gun. During the latter tests he had the opportunity to shoot down a Ryan BQM-34 Firebee drone with the cannon. This was about as close as anyone flying a Convair delta ever got to shooting down an opposing aircraft.

With such an advanced state-of-the-art aircraft available, it was not long before its capabilities were put into play in the area of record setting. On December 15, 1959, Maj. Joe Rogers pulled the cork and set a single engine world speed record of 1,525.95 miles per hour at 40,000 feet over Edwards Air Force Base. The record stood for many years. A year later the F-106A gave a demonstration of its long legs by flying 1,500 miles without benefit of refueling!

Even today, years after it was collecting those headlines, the F-106 still gets a share of the limelight. Example: Dateline, March 18, 1981, Otis Air Force Base, Massachusetts, "For the second time in six weeks, state Air National Guard F-106 fighters have intercepted Soviet reconnaissance planes along the East Coast, officials say. The latest interception came before dawn yesterday as two fighters, manned by graduate students of Northeastern University, scrambled to meet two Soviet planes."

In the fall of every other year the knights of the air appear at Tyndall AFB, Florida. In units of four aircraft each, they begin to flock in where Ponce de Leon once searched for the fountain of eternal youth. It is for a jousting match, every bit as keen a competition between warriors as were those matches in the medieval days of King Arthur. Now for weapons, however: instead of horse and lance, it is supersonic fighters and missiles. The four-plane groups are from United States and Canadian fighter interceptor squadrons and are selected to compete by means of rigorous fly-off competitions against their peers gathered from around the world. The competition is called the William Tell meet, named after the famous Swiss archer. The meet is held to objectively shake out the top guns of the fighter interceptor squadrons. It is played with live ammunition against target drones and scored electronically by experts. To see what went on at one of these meets when the F-106 Delta Dart was in its heyday we will look at the William Tell of 1972, a typical year.

From the angle of a typical fighter interceptor squadron, we will pick the 95th FIS stationed at Dover AFB, Delaware, at that time. Squadron Commander, Lt. Col. James A. MacDougald, has selected his flight commanders as the team. The team consisted of MacDougald himself, known as "Big Mac," Maj. Wesley D. (Robbie) Robertson, Maj. Henry (Trigger) Armstrong, Capt. Norman (Nuke 'Em Norm) Komnick, and, as an alternate, Maj. William (Wild Bill) Gillis. The nicknames, of course, were hoopla

This California ANG F-106A launches an AIM-4F Falcon (radar guided) during firing practice at Tyndall AFB, Florida. (Hughes Aircraft Company)

and hokum, but it was all in the competitive spirit of the contest to come. They arrived at the William Tell wearing top hats, ascots, monocles, white gloves and walking sticks, plus their flight suits, to further daunt their competition. This guise was taken from the squadron's insignia of a skull adorned with similar formal garb.

To hone their skills before the meet, the pilots performed daily practice missions, flying attack profiles similar to those used at the William Tell meet. The profiles were thoroughly briefed prior to each flight. As one wag put it, "The William Tell profiles are pretty much canned missions, which is understandable. There will be fifty-five fighter pilots shooting live ammunition and certain restraints are necessary to insure the F-106's and F-4's don't square off against each other."

Finally, meet time arrived, September 16–30. At Tyndall, the 95th FIS people set aside the tricky nicknames and garish dress to get down to the business of perhaps being named the best shooters in the Air Defense Command (ADC). In addition to the pilots, the meet would name the best aircrew/ maintenance, controller and weapons loading teams in each of the air defense weapons system categories. The crews were of vital importance to the pilot's success. He couldn't very well attack a target if his radar or weapons system malfunctioned.

In the case of the 95th, to preclude this, a thirty-man crew of maintenance people was sent to Tyndall. These included specialists in hydraulics, fuel system, attack radar systems, weapons loading and so on. Since the aircraft (four) were committed to the contest, and no substitutions were allowed, maintenance became very critical, and much midnight oil was burned assuring the perfection of the machines. On the fighters' arrival at Tyndall, each team had two days to shake down and peak its aircraft.

Finally, the shooting part of the meet was underway. The competition was wide and varied. In addition to the four pilots and F-106's of the 95th FIS, there were three teams of F-101 VooDoo's (one RCAF and two ANG), three F-102 teams (two ANG and one from Iceland) and two F-4 Phantom teams (Pacific Air Command and the Alaskan Air Command). There were also five teams flying F-106A's— the 95th's direct competition.

The meet was challenging. Aircrews would fire live ordnance on three of the four scheduled intercepts. To win required top-notch piloting skills and an aircraft honed to its maximum capabilities. If an intercept was missed, due to pilot error or equipment malfunction, tough stuff. There were no second chances. Not only was the pilot's performance scored, but also the performance of the ground-based

A low-level pass by a wing-tank-equipped F-106A at Castle AFB, California, in November 1966. Note stowed arresting hook and missile bay door outlines. (USAF)

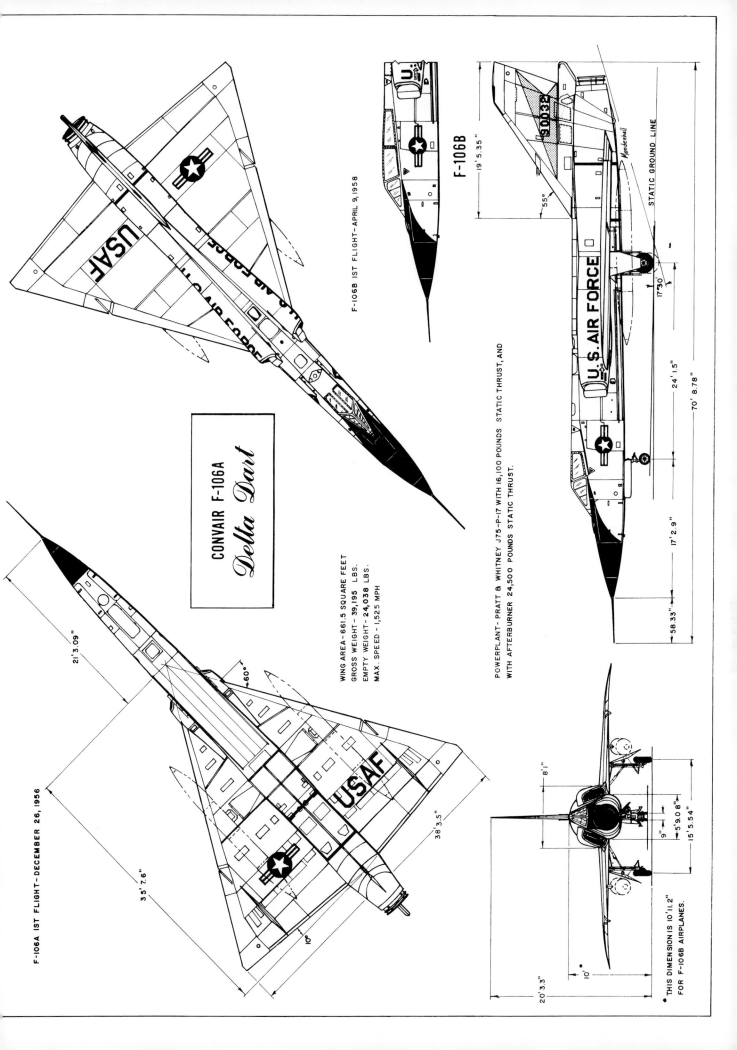

F-106B 1ST FLIGHT—APRIL 9, 1958

F-106B

CONVAIR F-106A
Delta Dart

WING AREA—661.5 SQUARE FEET
GROSS WEIGHT—39,195 LBS.
EMPTY WEIGHT—24,038 LBS.
MAX. SPEED—1,525 MPH

POWERPLANT—PRATT & WHITNEY J75-P-17 WITH 16,100 POUNDS STATIC THRUST, AND
WITH AFTERBURNER 24,500 POUNDS STATIC THRUST.

U. S. AIR FORCE

STATIC GROUND LINE

19' 5.35"

55°

17'3.0

24' 1.5"

70' 8.78"

58.33"

F-106A 1ST FLIGHT—DECEMBER 26, 1956

21' 3.09"

60°

USAF

35' 7.6"

38' 3.5"

10°

20' 3.3"

8' 1"

9"

5' 9.0 8"

15' 5.54"

10'

* THIS DIMENSION IS 10' 11.2"
FOR F-106B AIRPLANES.

radar operator, who guided the aircraft into intercept position. His job was not so glamorous, but was every bit as important for the mission's success. In this case, the radar operator not only guided the F-106 into an intercept position, but he did it within the strict rules set up by the managers of William Tell. To make matters tougher, he had to do this with four or more aircraft simultaneously.

Since real bombers, of course, could not be shot down as targets, the William Tell interceptors shot at specially designed drones, principally BQM-34A and TDU-25 targets, which were towed behind a very nervous F-101.

To simulate an electronic warfare environment, the F-106's dry fired against a B-57, T-33 or F-101 equipped with radar jammers and chaff dispensers. The target also tried to evade the attackers by turning, climbing or diving. To make it a little tougher, but to assure a keen edge of maintenance reliability, each aircraft had to fly when scheduled,

Displayed in front of the pointed radar nose of this F-106A are the 200 electronic black boxes which comprise the 2,520-pound MA-1 navigation and armament control system. The missiles are AIM-4F radar-guided Super Falcon missiles (standing on their tails) and AIM-4G infrared guided Super Falcons. (Hughes Aircraft Company)

or it was scored a miss. The competition was so keen that a contender, to have any chance of winning the William Tell, had to almost score a hit on each of the four missions flown.

In the case of the 106, one of the tests was to shoot down a target drone on a frontal intercept using the "snap-up" technique. This was where the radar controller vectored the F-106 in front of the target, about fifty miles out, to allow the pilot to acquire it on his cockpit radar, lock on and start to track it. The drone was at a somewhat higher altitude than the interceptor, so the pilot had to accelerate the aircraft to a specified supersonic speed, then commence a sharp pullup at a point designed to place him in a firing position just below and in front of the target. The F-106 could carry a small nuclear-tipped rocket during wartime, which it would probably fire at the target. Since Gulf Coast residents would certainly object to even the smallest of nuclear warheads going off around them, the F-106 fired an ATR-2A, an inexpensive training rocket that did everything but explode. Transmitters on the target and on the ground could track the rocket's journey to see if it came near enough to destroy the target if it had been of the nuclear variety.

The next test of the 106/pilot/radar operator team was to fire an infrared heat-seeking missile at a towed TDU-25B target drone that simulated a bomber. It was an uneasy position for the tow pilot to be in, though the cable *was* hundreds of feet long when fully deployed. The radar operator again vectored the pilot into a position to attack the target. This time a direct hit on the target had to be made to score. The third sortie was similar to the first except the altitude

separation of the drone and fighter-interceptor would be only 5,000 feet. The F-106 would attack the target head on and fire the dummy ATR-2A. The pilot would then pass by the drone, turn 180 degrees, get the target on the radar screen again, lock on and shoot the drone down with a guided missile. As in the second sortie, the missile had to hit the drone for it to count. The entire front, stearn, reattack sequence happened in just a few minutes.

The final sortie was really the most difficult. The radar operator would vector the aircraft into an attack position against a low-flying target that was doing everything it could to cause the interceptor an MI (missed intercept). This sortie was, of course, most like what a pilot would encounter in real war.

The first day of shooting took place, and the 95th FIS completed its first phase of the competition: the dry fire electronic countermeasures mission (ECM). The gate stealer, chaff and radar jammers gave them a pretty hard time. Armstrong and Komnick made perfect scores. Robertson had a radar failure while pitted against a fast moving F-101 with an unbelievable radar jammer. Not one pilot pitted against this champ was able to intercept. MacDougald also had problems, but of a more minor nature.

The first-round scores for the 95th were 1,935 points out of a possible 3,200. The team to beat at that point was the 2nd FIS from Wurtsmith, Michigan, with an impressive 3,020 points. This, along with some heavy scores from the other fighter groups, put the 95th in a bad position from which it never recovered. However, just to have been in the contest was an unquestioned honor.

March 1964 photo at Edwards AFB of an F-106A shows off the lines that got it dubbed the "Delta Dart."

The 95th's participation was filled with ups and downs during the remainder of the contest. Bad weather forced Komnick to dodge in and out of cloud formations, making his mission to fire an infrared missile unsafe. In a war he would have done it, but for a pilot to scrag himself during peacetime practice would have been ridiculous. A refly of the mission would have been allowed had a film pack in Komnick's radar not failed to run. Without it, he had no way to protest. He made up for it later when he totally destroyed a drone by a direct hit with a radar-guided missile. Instead of simply damaging the $100,000 drone, he sent the orange-colored target out of control and burning into the Gulf of Mexico. This was unusual, as some drones had been hit and recovered to fly as many as almost eighty times.

The meet finally ended, with the team from the frozen north, the 460th FIS from Grand Forks Air Force Base, North Dakota, winning the marbles in the F-106 category. They had acquired a total of 13,950 points out of a possible 16,800. The 95th had a total of 12,223 points—a good performance but, as mentioned earlier, a unit had to be able to have almost no problems to be in the running. Again, it shows that all groups that were selected to attend the William Tell meet were indeed first-class FIS defenders of the continent. The 95th was retired from active status in January 1973, as economy moves and general rearrangement of the Air Force took place. The FIS was later reactivated at Tyndall as the 95th Fighter Interceptor Training Squadron. Its mission was to train T-33 pilots and prepare them for entry into the F-106 squadrons.

Of course, with a hot new fighter aircraft that knocked the socks off just about anything else flying,

Hughes came to the forefront with a new weapons system for it, the MA-1. To do the tricks the designers had in mind took up more space and weight than the MG-10 that was used on the F-102A. The new MA-1 weighed in at 2,520 pounds, compared to the MG-10's 1,425 pounds. Spacewise, it was forty-five cubic feet versus the MG-10's 24.6 cubic feet. With its size and weight almost twice that of the MG-10, it had to be an improvement of like size, and it was.

The MA-1 was a fabulous electronic navigation and armament control system developed specifically for the Delta Dart. It was the Air Force's most automated electronic weapons system for manned aircraft at the time. It is still in use on the F-106 today, although it has been updated on several occasions. Its digital computer is capable of making 9,600 arithmetical calculations in one second, 6,250 decisions in one minute. Try that with the old pad and pencil! The MA-1 system computes SAGE target vectoring information and takes over almost total control of the F-106A during a combat intercept. It's able to guide the Six to its target, pinpoint the target's position, launch a missile attack and automatically bring the Six back to its base. It's easy living for the pilot, but it would be pure hell on an enemy who chose to attack. It doesn't even really need the ground control of SAGE. If it is given the speed and flight path of the target, the MA-1 will program the interceptor on its own to knock an intruder down. Its capabilities are, of course, all-weather.

All-weather? Well yes and no. Joseph Kovac, Jr., a SAC weatherman, had this to say about what all-weather meant to the interceptor squadrons:

"With data link even the pilot becomes redundant between gear-up and gear-down at the begin-

This three-quarter front view can only be labeled s-m-o-o-t-h. The slim fuselage housed a powerful J75-P-17 from Pratt & Whitney that punched out 24,500 pounds static thrust in afterburner. (USAF)

ning and end of the flight. The computer program in SAGE considered the terminal and alternate weather conditions during the intercept, and if not overridden by the IND, would terminate the operational employment when fuel state dictated a requirement to return to home base, make one missed approach and proceed to the nearest suitable alternate airfield for recovery.

"A manual override feature was necessary as the weather entered in the computer was the lowest expected for the next three hours. This was quite often an intermittent condition not expected to last for more than thirty minutes at a time. It would be difficult to justify the loss of an intercept sortie when the 'weapon' got an automatic break-away for fuel state after a lock-on, and the destination weather was, say, 2,000 feet scattered and visibility ten miles with a forecast of occasional variations to a ceiling of 800 feet obscured and visibility one mile in snow showers.

"The weather forecasters assigned to the SAGE direction centers were in regular hotline contact with the IND's to insure that the variability condition was not overridden when the poor weather was impending. They also carefully monitored the upper winds to insure that the narrow band of strong winds associated with the jet stream was not ignored by the computer. The data link input to the fighters was based on a trigonometric intercept solution that considered heading, airspeed and altitude of both interceptor and target, type of intercept tactics and type of weapons available, among other things. The 'offset' was adjusted to include the effects of wind throughout the attack curve.

"As the computer could control the position of the fighter, the wind forecast to affect the target was selected as a parameter. This is ok when both aircraft are in similar wind regimes. An investigation into the cause of some 'no kills' [misses] confined to one tactic revealed that the program was unsatisfactory. With the interceptor at 35,000 feet in a west-to-east jet stream at 130 knots, for example, and the target above 50,000 feet in winds from the northeast at seven knots, it was possible to run a 'perfect' solution and have the fighter miss by hundreds of miles. IND's were kept advised of the location and intensity of the jet streams and could initiate a manual override to use winds at interceptor altitudes when significant differences in speed and direction between fighter and target altitudes existed."

The F106A missile cargo is similar, but more advanced than that of the F-102A's. It consists of one AIM-2A Genie nuclear rocket and four Falcon missiles. The Genie isn't homing, but with a nuclear explosion in the enemy's flight path a direct hit is not all that necessary. The target aircraft would be downed with the detonation as far as 1,000 feet away! The additional four Super Falcons, two AIM-4F radar-guided missiles and two AIM-4G infrared-guided missiles completed the awesome weapon load—that is until the 20 mm General Electric Vulcan cannon was fitted to most missile bays in recent years.

The computer doesn't stop at hitting the enemy, it also has what is called a navigational mode, which includes continuous position determination through the tactical air navigation station (TACAN) and dead reckoning. It also has the feature

Flyby of F-106 with 360-gallon supersonic fuel tanks. The tanks provided a 2,700-mile range at 610 miles per hour at 40,000 feet. (USAF)

of automatic navigation to any of several preselected homing points. To make sure it all works, it has a built-in, five-minute self-test program. A high-capacity digital computer, automatic data link reception and automatic flight control for navigation, radar attacks and instrument landing approaches all make the F-106A/MA-1 combination a roaring success. It takes a great airframe to perform the mission, but it takes just as great an electronic system to control that performance with the precision that is required to make the whole combination a deadly menace to any enemy.

The electronic part is a bit on the mind-boggling side. The MA-1 consists of 200 black metal boxes packed with thousands of tiny electronic parts and nearly eight miles of wiring. It all comes into action with just the flip of a switch. It is magic carpet all the way. Take off, flip the switch and watch the system direct the attack, i.e., fly out to meet the target, launch the missiles and monitor the slick interceptor's trip back to its base, the pilot only taking over the controls as it sweeps over the numbers for a landing.

To be more specific about the computer, it is named the "Digitair" by its Hughes designers, and it is the brain of the Hughes electronic system. What happens is that the F-106A tells the computer what it is doing and the computer tells the F-106A what it should be doing. Any difference of opinion between the two is corrected through the automatic flight control system.

Air navigation in the F-106A is like watching a travelogue on a small home television. During a mission, the pilot follows his progress on an eight-inch tactical situation display screen that shows film strips of appropriate air navigation maps. The pilot keeps track of his aircraft by watching a small black delta wing symbol with a needle nose (the bug) move across the screen. An intercept under SAGE direction also presents the target and its location by means of an X bisected with an arrow. If the attack area is not covered by SAGE, then no arrow with an X appears on the screen; however, the attack is still controlled by automatic digital signals transmitted directly to the aircraft by ground data link stations. These signals give the pilot the same information otherwise supplied orally by ground controllers, only more crisply and quickly.

By use of either method of control, the F-106A is automatically directed by Digitair to a position where the pilot should be able to find his target on the MA-1 radar screen. The system even turns the interceptor onto an approximate attack course, and markers appear on the radar scope predicting the range, azimuth and elevation of the target aircraft. Once the target is obtained the pilot and the MA-1 press home the attack without further assistance from the ground-based SAGE or data link equipment.

If some of the equipment goes belly-up, the pilot can be directed by a controller in a ground-based Air Force radar station. In that case, the pilot simply follows the verbal directions he receives from the ground controller until he makes contact with the intruder.

The film strip, mentioned before, of the interceptor's home base area is inserted in the MA-1 system by the ground crewmen. Each strip shows all major ground references up to about a 400-mile radius of the operations base. Of course, when going from base to base the strip can be changed in accordance with the locale. Also, the strips cover the adjacent areas to that of the home base, and when the pilot nears the edge of his magic map he simply switches over to the next appropriate map on the strip. The delta-winged symbol (bug) showing the position of the F-106A is positioned on the screen by transmissions from TACAN (tactical air navigation station). TACAN also sends along to the fighter the latest weather information, such as wind direction and velocity, which helps the pilot and MA-1 maintain a proper intercept course.

The Hughes MA-1 system automatically computes this information and directs any necessary changes in course. Fuel consumption is also one of the parameters taken over by the computer and presented visually on the tactical situaton display screen. As fuel is used, a dark green shadow drifts from the edge of the scope and forms a circle around the bug symbol that represents the aircraft. The size, or diameter, of the circle represents the maximum reliable flight range of the F-106A at current altitude and speed. The closer to the bug the circle gets, the less range that remains.

On a scramble, as the F-106A rolls out of the alert hangar, the computer is churning with target information supplied by a SAGE direction center or data link control unit. By the time the interceptor passes the 5,000-foot mark, the pilot will have received the course, altitude and speed of his target. Also, he will know the rate of climb and course he will need to intercept it. Rather than flying the mission manually, he can switch to the fully automatic flight control mode and the MA-1 will direct the craft to the *offset point*. That is the most effective position from which to launch an attack. The pilot can watch the interceptors progress as the black bug, representing himself, crawls across the gray situation display screen toward the target.

The pilot selects the firing order of his armament, generally the nuclear-tipped Genie and then a salvo of the four Falcons. When the target is a nuclear-bomb-carrying adversary, there is no fooling around when the missile launch point is arrived at. It would take much too long to reach the weapons launch point a second time at the closing speeds that are involved.

As the offset point is reached, the MA-1 turns the Six on a lead collision course with the target, a position about forty-five degrees to the enemy's projected flight path. The computer then predicts the position of the bomber in relation to the fighter by displaying a target marker circle somewhere on the F-106A's radar scope. The target echo blip will appear inside the circle as soon as the interceptor comes within radar range of the enemy. Once the sharp bead of light pops up within the circle, the pilot triggers a switch that stops the search antenna oscillations, after which he manually points the antenna directly at the target by superimposing the now dormant antenna scope indicator on the target echo blip. He releases a switch that locks the F-106A on the enemy bomber. It's too late for evasive maneuvers by the target now. The Dart is closing fast, and the MA-1 system is keeping the F-106A locked on with tenacity as the range closes. The pilot pulls the "will to fire" trigger, which releases the missile load to the MA-1 fire control for automatic launching. The system computes the precise instant for the launch and, when satisfied, the missile bay doors snap open and with a fiery blast the missiles head off for the target at supersonic speed, Mach 3 in fact. An X appears on the radar scope notifying the pilot that the attack is over. The pilot immediately banks the Six over in an escape maneuver to clear the blast area that will surely develop in a few moments. He switches back to automatic flight control. This sets the aircraft's course toward one of the homing points that has been programmed into the MA-1's memory drum, a sophisticated magnetic tape recorder that stores navigational information for the pilot.

As the F-106A nears its base, the pilot notifies ground tactical control that he is about to execute a penetration letdown, and the F-106A descends automatically toward the ILS (instrument landing system) gate. As the F-106A enters the final approach, the pilot switches to the automatic instrument landing approach mode that keeps the interceptor in line with the runway while maintaining proper approach speed and rate of descent. Just over the threshold, the pilot takes control of the aircraft for the actual touchdown and rollout.

Considering the F-106A aircraft's longevity (the first flight was over twenty-five years ago), it is somewhat amazing that it is still around today. Two hundred seventy-seven were built and by mid-1982, 153 of them were still kicking around the Air Force and Air National Guard as first-line interceptors and full members of the SAGE team. These old aircraft fleshed out the Air National Guard with eighty-eight of the machines, in summer 1982, in the 102nd FIS, Otis AFB, Massachusetts; 144th FIS, Fresno, California; 120th FIS, Great Falls, Montana; 125th FIS, Jacksonville, Florida; and the 177th FIS, Atlantic City, New Jersey. The active F-106 first-line interceptors average in age from twenty to twenty-five years. McDonnell-Douglas has recently run an ad for F-15's by featuring drawings of the F-106A and acknowledging it as a superb fighter for its day but mentioning that it should now be replaced. The ad made a point of the fact that some of the Six's current pilots were younger than the plane itself!

This longevity, however, has also allowed some of the more mature pilots to amass a great number of hours in the type. One good example is Maj. Charles E. (Chuck) Townsend, who, by summer 1981, had completed 3,000 hours in the driver's seat of the F-106—a feat nobody else had yet attained. While time will see to it that others may also attain this record, that's still a lot of hours. It equates to seventy-five forty-hour weeks or a solid year and a half of work weeks sitting at the controls of that thing! Of course that is not really the way it is done. Townsend is currently a member of the 102nd FIS at Otis AFB, Massachusetts, an Air National Guard unit. His F-106A experience began in 1967 when he served as a squadron pilot on active duty. All total, he has over 3,500 hours in jets, which includes a tour in Southeast Asia, where he logged 128 combat hours in F-4C's.

The 177th FIG at Atlantic City, New Jersey, prepares for a routine intercept mission. (John Maene, Jr.)

△ CHAPTER VIII
△ *INSIDE CONVAIR'S DART*

△————————————THE CONVAIR F-106 DART, either A or B model, looks almost scorpionlike in stance when approached. It is because of the short nose-gear leg and small wheels and tires. Starting at the aircraft's front, the first thing one notices is the long, slender probelike tube that extends nearly five feet forward from the pointed nose of the black radome, much like the lance of some medieval knight charging into combat. This tube serves the purpose of a pitot tube, except in a much more sophisticated manner. The 58.33-inch, to be exact, protuberance is the air inlet for the central data computer (CADC). From this device true airspeed and altitude information is passed along to the cockpit instruments and the main aircraft computer. Being so slender and so important to the aircraft's operation, it is often painted with alternating red and white stripes for better visibility by the ground crew and attendant vehicle drivers.

At the root of this probe, the black nose extends rearward in a smooth, bullet-shaped cone. This sleek housing is of a dielectric plastic material, and inside it sits the movable radar dish, an antenna capable of scanning the sky ahead for both weather and enemy targets as it sends out and receives the bounce-back of its microwaves.

Directly behind the antenna, and enclosed by the faired aluminum fuselage, is the radar and MA-1 weapons system equipment, the electronic black boxes so often heard about because of their mystical powers. Of course there is nothing mystical about them. They are electronic circuits that process information and feed an output based on it to the pilot's radar scope or situation display screen. Certainly a color TV is every bit as complicated, but there is less of it. However, a television is not nearly so wrapped in enticing secrecy and therefore is considered mundane.

Aft of the radar transmitter and receiver equipment is the area termed the radar rack, which consists of a digital (Digitair) computer and its power supply. This controls the automatic fire control system, which can be ground-controlled, as well as the infrared system (IR system) that can seek and home in on heat-emitting signatures such as the tailpipe plume of a target's engines.

From that point, moving rearward through the fuselage, is the pilot's compartment, the heart of the aircraft, in which, in addition to the aforementioned electronics, are also found more black boxes. They are behind the pilot, on either side of him, and below him, filling in the volume not taken up with the nose gear and its hydraulic retraction mechanism. The various electronics bays contain the air data equipment for inflight sensing which, as mentioned before in connection with the nose probe, provides aircraft control equipment for target acquisition and attack under ground control. It also offers identification friend-or-foe equipment, navigational equipment and voice communication for landing and navigation equipment.

All in all, this mass of transistors, vacuum tubes, resistors, printed circuits, all the other electronics and what have you, weighs in at something over a ton and consists of over 200 of the innocuous little black boxes, each carefully designed for reliability, regardless of cost, and pushed to the sixties' outer limits of state-of-the-art in miniaturization. As always in aircraft design, next to functional capability, weight and size are of the utmost importance. In the case of the MA-1 system, it has been periodically updated to the latest standards.

As mentioned, this mass of electronic gear is wrapped completely around the pilot on all sides except the top, which is, of course, the canopy and windscreen. A short tour of the cockpit follows.

The cockpit is entered from the left side of the fuselage by means of a tubular steel ladder hooked over the cockpit edge. The pilot drops his back-type parachute into the seat and connects it to the seat

Left and right side views of the prototype F-106B two-seat trainer aircraft. It was higher in the cockpit area than the 106A to allow rear-seat pilot to see what was going on. From ground line to top of canopy was 7 foot 6 inches for 106B and 6 foot 6.8 inches for F-106A. (USAF)

survival kit. The chute firing lanyard is next connected to the ejection seat. The seat was needed for the pilot's well-being in the supersonic F-106. In the case of modern aircraft, even in the fifties, it meant some sort of ejection seat was needed as the old over-the-edge-of-the cockpit-with-a-lunge option was long gone. Try that maneuver in a hot jet and you were long gone, chopped up by the tail or the supersonic airflow. Therefore the F-106A, Cadillac of the Fighters, had what was called a supersonic seat. This meant the pilot could bail out at supersonic speeds. The seat was not Convair's product, but was the result of a lot of supersonic aircraft manufacturers working on the same problem. The initial seat design was not all that it could be, and during the 1965–67 era it was replaced in all aircraft by the "Weber" seat.

The first seats had not been designed and built for comfort. They folded in the middle, shoving the pilot's knees against his chest, grabbing and throwing his arms against his stomach and between his thighs. The canopy then blew off and the chair was fired into the airstream, stabilized by two booms that held the chair firmly and aerodynamically in a flight path that the pilot could physically tolerate after ejection. At 15,000 feet, the parachute was popped open and the seat fell away.

To get a seat that would work properly, many tests were run with rocket sleds at Holloman Air Force Base. These were accompanied by additional testing at Edwards. The tests verified that ejections up to nine hundred knots were survivable. Tests with humans aboard the rocket sleds were conducted thirty-five times to prove the system. The testers got so good at it that on one sled run, with a

dummy abroad, they reached Mach 1.4 on the ground, which was equivalent to Mach 2.5 at 30,000 feet. The ejection was so smooth that a cigarette pack in the dummy's flight suit pocket remained there throughout the test.

The cockpit has consoles running along either side of the ejection seat and, of course, the instrument panel ahead. The left-hand console contains the throttle lever, a fuse block, a spare fuse holder, anti-g-suit selector switch, fuel tank transfer switches, canopy opening and closing switch (both emergency and automatic), oxygen system controls, landing light switch, radar horizontal and scan control switches, weapons bay switches for arming missiles, an emergency hydraulic pump (the RAT again) and T-handle. The right-hand console holds the radio equipment, both navigational and communications. There are also various light switches.

The instrument panel with its flight instruments sits directly in front of the pilot. Many of the more important instruments, such as airspeed and altimeter, are of the vertical tape variety on the later aircraft of the fleet. Engine rpm and temperature gauges, as well as fuel and oil level gauges and automatic pilot controls, are also located here. The drag chute control handle is located on the upper left-hand section of the panel. It operates by pulling the handle for chute deployment and pushing it in, once on the ground, to jettison it. The chute usually is not jettisoned but pulled along behind the plane to the ramp. This makes it unnecessary for someone to go out on the runway or taxi strip to retrieve it.

In the center of the instrument panel, from top to bottom, is the radar scope, flight attitude control-

The first F-102B, 57-2507, was painted the usual gray with red nose section, wing tips and a wide bar on vertical tail. (USAF)

ler display, compass and, at the bottom near the floor, the tactical situation display. This is a large, circular screen on which a map is projected with symbols for the target as well as the F-106A aircraft itself superimposed on it. These symbols move about the map to show their position relative to the ground and to each other. High in the triangle formed by the windscreen is the optical sight for visual firing of missiles and the Vulcan 20 mm cannon now installed on some of the aircraft.

While the rudder pedals are conventional, the control stick is certainly not. From its central shaft that comes out of the floor, it forms a double handle U-shape. With both hands on the stick, the pilot controls not only the aircraft but the weapons and attack mode as well. The left handle of the stick contains at its top the RDR IR/EXP-LC/PUR switch. Protruding from the left-hand side of the handle is the auto search switch. On the inside of the handle, almost directly opposite, is the antenna elevation wheel. Lower on the handle is the radar/IR select button on the inside and the action switch directly behind it on the side opposite the pilot. The right handle, starting at the top, has the elevon trim switch, the nose-wheel steering and microphone buttons and the emergency direct manual button. Right below the top, away from the pilot, is the armament trigger. Below that is a second switch that is the manual mode trigger and, on some aircraft, the air refueling manual disconnect switch. In the center of the U is the hand control lock.

On the upper side of the fuselage, directly behind the pilot, is a 227-gallon fuel tank. On the F-

106B, with its tandem two-pilot cockpit, that tank size is reduced to 177 gallons. The instrumentation of the F-106B is similar, but more simple in the rear cockpit than the front cockpit. The instrument panel is nearly the same; the side consoles are somewhat less cluttered.

Directly behind the fuel tank is the air-to-air refueling hatch. Below it and extending at least a quarter of the length of the fuselage is the weapons and armament bay. In many respects it is more like the bomb bay of a medium bomber than a section of a fighter plane. It even has doors that open and close, similar to the main bomb bay doors of a World War II Martin B-26. The F-106A is an aircraft that, in the interest of speed, carries all of its ordnance internally, none of this hard spot stuff with missiles, gun packs and other assorted paraphernalia hung beneath the wings.

The idea was to make it a super clean aircraft, and super clean it is, and the performance shows it. It was *designed* as a very efficient interceptor aircraft. When built, it *looked* like a super efficient aircraft. And it *flew* like a super efficient aircraft. This cleanliness in design has kept it in good stead for twenty-five years as a first-line fighter and will probably sustain it in the first-line inventory for another several years into the eighties.

What went into the bomb-bay-like weapons bay? Well, there is enough destructive capacity in there to make whole squadrons of World War II aircraft pale in insignificance. It's all similar to the F-102A, except that, starting in the early seventies, a

This front view of an F-106A, taken at Edwards AFB September 24, 1969, makes the craft look very rugged with the big air scoops and wing tanks—both providing the ingredients needed to fire up the powerful Pratt & Whitney J75. (USAF)

Vulcan six-barrel, 20 mm cannon was added to the bottom of the weapons bay.

Topside of the aft fuselage are the vertical fin and rudder. Swept back at fifty-five degrees at the leading edge it is truncated at the top rather than forming the full triangle as did the fin and rudder of the F-102A. The area is as great as that of the F-102's; however, the fin leading edge was moved forward to retain the lost surface area. At the rear base of the fin are the speed brakes, two surfaces that split down the centerline of the aircraft and are pushed out at nearly right angles to the airflow by small hydraulic cylinders. When the speed brakes are open, they reveal the packed drag chute that is located at the base of the rudder. On the fin's leading edge are two short probes situated closely together. They are intakes for the rudder feel system of the flight controls. Unlike the F-102A, there is no UHF antenna near the top of the fin.

On the underside of the rear fuselage is an arresting hook that was retrofitted to all F-106's beginning in May 1963. This hook is used for emergency landings when the aircraft's brakes are disabled. The technique is very similar to that of the arresting gear

The 360-gallon Mach 2 rated drop-tanks on this F-106A are slanted downward with relationship to the wing. This is done so that at speed, with the wing at a nominal angle of attack, the tanks will present the least cross-sectional area to the airstream. (USAF)

used during Navy carrier operations, except the stopping is not quite so violent, as there is a whole runway ahead to use rather than the somewhat short deck of a carrier. Unlike the F-102 hook, this one is retractable. Also on the fuselage bottom is a compartment with a wind-driven emergency hydraulic pump (RAT) that can be deployed into the airstream to provide enough power to the controls to get home if the main hydraulic systems go out. At the front base of the vertical fin is the engine oil tank, containing 4.5 gallons of that vital engine lifeblood.

The aluminum alloy wings of the F-106A (and B) serve several purposes aside from being the lifting surfaces. They house the main landing gear struts when the gear is retracted (the fuselage houses the wheels). The wings also carry most of the aircraft's fuel internally, as well as serving as a hard spot mount for the two external fuel tanks and, lately, even for some missiles and chaff dispensers.

The structure of the sixty-degree swept-back wings is based around five forged one-piece spars in each wing. They are covered with machined alumi-

This front view of an F-106A was taken March 9, 1980, on the ramp at Offutt Air Force Base, Nebraska. It shows fine detail of such things as the clear vision canopy, wheel well doors, retraction linkage, landing lights mounted on wheel well doors and pylon-mounted wing tanks. (George R. Cockle)

num alloy skins with conical cambered leading edges. Inside each wing are four fuel tanks (the fourth one between the aft spar and the elevons is really a transfer tank). Near the leading edges, by the fuselage, are the number one tanks, which together hold 299 gallons. Aft of this tank are two wing spars separated by the space required for the retractable landing gear. Behind the rear-most spar of the landing gear well are tanks two and three, each pair holding 311 gallons and 424 gallons respectively. The two transfer tanks each hold 210 gallons. With the forty-gallon fuselage tank behind the pilot the total capacity internally (and this is considered over-loaded) for fuel in the F-106A is 1,514 gallons which, in addition to the tanks, also includes thirty gallons in the fuel lines.

When you think about it, the fuel *lines* of this fighter hold more fuel than the fuel *tank* of most automobiles. External tankage in the form of two supersonically rated drop tanks increase the fuel capacity by another 454 gallons making the grand total of usable fuel in the normal configuration 1,968 gallons or 12,792 pounds of JP-4. To convert gallons to pounds, figure on 6.5 pounds per gallon of JP-4 on a standard day. The B model's all-up fuel capacity is slightly less, 1,936 gallons or 12,584 pounds. This is

This pair of Sixes with 230-gallon subsonically rated drop-tanks open their speed brakes as they prepare for landing approach. Note conical camber on wing's leading edge. (USAF)

Closeup shot of the nose of 57-2547 from the 87th FIS from K.I. Sawyer AFB, Michigan. (George R. Cockle)

This F-106B comes from the "Big-Sky-Country" courtesy of the Montana ANG, 186th FIS. Photo was taken at Offutt AFB, Nebraska. (George R. Cockle)

due mainly to the smaller tank in the fuselage, but is somewhat offset by slightly larger wing tanks.

For control surfaces, the honeycomb structural elevons on the trailing edge are built in two sections. The wing is so thin that the outer section push rods and control mechanisms must be mounted in streamlined fairings that are exterior to the wing's lower surface.

The earliest F-106's still had wing fences similar to those used on the F-102 to control the flow over the wing. However, it was soon discovered that saw cuts (a slang term) in the leading edge would serve just as well and result in greater simplicity and less drag; so that method was soon adopted.

The main landing gear retracts inward, the struts going into the wings and the wheels being tucked, almost tire tread to tire tread, in the fuselage. Doors fitted to the struts cover the wells flush with the bottom skin of the wings. The wheels themselves are covered by fuselage doors, hinged at the fuselage centerline, that swing outward and upward to fair the wheel bays smoothly with the fuselage. Landing lights are attached to each gear strut and are ready for operation as soon as the main gear goes down. The main gear wheels themselves are quite small and contain very high air pressures. The tread of the main gear is a wide, fifteen feet 5.54 inches for easy ground handling, and the distance from the nose-wheel centerline to the main gear centerline is twenty-four feet 1.5 inches. The angle with the main

gear strut fully extended to prevent touching the afterburner nozzle on the ground during takeoff rotation, or flare, is seventeen degrees thirty minutes.

I recall one late afternoon, standing at the FAA station at Atlantic City, New Jersey, as six Air Guard 106's came swooping low over the field line astern. They had been on a surveillance mission out over the Atlantic. The pilots were all captains—airline captains, men who had learned their trade in the Air Force but now had gone on to the greener pastures of the commercial airlines. Pushing the sluggish transports around, while lucrative, did not offer the sense of being an airman that piloting the fighters did, so it was into the Convairs as "Weekend Warriors" to keep up the old feeling of masterful confidence known only to the fighter pilot. As they came across the field, line astern, then pulled upward into a steep climb into the cloud deck with afterburners booming and spewing flame, one could sense their exhuberance in riding this fastest of the Delta Dazzlers.

Aircraft are unusual in that sometimes they end up being used for missions for which they were not designed. There is nothing wrong with this, as it really is only a tribute to the excellence of the basic design. The F-106A was designed for the interception of enemy bombers. Those aircraft were considered large targets that would be moving over the poles, from Russia toward the North American continent, laden with destructive nuclear bombs. The

With a storm coming and remnants of the last snowfall on the grass behind the ramp, the F-106A is hunkered down and ready to take it. Photo was taken February 28, 1980, at Offutt AFB, Nebraska. (George R. Cockle)

mission of the F-106A was to scramble and get to the target at tremendous speed well before the bomber could do any damage to populated areas. It was intended to fire on and destroy the bombers in any kind of weather and then to return safely to base to await its next protective mission.

In the time frame the F-106A was designed for, it could accomplish that mission very well, had it ever have been required. However, as the threat changed from manned Soviet bombers to intercontinental ballistic missiles, it was decided that the high-performance interceptor was also able, with the proper pilot training, to engage in dogfighting with the enemy's fighter aircraft. One of the first steps was to add the Gatling gun 20 mm cannon to the plane's already lengthy list of armaments. The next step was to train the pilot in the art of air-to-air combat that went back to before World War II.

While the radar on the F-106A did not have as long a range as, say, the F-4, it was made up for by the close connection between the craft and the powerful SAGE ground radar. Other problems that the Dart had to live with, however, were lack of armor plating and rather vulnerable fuel tanks and systems. On the plus side was the great performance of the big delta wing at altitude when compared to the F-4. The F-106A did, however, lose out to the F-4 in a flyoff for a first-line fighter aircraft in 1961.

From the pilot's point of view, the Six, dogfightwise, is not too bad a fighter. A dogfighter has to be careful of the stall situation. The Six, being a delta, is not susceptible to stalls, but if it got into one, all hell would break loose as far as recovery. However, in a tight rolling turn it reacts in an almost explosive manner. With no question, the Six could act as a first-line fighter at high altitude as well or better than its contemporaries. By using the possibilities of energy management, the F-106 can still take on, with deadly adversarial aplomb, almost any fighter in the world and come out on top.

As the pilot's manual was used to outline the F-102's capabilities and usefulness, so will the quirks and special interest items of the Six now be spelled out.

In many respects the F-106A was like the F-102A in flying characteristics and capabilities (the F-

Drooped wing tips show on a Michigan ANG "Red Bull" F-102A as it heads upstairs. (George R. Cockle)

Aircraft photographer George R. Cockle's tour de force of an F-106B (57-2337) that happened onto the ramp at Offutt AFB, Nebraska, one day. There are enough details in these photos to satisfy even the most demanding scale fan. (George R. Cockle)

106A was originally the F-102B), so a rehash of the basic aircraft is not required. What *is* of interest are some of the F-106A features that were great improvements over the F-102A's.

One of the first things to be noticed is the air intake ducts, which are shorter than those of the F-102A. These ducts include a new feature, the variable ramp system, which allows for maintenance of optimum inlet stability over the wide range of speeds and altitudes within the aircraft's capability.

This stability is very important, as it matches the inlet airflow to the engine's demands or, as the flight manual puts it, "The variable ramp system provides optimum performance at full engine thrust and maintains inlet stability by adjusting the inlet duct air at higher Mach numbers." What the variable ramp intake actually does is reduce the incoming airflow to subsonic speeds at the engine face. This is critical at supersonic speeds in order to preclude compressor stall, or buzz, if the pressure is too high.

Extended speed-brakes of F-106A are held in position by hydraulic cylinders that are electronically controlled. Drag chute is nestled between them. (George R. Cockle)

Closeup of the underside of a Six shows the rugged, but somewhat intricate, landing gear struts. Note the dual wheel nose gear. Also shown clearly are the sturdy weapons bay doors as well as a part of the variable-ramp engine air intake. (George R. Cockle)

Decreased engine performance occurs if the pressure is too low. Duct cross-sectional area controls these factors.

The inlet area pressure is sensed in each inlet's throat by a pitot static probe. The signals from these probes are ultimately joined together by means of a shuttle valve before being fed to the ramp control unit, which in turn is controlled by the air data computer. The purpose of the shuttle valve is to cancel the effects of yaw. During a yaw condition, the left and right intake probes read different pressures due to the duct on the side, in the direction of the yaw, being blanketed by the fuselage, nose and cockpit. If the signals are not averaged, the variable ramps would operate independently of each other and aggravate the asymmetrical condition.

The variable ramp itself is a fairly complex piece of machinery. It consists of a nine-degree wedge that extends forward of the inlet openings. The wedges show clearly in photos of the F-106. Immediately behind these wedges is a variable angle ramp assembly located in each duct. Those assemblies are composed of three hinged, interlocked sections that are arranged to automatically control the duct area and shock wave pattern. This system provides the inlet matching to engine requirements. These ramp sections are driven to their appropriate positions by four hydraulic, motor-actuated jack-screws. Their positions can be anywhere from eight to thirty degrees from the aircraft centerline. At lower speeds they are wide open, but as the Six accelerates past Mach 1.25, the system is automatically energized.

The ejection seat was also revised for the F-106. It was made capable of the long sought after zero-zero operation. That meant the pilot could eject

The twin seat F-106B had full operational capability for launching of Falcons, or Genie nuclear missile, if the need arose. (USAF)

at zero speed and zero altitude with a good chance of making it safely to the ground. The handgrips, similar to those on the F-102 seat, are lifted to punch out of the aircraft after the canopy is jettisoned. The seat itself is fired with a high-impulse rocket that burns for approximately one-half second. It catapults the seat and pilot up the rails and into the air some 200 to 300 feet above the aircraft. About one second after the seat starts up the rails, the ejection seat ballistic system igniter fires, automatically opening the safety belt, actuating the seat/man separator, arming the chute deployment gun and releasing the firing lanyard from the parachute disconnect. Two seconds after the seat/man separation and three seconds after the seat starts up the rails, the deployment gun fires and pulls the chute from the pack. Full deployment of the chute is realized in another three seconds at an altitude of about 150 feet and several hundred feet down range from the ejection point. That's fast—six seconds from sitting in the aircraft to floating down under a chute.

At high altitude the same sequence happens, except that the pilot free-falls to below 15,000 feet

A first-class example of a 49th FIS F-106A. Eagle was green, with white head and feathers, with a yellow beak and lightning flash. (George R. Cockle)

This formation of three F-106A's, and a "B" in the slot, were from the 87th FIS, Minnesota ANG. Photos were taken in May 1969. The unit is now located at K.I. Sawyer AFB, Michigan. (Maj. Gen. Wayne C. Gatlin, Minn. ANG)

before the chute is automatically deployed for the long, slow float-down. For this type of ejection, the seats are also equipped with a chaff dispenser to reflect radar signals back to the ground stations. With radar, ground personnel can readily track the bailout and help to quickly find and retrieve the pilot from the boonies.

The F-106B two-man trainer is equipped with the same type of seats; however, they do not blow out together. After the canopy is jettisoned, the rear seat fires approximately one second before the front one to allow for separation between the front and rear occupants. Simultaneous ejection would likely result in a collision of two bodies above the craft and entanglement of their chutes.

The real hop-up to the increase in performance of the F-106A over the F-102 was the powerful Pratt & Whitney J75-P-17 engine, encased in a slender area-ruled (from the start) fuselage. With a sea level static thrust of 17,200 pounds without afterburner and 24,500 pounds with the burner lit off, it was a massive jump in power. The F-102A had only 11,700

pounds and 17,200 pounds for the corresponding numbers.

Looked at another way, the J75 put out as much thrust without afterburning as the J57 did *with* afterburning. As a result the Six had a top speed of 1,525 mph, versus the Deuce's 825 mph. Like the J57, the J75 is of twin-spool construction consisting of a split fifteen-stage axial-flow compressor, eight radially mounted combustion chambers, a split three-stage turbine and an afterburner incorporating a two-position exhaust nozzle.

The split multistage axial compressor is made up of an eight-stage low-pressure rotor and a seven-stage high-pressure rotor. The low-pressure rotor is connected by a solid shaft to the second- and third-stage turbine wheels. A hollow shaft around the low-pressure shaft mounts the high-pressure compressor section and the first-stage turbine wheel that gets the full shot of thermal energy from the eight burner cans. The high-pressure portion of the engine is governed by the throttle, while the low-pressure portion is totally independent of the pilot's control.

Afterburner blazing, this "Red Bull" from Michigan makes takeoff for home from Offutt. It can make the flight non-stop with the drop tanks. (George R. Cockle)

A compressor air bleed system is used to divert part of the low-pressure air overboard at low engine rpm. The bleed is actuated automatically by a governor driven by the low-pressure rotor and aids in starting, improves engine acceleration and prevents engine surging during low thrust operation.

An instrument that goes along with the engine is the in-flight jet engine analyzer that has been added to the later models of the F-106A. It indicates exhaust gas temperature (EGT), the temperature spread and engine life remaining. With the analyzer it is possible for the pilot to immediately recognize engine over-temperature and get a quick readout of the number of over-temperatures the engine has experienced. This is complete with warning flag if too many have occurred.

There are two different types of instrumentation in the F-106A: "round eyes" and "tape." The round eyes, in the early F-106's, consist of conventional round instrumentation. The tape instruments had not been fully developed when the first Sixes started coming down the assembly line. The vertical tape instruments have long since been considered superior to the round ones, as they reduce cockpit work load dramatically. Some of the round-eyed aircraft have also been converted to tape instrumentation. The performance advantages are great, but some maintenance people relate that the tapes are much more difficult to maintain and service.

In this and the previous chapter, the Six has been covered primarily from the standpoint of its improvements over the Deuce. It can be seen that the careful area-rule streamlining, the more powerful J75 engine, the improved fire control system (MA-1) and the zero-zero ejection system all have combined to make this one fine aircraft. It was a real aeronautical breakthrough when it first flew, more than twenty-five years ago. Constant updating has, until recent years, pretty much kept it that way, so that even today it is still somewhat of a threat to any enemy, no matter how sophisticated.

To illustrate how this has happened take again the case of the F-106A design, conjured up for the role of an all-weather interceptor and now considered a viable dogfighter. There are two main changes that contributed to the plane's new role: the increase in cockpit vision afforded when the heavy, wide, center frame was removed from the top side of the cockpit canopy and the addition of the Vulcan 20 mm cannon and an excellent gun sight in the cockpit.

The gun is a package that can be installed within the weapons bay. It can be recognized as a bulge about six inches high and about three feet long that shows on the bottom of the aircraft. Spent cartridges are kept internally within the missile bay. The shells are highly explosive and incendiary, and as few as twenty of them can knock a bomber out of

This California ANG F-106A sits on a ramp at Offutt AFB, November 29, 1980.

the sky. Not all F-106's can mount the cannon, but most of the newer ones are capable of it, particularly those with tape instrumentation.

Along with these design improvements, the other half of the combat equation is met with pilot training at the USAF Air Defense Weapons Center at Tyndall AFB, Florida. This training covers the matter of energy management so that at the high speeds and altitudes involved the pilot can outfight his adversary, even getting on his tail and flaming him in the fashion of the World War I and II fighters. Navy F-4D Phantoms are currently used as practice adversaries in this training.

Still, the mainstream area of the Six is that of all-weather operation. These flights, in bad weather, are of course IFR. However, in addition to getting from here to there in one piece, such as on an airliner, there is the matter of an enemy to be found and vanquished in bad weather. Two weather conditions that are very unfriendly to the pilot's accomplishment of this task are ice and thunderstorms. Both deadly enemies of any aircraft, these conditions usually can be circumvented by changing altitude or heading to avoid them. Not so on an intercept. Deviation from an attack flight path means not getting the target; as at today's speeds he will be long gone before the new attack path can be accomplished.

As in any aircraft, the pilot is warned to avoid areas of heavy icing and to climb and descend as rapidly through them as possible. In such conditions, erratic airspeed indications are common, as are ice buildups on the canopy and engine air inlets. However, with the anti-icing systems in operation, the F-106 can be flown safely in icing conditions. There are no wing or vertical tail surface anti-icing devices, as the aircraft has sufficient power to overcome increased drag from surface ice buildups. Surface ice will, however, decrease range as additional thrust is required to maintain flying speed. It is important to set the anti-icing features to work when icing is encountered so that the inlet ducts do not suffer so much icing that the engine power is decreased due to lack of air passing through the intakes. Worse yet, under such conditions, dangerous compressor stalls can be encountered.

Along with ice, rain can cause some problems for the aircraft as well as for the pilot. Repeated supersonic flights through rain can erode the radome, which must be inspected for damage after landing.

Thunderstorms are violent and have been known to rip aircraft apart. An airline captain wrote a book about flying in thunderstorms, entitled *Anvil of the Gods,* and the title he chose is just what a thunderstorm is. The flight manual says to accomplish thunderstorm penetration at 275-325 KIAS *unless* an intercept mission demands otherwise. In that case, the pilot can penetrate the storm at any speed up to the aircraft's supersonic maximum. Convair assures the pilot that the heavy g-loads he encounters will not exceed the interceptor's design limits at any speed and, further, that engine performance and

F-106A at moment of rotation at Offutt AFB April 18, 1981. (George R. Cockle)

aircraft control will be satisfactory during supersonic penetration of the storm. The pilot is warned, however, to be prepared for large roll and pitch rates, with the largest in the roll mode.

There is a difference between subsonic and supersonic penetration of storms, in that subsonically most of the pilot's corrections will be combating roll disturbances and supersonically most of his efforts will be correcting pitch problems. The airspeed indicator may also go screwy due to the pitot icing up. The windshield could ice up, also.

This information was all well and good in the pilot's manual but, in the real world, meteorologist Joe Kovac recalls, it all might not have just been that pat:

"There are few extraordinary weather constraints on the fighters. No airplanes are thunderstorm-proof yet. The use of fiber or nonmetallic compounds in the skin of modern-day airplanes has made them particularly susceptible to electrical charging in the atmosphere. In the early 1970's an F-106 out of McChord AFB, Tacoma, Washington, got 'zapped' in the nose by lightning. The heat of the stroke caused the outer skin of the aircraft forward of the cockpit to be blown off. Through skillful airmanship the pilot managed to recover safely. A few years later an F-106 out of Griffiss AFB, Rome, New York, was not so lucky. A strike in approximately the same location on the aircraft during departure caused a fatal accident when the pilot had insufficient airspeed and maneuvering room in showery weather conditions.

"Moderate to severe turbulence could certainly make a steady 'lock' on a target difficult. For a few years we were required to brief the altitude of the −55°C temperature as there had been some difficulties with the engine of the F-102 when the temperature was significantly colder. Icing at departure and approach altitudes could also ruin a pilot's day. Freezing rain collected as an icy layer on the surface of the aircraft on final approach drastically altered the lift and weight of the F-102 where power available would be insufficient to maintain the proper attitude and rate of descent. It was not as critical in the F-106 as there was usually enough extra ooomph! in the system to keep the plane from landing short."

Another little jewel besides the thunder, lightning and turbulence is hail. At high speeds it can really make a mess out of the radome and wing's leading edge. They look as if someone had spent the day at them with a ball-peen hammer.

Another all-weather problem area is extreme cold. The aircraft is perfectly capable of performing its mission under these conditions but here, man, pilot and ground crew must bear and overcome the rigors of the weather. The aircraft could give a damn! Takeoffs are, of course, possible on instruments with practically zilch minimums. If the pilot can keep on the runway to rotation speed, he's all set for the ascent on instruments with the afterburner booming him swiftly upstairs where there are no clouds. Coming back down through the stuff is pretty well handled automatically by the Hughes MA-1 system,

The F-106A shown here made the trip from Cape Code, Massachusetts, to Offutt AFB, Nebraska, in May 1981. ANG pilot proficiency is honed to the nth degree with this type of cross-country operation. (George R. Cockle)

which should bring the pilot out of the stuff over the numbers with time left for him to take control for the final landing flare, with normal airspeed and altitude.

An F-106 pilot usually gets about fifteen to twenty hours of flight time per month. It takes from six months to a year for him to really get acquainted with the plane and still, after no matter how many hours in it, there always seems to be something new he can learn. Setting out alerts, the pilots are expected to be able to scramble in five minutes. During the day, when wide awake, this is quite possible to do. However, making this time after being rousted out of a deep sleep is far more difficult and dangerous. A sleep-groggy head is no real match for the high-performance interceptor's bag of tricks if something goes awry.

Now, after twenty-five years of first-line defense, it is time for the old girl to go. Even though her airframe was upped in useful life from 4,000 to 8,000 hours (a real tribute to the integrity of the Convair design), she is rapidly just simply getting outdated.

The fire control system is quite obsolete, compared with present-day standards, as are the missiles, which are now well behind the times when it comes to capabilities, performance, knockdown power and antijamming devices. Also, general maintenance of the aircraft is becoming a problem, as many of the parts and components have long been out of production. This makes it necessary to make some of them from scratch, which takes forever and a day, compared with pulling them off the shelf.

The Air National Guard will soon inherit the F-106's from the Air Force (that is, the ones they have not already received). Perhaps from there they will continue to serve in that capacity until the late eighties, when they will be retired altogether. Rather than sitting in the sands of Arizona rotting away, it might be fitting that they too go the route of the F-102A in the Pave Duece program. Devoid of a man in the cockpit, and with all that airframe strength and speed, they would indeed make a worthy but extremely tough target for missile and fire control systems not even developed yet.

The New Jersey ANG shows up at Offutt April 18, 1981. Aircraft is in the taxi-for-takeoff phase of its visit. (George R. Cockle)

CHAPTER IX
△ THE DIFFERENT DELTAS

△————————THERE IS SOMETHING ABOUT A delta wing that looks like speed in a *stylish* sort of way. "Styles are bad things in engineering." So said Clarence L. (Kelly) Johnson in his October 2, 1953, SAE paper, *Airplane Configurations for High Speed Flight*. He was, at the time, pointing a derisive finger directly at the delta wing aircraft, both in the U.S. and in England. He was right, of course, from an engineering viewpoint. Styles in engineering are bad. However, in spite of this, on the bottom line, engineers are people. If anything in the world stirs people up, gets their juices flowing, and sometimes makes them act in ways directly opposite of common sense (and common sense is really what engineering is), it is style.

But what about aircraft, those beautiful form-follows-function contrivances designed by engineering science of the highest technology? Those products, we are assured, are carved from metal to the nth decimal point of positive pristine mathematical formula. In the age of the jet transport, Sud Aviation uncorked a style with its first flight of the Caravelle on May 27, 1955. Everyone else had been plodding along, putting the then-new turbojets where piston engines had dwelled not long before. This meant on the wings for multiengine aircraft. And why not? This was the true, unfettered path of evolution.

The *true* path was not without its problems, however. Like peas in a pod, the B-47, B-52, 707 and DC-8 all appeared with engines slung beneath their wings in their streamlined pods. American engineers were dead against mounting the engines in the wing roots, à la Comet, for fear of an explosion or other catastrophic turbine failure ripping up the wings' internal structure. That was good sound engineering.

There were also some fine engineering advantages to the pods, apart from the safety aspects. They were short, with no ducts through the wings either into or out of the engine and, therefore, they were optimum from an airflow standpoint. Further, the engines' weight under the wings tended to offset the upward bending moment caused by the wings' lift. Therefore, the wings' structure could be lighter while still safely adequate. Another advantage was that the engines were low and easily serviced and changed. New and different models of engines could also be added with a minimum of airframe modification and redesign.

To be sure, this style had some bad points: ingestion of foreign objects due to the low mounting position above the runway, breaking up of wing flaps to allow room for the powerful jet blast to escape from under the wings without structural damage and, of course, damage caused by high decibels of noise from the engines, which could cause fatigue to the surrounding metal.

Then came the new style. The French Caravelle transport mounted the engines on either side of the rear fuselage and got rid of the wing-related problems once and for all. The wings were now super clean and left alone to produce lift—their basic purpose. The engines were high out of the debris ingestion area. They were quieter, as they were behind the cabin, and from a safety standpoint they were well away from the main fuel tanks in the wings. It was a panacea, and they *looked* pretty sharp back there too.

The new style caught on (the French have always been great style setters) and overnight the rest of the industry was tumbling into the rear engine barrel along with the sexy French Caravelle. Everything, from the smallest to the very largest aircraft, was affected. The executive twin-jets, the North American Sabre-Liner, the Lear-Jet and the Fan Jet Falcon went the rear-mount route.

In a design landslide, at the same time, the rear engine style caught on in the design of transport aircraft in the United States, England and Russia. In the U.S., the Douglas DC-9, as well as the Boeing 727, sprouted rear engines. England followed the style with the BAC 111, Hawker-Sidley Trident and, for very good measure, came up with the four-engines-in-the-rear BAC VC-10 and Super VC-10, an airliner with the superlative distinction of having never crashed or taken a life. Russia, not to be outdone in following the new style, built the IL-62, a spittin' image of the VC-10. She also came up with the TU-154 trijet and TU-134, both with rear-mounted engines. Almost all these aircraft also had T-tails, another style that seemed to fit well with the rear-mounted engines.

But the rear engines and T-tail design was found not to be the complete panacea it had looked like originally. The T-tail tended to become ineffective during high angles of attack when the wing blanketed it, causing an irrecoverable phenomena known as the deep stall. This happened to the ill-fated BAC 111 prototype. Automatic stick shakers were soon installed to prevent that condition. Without the download of the engines, the wings had to be built heavier for strength and at the same time the rear fuselages had to be beefed up to support the engines and their thrust loads. Of less importance, but still significant, was the difficulty in gaining access to the high-mounted engines for service as well as for c.g. control, with so much of the aircraft's weight located aft.

The point of the foregoing discussion is to illustrate that style can affect even so calculated a discipline as aeronautical engineering. Regardless of the subject, style is new, tantalizing and almost impossible to ignore. That's a quirk of mankind and it will probably always be.

So it was that Convair's initial interest in Dr. Alexander Lippisch's delta wing aircraft was due to its potential as a style setter. It looked fast and, early on, not only Convair's designers sensed this, but so did others. It was the same old story. If it works, is different and can stir the viewer's imagination, you have the makings of a significant trend, or style, on your hands.

To deal with the delta is to deal with the realm of high-speed flight. The delta style, as Kelly Johnson

The North American B-70 was the delta wing brought to its zenith with United States aviation technology. Meant to be an intercontinental bomber, two copies of the aircraft were built before it lost out to the ICBM method of continental defense. (Collect Air)

called it, quickly caught on in places other than Convair engineering. Even though Johnson was not enamored of it at first, it wasn't too many years before he adopted it in modified form for the high-flying YF-12A that evolved into Lockheed's SR-71A Blackbird. The first flight of the type was on April 26, 1962. It was quite a bird. It could move rapidly along at 2,200 miles per hour at 86,000 feet. When Johnson finally decided to go with the delta, he certainly went all the way and now, almost twenty years later, no one has really ever come up with anything that can match the craft's fantastic performance.

Douglas also took a crack at the delta planform and by January 23, 1951, had the XF4D-1 Skyray prototype in the air. By October 3, 1952, the Navy shocked the hell out of the Air Force (and Convair) by grabbing the world speed record at 753 miles per hour. The English aeronautical types took heed of what was going on and came up with the spiffy little Gloster Javelin F. (A.W.) 1 fighter. They flew the prototype for the first time on November 26, 1951. Avro, after trying out the idea on a couple of small prototypes, opted to build its V-bomber in the delta form. The big Type 698 Vulcans are still around today, ready to carry nuclear bombs to about any target that they are sent to. The English also built several other experimental designs, a couple that were even supersonic, using the triangular planform.

When the time came for the U.S. to design a super bomber that would last into the twenty-first century, the delta again won out in the competition. A supersonic giant to replace the B-52 was North American's B-70 Valkyrie. It was large. Its overall length was 196 feet, versus the B-52's 157 feet seven inches. Its delta wing spanned only 105 feet. However, due to the triangular shape it provided great wing area with the short span. It was built to go Mach 3, pushed along by six General Electric YJ93-

The cranked arrow (really a modified delta) wing of the F-16XL shows up well in this artist's rendering of the future General Dynamics fighter. The aircraft will be designated F-16E in production. (General Dynamics)

GE-3 engines with 31,000 pounds static thrust each when in afterburner. The ICBM missile nosed it out of contention as America's defender of the future, but not before two B-70's were built, the first flying in September 1964. From a military aircraft standpoint, the B-70 was the last of the deltas for the United States.

In more recent years the French seem to have stuck with the delta shape as the way to go more so than any other country. There has been a whole series of Dassault-Mirage fighters that have used the triangular wing, culminating in the new and now prototype Mirage 2000 and 4000 designs. The Mirage 2000 is a single engine design, while the 4000 is a twin-engine design. Both are highly reminiscent of the F-106A. In fact, they are probably much like what the F-106A would be today if it had the benefits of the technology of the seventies instead of that of the fifties. The Mirages are obviously first-line fighters, and they will certainly still be around well past the year 2000.

The Israeli Kfir is a direct derivative of the Mirage design. It is powered by a General Electric J79-17, and is that nation's first-line fighter. It has shown itself off very well in the aerial warfare over the Mideast desert during recent years. Sweden has made use of the delta, though in a very modified version, for many years in its Draken fighter design.

Today, even Convair is once more looking at the delta planform, almost coming full circle back to the F-106 after its highly successful straight-wing design F-16. The new aircraft is labeled the F-16XL and has what is called a cranked arrow planform. That means, when translated, that it is a delta with a kink in the leading edge. The design calls for stretching the F-16 fuselage fifty-four inches to accommodate the new delta's long wing chord. The empty weight of the fighter goes up to a projected 17,402 pounds from the standard F-16's present weight of 15,137 pounds. But that big delta wing with loads of area takes the weight gain in stride and, as it turns out, the F-16XL has a short takeoff distance of only 1,640 feet, compared with the standard F-16's 2,425 feet. Not only that, the large wing area also provides underwing mounting for almost double the armament stores that the standard F-16 can carry.

The design is being studied for use as both a hot-shot combat fighter and a ground attack aircraft. Completion of the aircraft is projected for the early nineties. Speed of the new design will be in the Mach 2.2 range, so it sounds like a first-run contender for a contract. While it is still too early to say if the delta F-16XL will make it into production, with the delta's past track record it would not be surprising.

The fighter and bomber business has no exclusive rights to the delta design. Supersonic transports also quickly shook out their designs to be strictly delta. The two flying examples, the TU-144 and the Concorde, are of course both deltas. Back when the competition was underway for the U.S. SST, manufacturers in general favored the delta design in their proposals. The winning proposal was that of Boeing, who had fielded a massive swing-wing design, for the development contract for the United States supersonic transport. Soon after the Boeing people got down to business on the SST design, they revised their design to incorporate a delta wing.

The aircraft covered here are only teasers of what the delta wing is capable of in the high-speed flight ranges. For openers, take a look at the wing on the space shuttle. It is clear that the delta, with its great attributes in the supersonic ranges, even hypersonic ranges, will be around in the far future as new fighters, bombers, transports and space vehicles are designed and developed.

Yes, the triangular Greek letter is Delta, and it means difference in engineering calculations. In aircraft design it means . . . *what a difference!*

CHAPTER X
△ THE DELTA DATA BANK

△—————————THE MATERIAL IN THIS CHAPTER IS ARRANGED to provide a concise source of dimensions, specifications and performance data for the Convair delta-winged airplanes. The aircraft are covered in chronological order by date of each type's first flight. Also included is a complete listing of the service serial numbers of the aircraft.

Convair XF-92-CO (ex XP-92-CO) Model 7

While it never got beyond the preliminary design stage, this was the original Convair study for a very high-speed interceptor. It was begun in 1945, and certain planned items about the aircraft are known.

Configuration: The design began as a ram-jet-powered semi delta-winged aircraft with a butterfly tail. It evolved, on paper, into a pure, tailless delta-winged machine.

Powerplant: Westinghouse J30-WE turbojet, providing 1,560 pounds static thrust plus six 2,000-pound static thrust nitromethane rockets. Combined with the jet engine, they provided a total of 13,560 pounds of static thrust.

Maximum Speed: 825 miles per hour, or Mach 1.25 at 50,000 feet

Armament: Four 20 mm aircraft cannon

Range: Ten minutes at cruise and five minutes at full combat speed

While the program was active it was determined a flying mock-up of a delta wing was needed to try out the concept. This became the XF-92A.

Convair XF-92A-CO (Model 7002)

First Flight: September 18, 1948

Number Built: 1

USAF Serial Number: 46-682 (46-683 and 46-685 were also issued for the 7002 program, but were soon canceled.)

Span: 31 feet 3 inches

Wing Area: 230 square feet

Length: 42 feet 5 inches (with afterburner), 41 feet (without afterburner)

Height: 17 feet 8 inches

Powerplant: Allison J33-A-29 turbojet, fitted with an afterburner providing 7,500 pounds static thrust and

8,200 pounds static thrust with afterburning (1951). Allison J33-A-23 turbojet, providing 4,600 pounds static thrust or 5,400 pounds static thrust with water and methanol injection (1948).

Maximum Speed: 630 miles per hour (Mach 0.95) at 45,000 feet

Crew: 1

Armament: None

Empty Weight: 8,500 pounds

Gross Weight: 15,000 pounds, when loaded with 295 gallons of fuel and fitted with afterburner. 13,000 pounds without afterburner.

This aircraft, with its sixty-degree delta wing, was a flying mock-up of the XF-92 aircraft. As such, it was the first powered delta wing to fly. The afterburner-fitted version was used for most of the formal flight test program. To speed up assembly of the test aircraft, components of five other aircraft were used in its construction.

Convair XF2Y-1 Sea Dart (Model Y2-2)

First Flight: April 9, 1953 (The aircraft was launched on San Diego Bay December 16, 1952, for taxi trials.)

Number Built: 1

USN BuAer Number: 137634

Span: 33 feet 8 inches

Wing Area: 563 square feet

Length: 52 feet 7 inches without nose probe, 56 feet 4.5 inches with nose probe

Height: 16 feet 2 inches with hydroskis retractred, 20 feet 9 inches with twin hydroskis extended

Powerplant: Two Westinghouse J34-WE-42 turbojets, providing 3,400 pounds static thrust each. The aircraft was later fitted with two Westinghouse J46-WE-12B turbojets with afterburners. Static thrust was raised to 4,600 pounds and 6,000 pounds with afterburner, each engine.

Maximum Speed: Unknown, due to aircraft being fitted with temporary J34 engines without afterburning. The high-speed tests were terminated by the time the J-46's were fitted.

Crew: 1

Armament: None

Empty Weight: 12,652 pounds

Gross Weight: 16,527 pounds with 630 gallons of fuel

This aircraft was the first of five Sea Darts built and also the first to fly. It was equipped with both single and twin hydroskis, each system tried with many variations, in an effort to find a solution to the heavy pounding that occurred during takeoff and landing.

Convair YF2Y-1 Sea Dart (YF-7A after 1962)

First Flight: Early 1954

Number Built: 4

USN BuAer Numbers: 135762, 135763, 135764 and 135765

Span: 33 feet 8 inches

Wing Area: 563 square feet

Length: 52 feet 7 inches without nose probe, 56 feet 4.5 inches with nose probe (This dimension is provisional, as various nose probes were used in the test program that were either shorter or longer.)

Height: 16 feet 2 inches with hydroskis retracted, 20 feet 9 inches with hydroskis extended

Powerplant: Two Westinghouse J46-WE-12B turbojets with afterburners fitted. Dry static thrust was 4,600 pounds and with afterburning was 6,000 pounds, each engine.

Maximum Speed: 695 miles per hour at 8,000 feet and 825 miles per hour at 30,000 feet

Crew: 1

Armament: None

Empty Weight: Approximately 17,500 pounds

Gross Weight: 21,000 pounds with 630 gallons of fuel

Takeoff Run: 5,500 feet

Landing Distance: 1,000 feet

Rate of Climb: 132 miles per hour

Service Ceiling: 42,500 feet

These four aircraft were all fitted with twin hydroskis and the paint schemes were a solid navy blue. Aircraft 135762 exceeded Mach 1 in a shallow dive on August 3, 1954.

Convair F2Y-1 Sea Dart

Number Built:0

Number Ordered: 14

USN BuAer Numbers: 135766 through 135773, 137635, 138530 through 138534.

These aircraft were ordered when it appeared the Sea Dart might be a viable Navy first-line fighter. They were to be the first production batch, and the design had once more reverted to an improved single hydroski.

Convair XF2Y-2 Sea Dart

Number Built:0

USN BuAer Number: None issued

These aircraft were to be based on the F2Y-1 Sea Dart but, in light of the lack of success with the Westinghouse engines, Convair decided to go to the more powerful Pratt & Whitney J75 with 15,000 pounds static thrust, or the Wright J67 with 12,000 pounds thrust. In either event, only one engine would have been used. An improved single hydroski was also planned. The Navy, discouraged with the problems that had been encountered in the Sea Dart program, was not interested in pursuing this one even though the USMC was envisaged as the recipients of the new fighters.

Convair YF-102-CO-Delta Dagger (Model 8-80)

First Flight: October 24, 1953

Number Built: 2

USAF Serial Numbers: 52-7994 and 52-7995

Span: 37 feet

Wing Area: Approximately 375 square feet

Length: 52 feet 6 inches without nose probe, 57 feet with nose probe

Height: 18 feet

Powerplant: Pratt & Whitney J57-P-11 with 10,200 pounds static thrust and 14,500 pounds with afterburner

Maximum Speed: Approximately 750 miles per hour

Crew: 1

Armament: While designed for the Hughes Falcon missiles, these aircraft carried no armament as they were used only for flight tests.

Empty Weight: Approximately 16,500 pounds

Gross Weight: 23,000 pounds

The two test aircraft were scaled up wherever possible from the XF-92A at a ratio of 1.22:1. They were a disappointment to both Convair and the Air Force, as they were unable to go supersonic in level flight as had been desired. Number 52-7994 crashed eight days after its first flight. Number 52-7995 made it into the air in January 1954, but was unable to pass Mach 1. It was returned to Convair for installation of some area rule bulges on the aft fuselage and a lengthened nose. While improved, it was still unable to exceed Mach 1.

Convair YF-102-CO Delta Dagger (Model 8-82)

First Flight: March 1954

Number Built:8

USAF Serial Numbers: 53-1779 through 53-1786

These eight aircraft were the same as the previous

Model 8-80, with only minor detail changes. Dimensions and performance were the same.

Convair YF-102A-17-CO Delta Dagger (Model 8-90)
First Flight: December 20, 1954
Number Built: 4
USAF Serial Numbers: 53-1787 through 53-1790
Span: 38 feet 1.6 inches
Wing Area: 661.5 square feet
Length: 68 feet 3.3 inches
Height: 18 feet
Powerplant: Pratt & Whitney J57-P-23 with 10,000 pounds static thrust and with afterburner 17,200 pounds of static thrust
Maximum Speed: 825 miles per hour (Mach 1.25) at 40,000 feet
Crew: 1
Armament: While built to use the Hughes Falcon missiles these aircraft were still considered developmental and were therefore unarmed.
Empty Weight: 19,900 pounds
Gross Weight (normal): 27,700 pounds
Gross Weight (maximum): 31,500 pounds

These aircraft were the reworked YF-102 design featuring Whitcomb area rule, which brought about an increased nose length, rear fuselage bulges, a longer span and introduction of the sharp, pointed supersonic canopy. Plane 1787 was the forerunner of these, and in the colorful red, white and blue paint scheme posed for the aviation press as the delta that could go supersonic.

Convair F-102A-CO Delta Dagger (Model 8-10)
First Flight: Early 1955
Number Built: 875
USAF Serial Numbers: F-102A-5-CO 4 built 53-1791 through 53-1794, F-102A-10-CO 3 built 53-1795 through 53-1797, F-102A-15-CO 5 built 53-1798 through 53-1802, F-102A-20-CO 9 built 53-1803 through 53-1811, F-102A-25-CO 7 built 53-1812 through 53-1818, F-102A-30-CO 13 built 54-1371 through 54-1383, F-102A-35-CO 17 built 54-1384 through 54-1400, F-102A-40-CO 7 built 54-1401 through 54-1407, F-102A-41-CO 23 built 55-3357 through 55-3379, F-206A-45-CO 47 built 55-3380 through 55-3426, F-102A-50-CO 38 built 55-3427 through 55-3464, F-102A-51-CO 16 built 56-957 through 56-972, F-102A-55-CO 72 built 56-973 through 56-1044, F-102A-60-CO 92 built 56-1045 through 56-1136, F-102A-65-CO 97 built 56-1137 through 56-1233, 4 built 56-1317 through 56-1320, F-102A-70-CO 41 built 56-1234 through 56-1274, 11 built 56-1321 through 56-1331, F-102A-75-CO 42 built 56-1275 through 56-1316, 98 built 56-1332 through 56-1429, F-102A-80-CO 89 built 56-1430 through 56-1518, F-102A-90-CO 86 built 57-770 through 57-855, F-102A-95-CO 54 built 57-856 through 57-909
Span: 38 feet 1.6 inches
Wing Area: 661.5 square feet
Length: 68 feet 1.8 inches
Height: 21 feet 2.5 inches
Powerplant: Pratt & Whitney J57-P-23 or -25, providing 11,700 pounds static thrust and 17,200 pounds static thrust with afterburner
Maximum Speed: 825 miles per hour (Mach 1.25) at 40,000 feet
Crew: 1
Armament: 6 Hughes GAR-1D (AIM-4A) Falcon radar-guided missiles, or 6 Hughes GAR-2A (AIM-4C) Falcon infrared-guided missiles, or 6 Hughes GAR-3A (AIM-4F) Super Falcon radar-guided missiles, or 6 Hughes GAR-4A (AIM-4G) Super Falcon infrared-guided missiles, or Hughes radar-guided Nuclear Falcon missile and 24 folding-fin 2.75-inch unguided missiles in the weapons bay doors
Empty Weight: 19,050 pounds
Gross Weight (normal clean): 27,700 pounds
Gross Weight (maximum): 31,500 pounds
Range (internal fuel): 1,350 miles
Combat Radius (internal fuel): 400 miles
Initial Climb: 13,000 feet per minute
Service Ceiling: 54,000 feet

Starting with 55-3357, the vertical fin was heightened, larger air brakes fitted and the intake ducts were improved for airflow and to lower cockpit noise. Starting with 56-1317, the cambered wing was added, which resulted in a 4,200-foot increase in maximum combat ceiling plus a Mach .06 speed increase at 50,000 feet. The early models were also brought up to standard with provisions added for drop tanks and addition of an updated fire control system. This constant modernization program continued throughout the life of the aircraft. They were finally struck from USAF inventory and given over to the Air National Guard. Small numbers of these aircraft also went to the Greek and Turkish Air Forces.

Convair/Sperry QF-102A-CO Delta Dagger (Target Drone)
During the development of the McDonnell-Douglas F-15 Eagle, several of the F-102A-CO's were modified with suitable equipment by Sperry so that they might be flown without pilots aboard, though the cockpits could still be manned if so desired. These aircraft provided high-speed maneuvering targets for the F-15 program.

Convair/Sperry PQM-102A-CO Delta Dagger (Target Drone)
These modified F-102A-CO's are used in the Pave Deuce program for high-speed, full scale targets in anti-aircraft missile training. They are not equipped to accept pilots. They are used for ground-to-air missile training at the White Sands, New Mexico, test facility and for air-to-air training at Tyndall Air Force Base, Florida.

Aircraft from practically every dash number have been or will be converted, over 200 in all.

Convair TF-102A-CO Delta Dagger Trainer (Model 8-12)
First Flight: November 8, 1955
Number Ordered: 198
Number Built: 111
USAF Serial Numbers: TF-102A-5-CO 4 built 54-1351 through 54-1354, TF-102A-10-CO 5 built 54-1355 through 54-1359, TF-102A-15-CO 5 built 54-1361 through 54-1365, TF-102A-20-CO 3 built 54-1366 through 54-1368, TF-102A-25-CO 2 built 54-1369 through 54-1370, TF-102A-26-CO 3 built 55-4032 through 55-4034, TF-102A-30-CO 8 built 55-4035 through 55-4042, TF-102A-35-CO 1 built 54-1360, 8 built 55-4043 through 55-4050, 7 built 56-2317 through 56-2323, TF-102A-36-CO 6 built 55-4051 through 55-4056, TF-102A-37-CO 3 built 55-4057 through 55-4059, TF-102A-40-CO 12 built 56-2324 through 56-2335, TF-102A-41-CO 18 built 56-2336 through 56-2353, TF-102A-45-CO 26 built 56-2354 through 56-2379, TF-102A- -CO 87 56-2380 through 56-2466 (not built)
Span: 38 feet 1.6 inches
Wing Area: 661.5 square feet
Length: 63 feet 4.5 inches

Height: 20 feet 7 inches
Powerplant: Pratt & Whitney J57-P-23 or -25, providing 11,700 pounds static thrust and 17,200 pounds static thrust with afterburner
Maximum Speed: 646 miles per hour
Crew: 2
Armament: None usually carried, but could carry same as F-102A
Empty Weight: 20,731 pound
Gross Weight (normal clean): 28,978 pounds
Gross Weight (maximum): 32,104 pounds
The TF-102A was very similar to the F-102A from the leading edge of the wing rearward. However, a new side-by-side seating arrangement was provided for the instructor pilot and student in the forward fuselage area. Starting with 56-2336, the cambered wing was added. The high performance of the F-102A required that the trainer be built so that the new pilot could transit safely. For this reason Greece and Turkey also received a few TF-102A's to train their pilots for the F-102A's they had acquired in their inventories. These aircraft went through several modification update programs before being turned over to the Air National Guard. The aircraft, while not supersonic in level flight, was capable of Mach 1 in a slight dive.

Convair F-102B-CO Delta Dagger (Model 8-24)
This aircraft designation was not used for actual hardware. The F-102B-CO became so different by the time the Convair designers had finished with it that it was given a new designation, F-106A-CO. Differences included: the fuselage was redesigned to conform to the Whitcomb area rule; the cockpit was moved forward; twin nose wheels were added; and there was a changed main gear. The fin and rudder were also modified in shape to a truncated triangle. The only thing left of the F-102 was the basic wing, and even that was changed after the first few models. For more information, see Convair F-106A-CO.

Convair XFY-1 Pogostick
First Flight: (VTO) August 1, 1954 (full transition) November 2, 1954
Number Built: 3 (The first unit was used for static airframe tests.)
USN BuAer Numbers: 38648, 38649, and 38650
Span: 27 feet 7.75 inches
Wing Area: 355 square feet
Length: 34 feet 11 inches
Height: (tail span) 22 feet 7 inches
Powerplant: Allison YT40-A-14 turboprop engine with 5,850 ehp
Maximum Speed: 500+ miles per hour
Crew: 1
Armament: None (If aircraft had been developed, 20 mm aircraft cannon would have been mounted in the wingtip pods.)
Empty Weight: 11,742 pounds
Gross Weight: 16,250 pounds
These aircraft were direct competitors of the Lockheed XFV-1 VTO aircraft. They were intended to take off straight up, with no provisions made for a conventional landing or takeoff. The Lockheed craft did have a jury-rigged conventional gear, but the XFY-1 performed all its flight testing from the tail-sitting position. Initial flight tests were performed with the craft suspended by cables from the roof of a blimp hangar.

Convair XB-58-CF Hustler (Model 4)
First Flight: November 11, 1956
Number Built: 2
USAF Serial Numbers: 55-660 and 55-661

Span: 56 feet 10 inches
Wing Area: 1,542 square feet
Length: 96 feet 9 inches
Height: 31 feet 5 inches
Powerplant: 4 General Electric J79-GE-1 turbojets with 10,500 pounds static thrust and 15,600 pounds static thrust with afterburner
Maximum Speed: 1,321 miles per hour at 63,150 feet
Crew: 3 (pilot, bombardier/navigator, defense systems operator)
Armament: None
Empty Weight: 55,560 pounds
Gross Weight: 163,000 pounds (maximum takeoff combat weight)
Range: 5,028 miles
These aircraft were the initial test vehicles for the airframe and were test flown without the weapons pod slung underneath. They were used to explore the aircraft's flight envelope.

Convair YB-58A-CF Hustler
First Flight: Unknown
Number Built: 11
USAF Serial Numbers: 55-662 through 55-672
These aircraft were prototypes of those Convair expected to build in production. Dimensionally, they were the same as the XB-58-CF models. They were fitted with improved engines as they became available, those being J79-GE-5's or 5A's with 15,600 pounds of static thrust in afterburner. These planes were later brought up to production standards of the B-58A-CF models.

Convair B-58A-CF Hustler
First Flight: September, 1959
Number Built: 86
USAF Serial Numbers: B-58A-10-CF 36 built 59-2428 through 59-2463, B-58A-15-CF 20 built 60-1110 through 60-1129, B-58A-20-CF 30 built 61-2051 through 61-2080
Span: 56 feet 10 inches
Wing Area: 1,542 square feet
Length: 96 feet 9 inches
Height: 31 feet 5 inches
Powerplant: 4 General Electric J79-GE-5A, -5B, or -5C single shaft turbojets with 10,500 pounds static thrust and 16,000 pounds static thrust with afterburning
Maximum Speed: 1,321 miles per hour at 63,150 feet, 610 miles per hour at sea level
Crew: 3 (pilot, navigator/bombardier, defense systems operator)
Armament: Nuclear weapons in the underslung pod plus a General Electric Vulcan 20 mm aircraft cannon in the tail barbette
Empty Weight: 55,560 pounds without weapons pod
Combat Gross Weight: 163,000 pounds
Maximum Weight with Aerial Refueling: 177,000 pounds
Range: 5,028 miles (plus more with aerial refueling)
Combat Radius: 1,750 miles
Cruise Speed: 610 miles per hour
Rate of Climb: 17,830 feet per minute
Combat Ceiling: 64,800 feet
Zoom Climb Altitude: 85,360 feet
These aircraft were the production run of B-58A Hustlers and were assigned to the 43rd and 305th SAC Bomb Wings. They were withdrawn from service in early 1970.

Convair NB-58A-CF Hustler

This aircraft was one of the YB-58A-1-CF's that was used as an engine test bed by replacing the weapons pod with a General Electric J79-GE-3 turbojet.

Convair RB-58A-CF Hustler

First Flight: Unknown
Number Built: 17
USAF Serial Numbers: 58-1007 through 58-1023
These aircraft were originally YB-58A-10-CF's, but were converted to RB-58A-10-CF's with a reconnaissance pod instead of a nuclear weapons pod.

Convair TB-58A-CF Hustler (Trainer)

First Flight: May 10, 1960
Number Built: 8
USAF Serial Numbers: 55-661, 55-662, 55-663, 55-668, 55-670, 55-671, 55-672, 58-1007
These aircraft were converted to operational trainers by changing the second crew station (navigator/bombardiers) to a cockpit for pilot instruction. Seat positions were in tandem.

Convair B-58B-CF Hustler

Number Built: 0
USAF Serial Number: 60-1109
This aircraft was to represent improvements in the development of the B-58A before it was canceled.

Convair B-58D-CF Hustler

This was a design study for a heavily armed interceptor version of the B-58A. Super fighter!

Convair B-58E-CF Hustler

This was a design study for an even more advanced version of the Hustler than the B-58B, probably using chemical fuels for Mach 3 speeds.

Convair F-106A-CO Delta Dart (Model 8-24)

First Flight: December 26, 1956
Number Built: 277
USAF Serial Numbers: F-106A-1-CO 17 built 56-451 through 56-467, 18 built 57-229 through 57-246, F-106A-65-CO 3 built 57-2453 through 57-2455, F-106A-70-CO 5 built 57-2456 through 57-2460, F-106A-75-CO 5 built 57-2461 through 57-2465, F-106A-80-CO 12 built 57-2466 through 57-2477, F-106A-85-CO 8 built 57-2478 through 57-2485, F-106A-90-CO 21 built 57-2486 through 57-2506, F-106A-95-CO 13 built 58-759 through 58-771, F-106A-100-CO 27 built 58-772 through 58-798, F-106A-105-CO 30 built 59-001 through 59-030, F-106A-110-CO 29 built 59-031 through 59-059, F-106A-120-CO 27 built 59-060 through 59-086, F-106A-125-CO 25 built 59-087 through 59-111, F-106A-130-CO 24 built 59-112 through 59-135, F-106A-135-CO 13 built 59-136 through 59-148
Span: 38 feet 3.5 inches
Wing Area: 661.5 square feet
Length: 70 feet 8.78 inches
Height: 20 feet 3.3 inches
Powerplant: Pratt & Whitney J75-P-17 twin-spool turbojet, rated at 17,200 pounds static thrust and 24,500 pounds static thrust with afterburner
Maximum Speed: 1,525 miles per hour (Mach 2.31) at 40,000 feet
Crew: 1
Armament (typical): 1 AIR-2A Douglas Genie Nuclear Rocket, or 1 AIR-2G Douglas Genie Nuclear rocket, or 2 AIM-4E or 4F Hughes Super Falcon radar-guided missiles, or 2 AIM-4G Hughes Super Falcon infrared-seeking missiles, or 1 Internal 20 mm General Electric M-61 multibarrel cannon with 75 rounds. (Some F-106's only)
Empty Weight: 23,646 pounds
Maximum Takeoff Weight: 38,250 pounds
Range: 2,700 miles with maximum fuel in external tanks at 610 miles per hour at 41,000 feet
Combat Radius: 575 miles with internal fuel
Initial Climb Rate: Approximately 30,000 feet per minute
Zoom Climb Altitude: 70,000 feet
Normal Service Ceiling: 57,000 feet
Maximum Maneuvering Speed: 1,255 miles per hour (Mach 1.9) at 40,000 feet

This model was originally the Convair F-102B-CO, but so many modifications were made that it was redesignated the F-106A series. The cockpit was moved forward and the nose lengthened, with the fuselage designed from the very beginning to conform to the Whitcomb area rule. This made it much slimmer. Twin nose wheels were added, and the main gear was somewhat modified. Finally, the wing fences were removed and slots, or saw cuts, were placed on the leading edge to prohibit the spanwise flow of the boundary layer. These aircraft continue to serve with a few FIS's of the USAF as well as the Air National Guard. It is a fully automatic part of a weapons system, able to fly an intercept mission from takeoff to destruction of its target and back to base again, flared for landing, all automatically. To keep the aircraft up-to-date, many modifications have been made, including supersonic ejection seats, improved fire control systems as they have been developed, a head-up instrument display as Model 8-31. Also, supersonic drop tanks, a clear cockpit canopy and 20 mm Gatling guns have been added.

Convair F-102C and D-CO Delta Dart

These aircraft were one-of-a-kind types that were enlarged in the nose area to accommodate a larger radar dish. They were modified from production aircraft. One other advanced design of the F-106 was the "design only" version, which had a canard fitted to the forward fuselage for better maneuverability.

Convair F-106B-CO Delta Dart Trainer (Model 8-27)

First Flight: April 9, 1958
Number Built: 63
USAF Serial Numbers: F-106B-1-CO 41 built 57-2507 through 57-2547, 5 built 58-900 through 58-904, 17 built 59-149 through 59-165
Span: 38 feet 3.5 inches
Wing Area: 661.5 square feet
Length: 70 feet 8.78 inches
Height: 20 feet 3.3 inches
Powerplant: Pratt & Whitney J75-P-17 twin-spool turbojet rated at 17,000 pounds static thrust and 24,000 pounds static thrust with afterburner
Maximum Speed: 1,525 miles per hour
Crew: 2
Armament: None, unless desired. In that case, same as F-106A-CO.
Empty Weight: 25,141 pounds
Gross Weight: 40,078 pounds
Range: 1,700 miles with drop tanks
These aircraft are trainers for the F-106A and are fully operational if the need should arise. They are updated to Model 8-32 standards.

BIBLIOGRAPHY

Air Progress. Monthly, 1953 to 1975.

Air Progress. *World's Great Aircraft.* Los Angeles: Petersen Publishing Co., 1972.

Andrade, John M. *U.S. Military Aircraft Designations and Serials Since 1909.* England: Midland Counties Publications, 1979.

Carson, Capt. Don, and Drendel, Lou. *F-106 Delta Dart In Action.* Carrollton, Tex.: Squadron/Signal Publications, 1974.

Cross, Roy. *Supersonic Aircraft.* New York: Hanover House, 1956.

Cross, Roy, and Green, William. *The Jet Aircraft Of The World.* Garden City, N.Y.: Hanover House, 1957.

Fahey, James C. *USAF Aircraft 1947–1956.* Falls Church, Va.: Ships and Aircraft, 1956.

Gunston, Bill. *Modern Military Aircraft.* New York: Crescent Books, 1978.

Hall, R. Cargill. "To Acquire Strategic Bombers—The Case of The B-58." *Air University Review,* Vol.XXXI, No.6, pp. 3–20, 1980.

Hall, R. Cargill. "The B-58 Bomber-Aeronautical Innovation for Supersonic Flight." History lecture delivered at 19th Aerospace Sciences Meeting, 1981, St. Louis, Mo.

Holder, William G. *Convair F-106.* Fallbrook, Calif.: Aero Publishers Inc., 1977.

Hull, Tom. "Sea Dart." *Naval Aviation News,* pp. 40–45, January, 1981.

Jones, Lloyd S. *U.S. Bombers.* Fallbrook, Calif.: Aero Publishers, 1974.

Jones, Lloyd S. *U.S. Fighters.* Fallbrook, Calif.: Aero Publishers, 1975.

Jones, Lloyd S. *U.S. Naval Fighters.* Fallbrook, Calif.: Aero Publishers, 1977.

Long, B. J. "Sea Dart—U.S. Navy XF2Y-1 and YF2Y-1 Experimental Supersonic Seaplanes." *American Aviation Historical Society Journal,* pp. 3–12, Spring 1979.

Matt, Paul R., and Robinson, Bruce. *United States Navy and Marine Corps Fighters 1918–1962.* Fallbrook, Calif.: Aero Publishers, 1962.

Munson, Kenneth. *Fighters—Attack and Training Aircraft.* New York: The Macmillan Co., 1966.

Munson, Kenneth. *Bombers—Patrol and Transport Aircraft.* New York: The Macmillan Co., 1966.

Palmer, Henry R., Jr. *Remarkable Flying Machines.* Seattle: Superior Publishing Company, 1972.

Robertson, Bruce. *United States Army and Air Force Fighters 1916–1961.* Letchworth, Herts, England: The Garden City Press, Ltd., 1961.

Robinson, Douglas H. *The B-58 Hustler.* New York: Arco Publishing Company, Inc., 1967.

Sekigawa, Eiichiro. *German Military Aircraft In The Second World War.* Tokyo: Aireview, 1958.

Shortal, Joseph Adams. *A New Dimension—Wallops Island Flight Test Range— The First Fifteen Years.* Washington, DC: NASA Scientific and Technical Information Office, 1978.

Taylor, John W. R. *Janes Pocketbook of Experimental and Research Aircraft.* New York: Collier Books, 1976.

Wagner, Ray. *American Combat Planes.* Garden City, N.Y.: Hanover House, 1960.

Wings and Airpower. Monthly, 1971 to date.

INDEX